Aunt Phil's Trunk: Volume 2

An Alaska historian's collection of treasured tales

By
Phyllis Downing Carlson
Laurel Downing Bill

Laurel Downing Bill

Dec. 20, 2014

Laudon Enterprises
Anchorage, Alaska

www.auntphilstrunk.com

The front cover design by Kristy Bernier of Palmer, Alaska, features Phyllis Downing Carlson, aunt of Laurel Downing Bill, prior to her death in 1993.

Carlson grew up in Alaska and wrote numerous magazine and newspaper articles about the state she loved.

Also on the cover, from left: Juneau 1914 with courthouse in background, Alaska State Library, Skinner Foundation Collection, ASL-P44-03-022; Judge James Wickersham, Alaska State Library, Wickersham State Historic Site, ASL-P277-007-107; Wyatt Earp's saloon in Nome, University of Washington, Eric A. Hegg Collection, HEG425; and Klondike Kate Rockwell, University of Alaska Fairbanks, Barrett Willoughby Collection, UAF-72-116-334.

The back cover photograph was taken by Walter Saxton of Harlingen, Texas.

International Standard Book Number 1-57833-343-1
Library of Congress Control Number 2006908361

Printed and bound in the United States of America.

First printing 2007
Second printing 2008

DEDICATION

I dedicate this book to Aunt Phil's stepchildren, grandchildren, great-grandchildren and their families; to Aunt Phil's sister, Jean Downing Anderson of Seward; to my brothers and sisters, their families and all our cousins. I also dedicate the work to my husband, Donald; son Ryan; and daughter Kim and her husband, Bruce Sherry. Thank you so much for believing in me.

Lastly, I dedicate this collection of historical stories to my grandchildren, Sophia Isobel Sherry, not quite 2 years old at the time I wrote this volume, and Maya Josephine Sherry, born midway through the writing of Volume 2. These delightful little girls remind me daily of the need to preserve our past for their future.

ACKNOWLEDGMENTS

I owe an infinite debt of gratitude to the University of Alaska Anchorage, the University of Alaska Fairbanks, the Anchorage Museum of History and Art, the Alaska State Library in Juneau, the Z.J. Loussac Public Library in Anchorage, the Seward Community Library and the University of Washington for helping me collect the photographs for this book. Without the patient and capable staffs at these institutions, the following pages may not have been filled.

I also want to extend a heart-felt thank you to Robert DeBerry of Anchorage for his excellent attention to detail as he readied for publication the majority of the historical photographs that appear in Volume 2 of Aunt Phil's Trunk. And I am extremely grateful to Nancy Pounds of Anchorage for slaving away with her eagle eyes to carefully proofread the pages.

My family deserves medals, as well, for putting up with me as I chased down just the right photographs to go with Aunt Phil's stories, poured over notes and the collection of rare books that make up Aunt Phil's library and sat hunched over my computer for hours blending selections of Aunt Phil's work with stories from my own research.

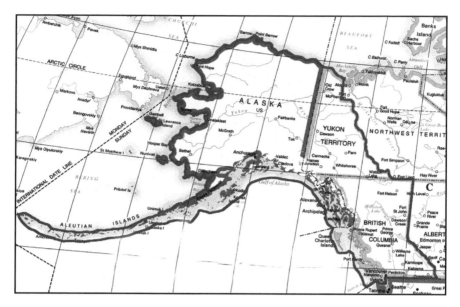

"Aunt Phil's Trunk: Volume 2" tells of various adventurers who traveled through Alaska and the Yukon Territory of Canada and settled in the Great Land. It continues from the Klondike Gold Rush at the turn of the 20th century and spotlights how law and order came to the Last Frontier, how rugged individuals set up a postal system and much, much more.

Phyllis Downing Carlson, who arrived in Cordova, Alaska, in 1914 at the age of 5, lived and loved the history about which she wrote.

FOREWORD

This book contains a collection of Alaska history stories written by my aunt, Phyllis Downing Carlson, as well as stories written by me that came from tidbits found among the notes and rare books I inherited when she died in 1993.

Born in 1909, Aunt Phil moved to Alaska in 1914 and lived the history so richly described in her work. She grew up in Cordova, where her father worked on building the railroad to the Kennecott copper mines; he then served as the conductor aboard the Copper River and Northwestern Railway. Phyllis graduated with a class of seven from Cordova High School in 1928, then studied journalism at the University of Washington and earned a teacher's certificate from Central College of Education in Ellensburg, Washington.

Aunt Phil landed her first job, which paid a whopping $150 a month, at Cooper Landing on the Kenai Peninsula. The new teacher kept the Yukon stove stoked in the little log schoolhouse and worked around cases of milk and staples stored for the winter.

After three years in the isolated community of 30, a widowed father of three of her pupils put an end to her single days. Carl Carlson moved her to the village of Tyonek, across Cook Inlet from Anchorage, and Phil again taught school in 1935 while Carl ran the village sawmill and served as postmaster.

The young bride met Tyonek Chief Simeon Chickalusion, who spoke English, Russian and his Native tongue. She later wrote an article, titled "The Tribe That Kept Its Head," about the chief and residents of Tyonek that ranked as one of the best articles submitted in a 1967 Writer's Digest contest. Years later, the village invited her back to a potlatch to share stories of the chief with the village young people.

The Carlsons moved to Anchorage in 1939, where Carl helped build Fort Richardson. The couple pitched a tent at Fifth Avenue and Denali Street and started framing a house over the tent. When they completed their home, they took down the tent and dragged it out the front door.

As a child, Alaska historian Phyllis Downing Carlson skipped down the dirt streets in Cordova, pictured here in 1919.

Phyllis Downing Carlson, who grew up in Cordova, taught school in the Native village of Tyonek in 1935. The village looked much like this photograph taken in 1898. She befriended Chief Simeon Chickalusion and was invited back to a potlatch when the village relocated after the village flooded during the 1960s.

After World War II, the couple moved to Cordova, where Aunt Phil honed her journalism skills. She produced her own radio show, "Woman to Woman," and conducted countless interviews that eventually led her to research Cordova's history through the local newspaper's archives.

"Oh, I had a wonderful time," she later recalled. "They had a real storehouse."

Her popular radio show led to the compilation of entertaining articles about Alaska, and for more than 40 years, Aunt Phil researched and wrote award-winning pieces as she moved about the state. Her stories appeared in a multitude of publications, including Alaskana, Alaska Journal, Alaska Sportsman, The Anchorage Times and Our Alaska.

She settled back in Anchorage from Kodiak after the Good Friday earthquake of 1964, and Phil spent so much time researching and talking with librarians at the Z.J. Loussac Public Library, they hired her. People said she didn't need to use the card catalog, because she knew the location of every volume.

"I don't remember faces," she said. "But I remember what I looked up for people."

The Alaska Press Women chose Aunt Phil for its Woman of Achievement Award in 1988. The organization cited her as an authority on Alaska history, recognized throughout the state by writers, researchers and politicians alike.

As a retiree, she served on a variety of boards, including the Anchorage Bicentennial Commission, Historical Landmarks Preservation Commission, State Historical Society and Alaska Press Women.

When she passed away in 1993, her treasured tales landed in my hands. As providence would have it, I, too, am a writer and lover of Alaska history. And since Aunt Phil was one of my favorite relatives, I feel it a privilege to perpetuate her work.

My Alaska roots stem from both sides of my family. My father, Richard Allie Downing – Aunt Phil's younger brother – was born in Cordova in 1916. Not only was his father a part of the railroad history there, but his grandfather, John Couch Downing, had witnessed the staking of gold claims around the area many years before when he sailed as the captain of the *Excelsior* and the *Portland*, both famous steamships that carried news of the riches found in the Klondike back to San Francisco and Seattle in July 1897.

My mother's grandfather, Robert Burns Mathison, arrived in Hope from Texas in 1898 and helped establish that little mining town. He pulled a small fortune out of Resurrection Creek and Chickaloon River and built a sawmill and mercantile. His son, Robert Lewis Mathison, married my grandmother, Inez Lee Brown, who traveled to the small community to work for her uncle, Charlie Shields, after being widowed in Kansas.

From that union came my mother, Hazel Isobel, and her identical twin, Hope Alisabeth, born at the Anchorage railroad hospital in 1920. The twins spent summers in Hope and winters in Seward, where they graduated high school in 1938.

My parents met at the University of Alaska Fairbanks, married in 1941, and settled in Fairbanks to raise their family. I was the fourth of their children born at old St. Joseph's Hospital, in 1951, following brothers Richard Ellsworth and Michael Woodrow and sister Meredith Lee.

I grew up between that gold-rush town and Juneau, where we moved after my father became the first commissioner of Public Works when Alaska became a state in 1959. That's where my younger sister, Deborah Lynn, was born in 1965 – shortly after my mother christened the Taku, the Alaska Marine Highway System's second ferry.

In 1973, I married and then spent 22 years in King Salmon with my fisheries biologist husband, Donald Bill. I worked for Bristol Bay Telephone Cooperative Inc. and raised two children, Kimberly and Ryan, and a foster daughter, Amie Morgan.

When the children graduated from Bristol Bay High School, and Don retired from the Alaska Department of Fish and Game, we moved to Anchorage. I went back to school in 1999, at the tender age of 48, and learned that I had a passion for writing. I earned a bachelor's degree in journalism in May 2003 from the University of Alaska

Anchorage and have spent the past few years writing my own award-winning articles for various Alaska newspapers and magazines while working on this labor of love.

Condensed versions of articles found in "Aunt Phil's Trunk" appeared in The Anchorage Chronicle, a weekly newspaper published by Alaska Newspapers Inc., from July 2002 until the paper closed its doors on Dec. 31, 2004. The Senior Voice, a monthly Alaska newspaper, picked up the column in February 2005 and it continues to appear in that publication.

I truly hope you enjoy this volume packed with Aunt Phil's articles and other stories that came from research jotted down in piles of notebooks, countless lined tablets and in the margins of rare books.

- Laurel Downing Bill

Charles, left, and Robert L. Mathison, maternal grandfather of Laurel Downing Bill, walk away from the Pacific Coast Trading Company and U.S. Mineral Surveyor and Assaying Office in Seward around 1906. The brothers, who mined with their father, Robert Burns Mathison, prospected around the gold-rush town of Hope.

TABLE OF CONTENTS

EARLY ALASKA

1

SUMMARY OF VOLUME 1

"Aunt Phil's Trunk: Volume 2" picks up where Volume 1 ended – about 1900. Following is a brief review of the material offered in the first collection to help readers get a jump-start on Volume 2.

Ancestors of modern-day Alaska Natives lived in skin huts similar to these on the shore of a village in Siberia.

Recap of early Alaska

After dinosaurs, bison and woolly mammoths roamed the Great Land, successive waves of settlers from Asia crossed the Bering Land Bridge, a broad expanse of temporarily exposed tundra that is today under 300 hundred feet of water. These ancestors of modern-day Alaska Natives, who arrived as early as 30,000 to 10,000 years ago, established maritime villages that evolved over the centuries into productive hunting and fishing settlements.

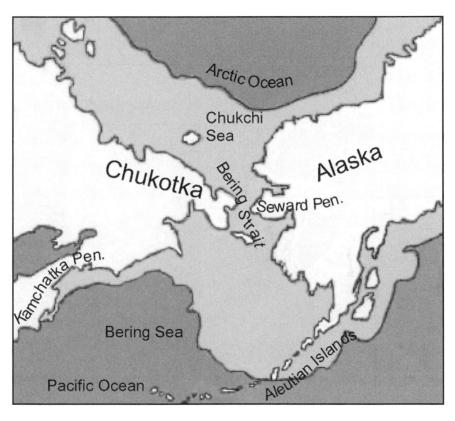

During the last ice age, which occurred around 12,000-15,000 years ago, the shallow seas now separating Asia from North America near the present-day Bering Strait dropped about 300 feet and made a 1,000-mile-wide grassy, treeless plain that linked the continents. Called the Bering Land Bridge, or Beringia, after Vitus Bering, this gateway allowed humans to enter the Americas. Plants and animals also migrated both directions across this grassland.

When European explorers rounded the coasts of Alaska in the early 18th century, they discovered the country inhabited by Eskimos in the north, west and Prince William Sound areas; Aleuts in the southwest; Athabascans in the interior and Cook Inlet areas; and Tlingit and Haida Indians in the southeast.

In 1728, Danish-born navigator Vitus Bering, sailing for the Russian Navy of Czar Peter the Great, made his way through the narrow waterway that separates the Seward Peninsula of Alaska from the Chukotka Peninsula in Siberia. He came close to the Alaska coast, but bad weather prevented him from making an official sighting.

He mounted a second voyage to Alaska with an additional ship in 1741. The first sighting took place on July 15, when the *St. Paul*, under the command of Bering's second-in-command, Aleksei Chirikov,

The portrait on the left is what historians for centuries believed was a resemblance to Vitus Bering, the Dane who first spotted Alaska in 1741. However, after a forensic reconstruction of the explorer's face, based on Bering's remains found in 1991, the bust on the right shows different facial features. It now is thought that the portrait is of Vitus Pedersen Bering, uncle to Bering's mother. The bust was created by V.N. Zvyagin, Institute of Forensic Medicine, Moscow.

reached Prince of Wales Island. Bering's own ship, the *St. Peter*, sighted Mount St. Elias and Kayak Island the next day.

Bering and many of his companions died of scurvy during the trip, but some survivors returned to Russia with pelts of fox, fur seal and sea otter. News spread fast, and soon Russian adventurers began pouring into Alaska to trap furs. By 1745, hunting and trading vessels from Siberia were obtaining fur pelts from the Aleuts along the Aleutian Chain.

The Russian traders, unskilled in hunting sea mammals, used bribery and coercion with the Aleuts, often taking hostages and demanding their ransom be paid in fur. The Aleuts repeatedly resisted. Aleuts on Unmak and Unalaska destroyed four Russian vessels in 1763. But the fur traders quashed that opposition, and by 1784, Grigorii Shelikhov had founded the first permanent white settlement in Alaska on Kodiak Island.

Europeans come north

The French, Spanish and English governments also were eager to share in Alaska's bounty. After two voyages – one that mapped

Once abundant in Alaska's Aleutian Islands, the fur seal population dropped drastically when greedy Russian fur traders arrived on the scene in the late 1700s.

NATIVES OF PRINCE WILLIAMS SOUND.

Published by J.Robins & C.Albion Press London.

This engraving of Alaska Natives encountered in Prince William Sound is based on the voyage of Capt. James Cook in 1778.

Tahiti and New Zealand and the other to prove that Terra Australis Incognita, the continent that people imagined was in the southern hemisphere to balance the earth, did not exist – English Capt. James Cook headed north. He set sail in 1776 aboard his 462-ton *Resolution* to find the fabled Northwest Passage, a trading route across the top of North America, from Europe to the Orient. He hoped to claim a £20,000 prize offered by Britain, following almost 300 years of unsuccessful expeditions, to anyone locating this important route.

Cook was instructed to avoid conflict with navigators of other nations who already had claimed land and not to go ashore where any other country's presence was noted. He reached and explored Alaska's foggy coastline in 1778 and described the scene in his published journal account for May 19 that year:

"On Eastern shore we now saw two columns of smoke, a sure sign that there were inhabitants.

"About noon, two canoes, with a man in each, came off to the

Two men in canoes paddled out to meet Capt. James Cook when he sailed along Alaska's coast in May 1778. Alaska Natives built and used canoes, like the one pictured above in the late 1890s, to travel on the country's waterways.

ship, from near the place where we had seen the smoke the preceding day. ... These men, in every respect, resembled the people we had met within Prince William's Sound, as to their persons and dress. Their canoes were also of the same construction. One of our visiters (sic) had his face painted jet black. ... Also smoke seen upon the flat western shore this day, from whence we may infer that these lower spots, and islands, are the only inhabited places."

On June 1, Cook sent two boats farther north, and when they returned, the explorers reported that the waters narrowed. Cook then made a conclusion:

"... all hopes of finding a passage were now given up."

However, he named the waters to the east "River Turnagain" and claimed the land for England.

"... In the afternoon I sent Mr. King again, with two armed boats, with orders to land, on the Northern point of the low land, on the South East side of the river; there to display the flag; to take possession of the country and river, in His Majesty's name; and to bury in the ground a bottle, containing some pieces of English coin, of the year 1772, and a paper, on which was inscribed the names of our ships, and the date of our discovery."

Before Western contact, Alaska's Natives wore clothes made from animal skins and fur. These four girls dressed in skins are all wearing cloth sacks, perhaps for berry picking, that might have been taken in trade for something found in Alaska.

Cook established that there was no land connection between the Asian and North American continents. And he and his expedition produced maps that set the navigation standard for the next century.

"The Russian Empress Catherine, unnerved at this intensive British survey of territory she considered her own, ordered Cook's journal translated into Russian as soon as it was published," according to a Public Broadcasting System Website.

Anxious to protect their interests in the New World, the Spanish sent several expeditions up the coast, including the 1779 voyage of the *Princesa* and *Favorita*, under the command of Ignacio Arteaga. At Nuchek Bay, they claimed possession of the territory in the name of the King of Spain, and then sailed back to California. French explorer Comte de La Perouse sailed north to Lituya Bay and claimed possession of that land for France.

Russia's rivals soon became distracted by politics and geography and could not continue pursuing exploration and settlement in

Alaska. During this time, the French faced a revolution at home, the British lost the American colonies and the Spanish could not hang on to their New World holdings in South America. The Russians, who'd arrived first, basically won the race to claim Alaska.

The Russian era

As Russia took hold of the coast of Alaska, exploitation of Alaska Natives continued. When Russian merchant Grigorii Shelikhov arrived at Kodiak Island in 1784 with three vessels, 4,000 Koniag Natives met his ships and demanded that the Russians leave immediately. The Russians fired cannons at them and destroyed Koniag homes after negotiations failed.

Shelikhov further extended his authority by setting up political districts in the Kodiak region and building a fur-harvesting labor force of Alaska Natives. And although the Russian government conducted an inquiry into his brutal methods of subduing the Native population, he was never charged with any crime.

This Russian cannon stood in front of the Erskine House, the oldest house in Alaska, in Kodiak. It's rumored to have been presented by Russian Empress Catherine.

Disorganized and greedy, Russian fur traders soon depleted the stock of furbearing animals in many areas and killed or enslaved large numbers of Aleuts. In an attempt to bring order to Russian America, Czar Paul I chartered the Russian-American Company in 1799 and granted it a monopoly on trading.

Under the leadership of Alexander Baranof, who led the company from 1800-1817, the Russians increased the fur harvest substantially as Baranof established new settlements. New Archangel, which later became Sitka, was founded in 1799. And although Tlingit Indians destroyed the fort in 1802, Baranof rebuilt it in 1804 and made it the capital of Russian America.

During the first half of the 19th century, the British Hudson's Bay Company and American traders also were active in Alaska. The rights of traders and many current boundaries of Alaska were established by treaties between Russia, Great Britain and the United States between 1824-1825.

Settlements continued to develop as the Russians built iron foundries and schools, developed coal mining, established trading routes, farmed and raised sheep. But by the mid-1860s, as a result of the Crimean War and contacts with American businessmen in San Francisco, the Russian government authorized Edouard de Stoeckl, a

Alexander Baranof befriended Sitka head chief Skautlelt. The Russian gave the chief many gifts, including this brass replica of the Russian Coat of Arms.

He also handed him an open letter stating: "... Baranof had witnessed that the grounds occupied by the Russian fort were voluntarily ceded by the chief and his clan for a remuneration, and that the chief had expressed his devotion to Russia, for which the Russians promised to provide him with the necessary supplies and to defend him from attacks of neighboring hostile peoples," according to the Alaska State Museum.

Russian diplomat in the U.S. delegation, to broach the subject of selling Alaska to the United States rather than lose it to the British in the event of another war.

Alaska becomes U.S. Territory

U.S. Secretary of State William H. Seward, an expansionist who saw the region as strategically important, negotiated the purchase of Alaska, and on March 30, 1867, a treaty of cession was signed by Russia and the United States. After ratification by the U.S. Senate, Russia handed Alaska over to the United States for $7.2 million in a ceremony at Sitka on Oct. 18, 1867.

Americans quickly occupied Alaska and took control of the assets of the Russian-American Company to trade along the Yukon River and to exploit the fur seal trade. During the early years of U.S. control, some people called Alaska "Seward's Folly" because they thought the region was useless.

Many Natives in remote Alaska villages were unaware that their homeland was claimed by Russia and then purchased by the United States.

2

MYTH SURROUNDS ALASKA'S PURCHASE

The amount of the check issued to Russia by America for the purchase of Alaska was $7.2 million. That sum is a fact. But some people think the check included a payment to Russia for favors bestowed upon a beleaguered Union during the American Civil War.

The Russian fleet, commanded by Admiral Lisovski, sits in the New York harbor on Oct. 17, 1863. This sketch appeared in Harper's Weekly, A Journal of Civilization.

Since the first printing of "Aunt Phil's Trunk: Volume 1" in 2006, a reader shared that some historians argue Alaska cost little more than $1 million and the rest of the money was a payment to Russia for sending its fleet to the East and West coasts during the Civil War.

That opinion led to the following research, which sheds new light on the purchase price of the Great Land.

"During the Civil War, Great Britain and France threatened to recognize the Southern Confederacy and disregard the blockade imposed by the North. The Czar of Russia sent the Russian navy (in 1863) to put on a friendly demonstration in both our eastern and western ports," wrote Mariette Shaw Pilgrim in her book, "Alaska, Its History, Resources, Geography, and Government."

"The expense item for this demonstration amounted to $5,800,000, but since no legal provision had been made for its payment, it was added to the purchase price of Alaska, thereby making it appear that the United States had paid the sum of $7,200,000 for this great northern territory, when the actual purchase price was $1,400,000."

The opinion that the United States paid the Russians to sail to America and show its support for the Northern cause was widely held after Alaska's purchase in 1867. The legend surrounding Russia's show of force to bolster the Union grew and persisted for decades – only to be completely demolished when historic research into the Russian archives finally brought to light the Czar's secret order to his fleet.

According to Tom Delahaye in his paper titled, "The Bilateral Effect of the Visit of the Russian Fleet in 1863," Czar Alexander II's reasons for wanting to send the Russian fleet off to America are related to a complicated European situation that began long before the Civil War. The basis for Alexander's action was a Polish insurrection.

The Poles were demanding social and political reforms. And France and England agitated for the Poles, thus aggravating the Russians.

Hugh Seton-Watson, in "The Russian Empire: 1801-1917," claimed that "the traditional sympathy of both French and British public opinion for Poland expressed itself with great fervor. ..." The European

Czar Alexander II sent the Russian fleet to America in a strategic move during 1863.

powers gradually moved closer to war.

Russia's refusal to consider Polish independence continued along with Franco-British agitation. In "The American Impact on Russia: 1784-1917," Max M. Laserson wrote that the French and British put unrelenting pressure on the Russians:

"... humiliating notes from these two powers rained on St. Petersburg between April and July 1863, in which Russian rejection of Polish independence was branded as an act that placed Russia outside the civilized world. ..."

Russians worried about fleet

By summer 1863, it appeared that war was inevitable. However, the Russian fleet was weak, so Russian General-Adjutant Krabbe submitted to the emperor a contingency plan for the navy.

"The fleet was very weak, even weaker than it appeared on paper," wrote F. A. Golder in "The Russian Fleet and the Civil War."

"It was made up of a small squadron in the Pacific, seven war vessels of various descriptions at Cronstadt, and a frigate in the Mediterranean. They were all, or nearly all, of wood, and although they had engines, the principal means of motion was still the sail, the orders being that steam should be resorted to only in case of urgent necessity."

Krabbe claimed that the fleet could be best utilized by preying on British and French commerce. He also realized that "if the fleet remained at home it would probably be blocked in; it was therefore necessary that it should be sent away to some place more conveniently situated for the purpose in mind."

Krabbe submitted his proposal to Alexander II, and on July 7, 1863, the Czar accepted the proposal. Admiral Lisovski was ordered to lead the fleet out of the Gulf of Finland and "proceed directly to New York." Krabbe also told Lisovski to try to keep all the ships in New York Harbor, if the Americans permitted it. Rear Admiral Popov's fleet was sent to San Francisco.

This sketch depicting the reception of the Common Council Committee in New York by Admiral Lisovski onboard the flagship *Alexander Nevski* appeared in the Oct. 17, 1863, issue of Harper's Weekly, A Journal of Civilization.

The Russian flagship, *Alexander Nevski,* arrived in New York harbor on Sept. 24, 1863, in the middle of the Civil War.

The war had become bogged down and neither side was able to make significant advances. The Union had just defeated Confederate forces at Antietam. The South also had been defeated at Gettysburg. Both victories raised hopes for a Union triumph and a quick end to the war. But the cost in human lives for these victories was high. With these high costs for the Union, and continued persistence by the South, enthusiasm from the victories began to fade.

Union needs morale boost

Howard L. Kushner, in his article "The Russian Fleet and the American Civil War: Another View," wrote:

U.S. President Abraham Lincoln welcomed the morale boost that the Russian fleet brought with its arrival in New York City in 1863.

"By early September 1863, the jubilation in the North over the victory at Gettysburg began to wane. Reports persisted that two ironclad rams being built at Laird's in Liverpool for the Confederates were completed and about to be released to batter the Union blockade."

Times were desperate for Lincoln and his Union. Victories were essential to help boost their spirits. Union morale was not helped by the actions of Britain and France. Both countries had declared neutrality. The neutrality, though, was very pecu-

liar, because it meant interference by these countries
when it best served their
national interests.

In Britain, the ruling
class sympathized with the
Union's idea of freeing the
slaves. But Lincoln aban-
doned that idea at first in
order to keep Southern border states in the Union. By
doing that, Lincoln lost the
support of the British ruling
class, which wanted to see
an end to slavery. It was not
difficult for the British aris-
tocracy to stop supporting
the Union. They had always
feared the growing power of
the United States.

Napoleon III had interests in Mexico and openly
negotiated business with the Confederates.

With the nation split, it
seemed less of a threat to Britain. Neutrality was the appropriate
course for the British. Historian Thomas A. Bailey supports the idea of
neutrality for Britain's self-interest. He claims that since "her Britannic
Majesty's possessions in North America would be more secure" with
a divided United States, Britain refused to get involved in the conflict.
The Northerners regarded this "cold neutrality as hardly less than
veiled hostility."

France also decided to remain neutral in the American conflict.
The neutrality, though, was like the British non-interference. France
openly negotiated with the Confederates. Napoleon III had interests
in Mexico. These interests were protected best by the United States'
inability to divert any attention from the war. French negotiations
with the Confederates gave the South some credibility and only made
the war effort for the North more difficult.

The actions of Britain and France were damaging to the Union war effort. Their neutrality was superficial in nature and changed at their own convenience. The North was alone in its fight for survival.

With the actions of these two countries, morale was low in the North and a foreboding mood spread over the region in the autumn of 1863.

Russian fleet arrives on America's shores

The Russian fleet arrived in New York and San Francisco harbors like a ray of sunshine over the horizon, according to Delahaye. It was the saving grace the Union needed. Oliver Wendell Holmes, referring to Alexander sending the Russian fleet to America, said he was "our friend when the world was our foe."

In "Europe and the American Civil War," Donaldson Jordan and Edwin Pratt claimed "Europe and the North saw this visit of the Russian fleet as a significant demonstration of Russian friendship for the Union in its hour of need." The incident had a lasting impact on Russian-American relations.

The arrival of the fleet delighted the Lincoln administration. Bailey wrote that "the morale of the United States received a definite boost at a time when it needed stimulants. ..."

An excerpt from the diary of Secretary of the Navy Gideon Welles in "Lincoln and the Russians" is an example of the jubilation felt by many Americans. He wrote:

"In sending them (the fleet) to this country there is something significant. What will be its effect on France and the French policy we shall learn in due time. It may be moderate; it may exasperate. God bless the Russians."

The arrival of the fleet meant hope for the Union, and therefore the Americans were ready to show their gratitude to the Russians. A reception was held in New York City, and then the Russian visitors were paraded down Broadway where American and Russian flags were displayed. Tiffany and Company decorated its building with a huge banner that stretched from the roof to the sidewalk. Cheering New Yorkers lined Broadway as the Russians rode by in carriages.

A sketch of the huge parade down Broadway, held in honor of the Russian fleet, appeared in the Oct. 17, 1863, issue of Harper's Weekly, A Journal of Civilization.

On Nov. 5, New Yorkers gave the Russians a ball at the Academy of Music. It was a very important affair attended by leading society people. Harper's Weekly ran several pages of illustrations of the dancing ladies and their Russian partners. A Harper's Weekly reporter commented that "the Russian guests from the fleet were worn out by the expressions of friendship and affection extended to them."

During all of the balls and banquets, each country toasted the other. Alexander was hailed as the emancipator of the serfs and the friend of America. Lincoln was toasted as the friend of Russia. Golder pointed out an interesting fact about the celebrations:

"All references to the European situation (i.e., Poland) were purposely avoided. This was good diplomacy, for on the one hand it concealed the real purpose of the visit, and on the other it strengthened the Americans in their belief that the fleet came especially for their benefit. The fact that this idea still has such strong hold on our country shows how skillfully the game was played."

It is not clear if the Russians purposely intended to hide the reasons for their visit. It seems very probable that many Americans suspected their true motives, but wanted to think otherwise to help the morale of the Union.

Russia's motives examined

Several articles in journals have been published that analyze American public opinion during the time the fleet arrived in America. The survey of opinions was done by researching editorials in newspapers across the country.

Bailey, in his journal article titled "Notes and Documents: The Russian Fleet Myth Re-examined," made a very concise survey of opinions. Bailey commented that "there was not consistency: different theories might be mentioned by the same editor on succeeding days."

Bailey concluded that the most popular reason for the landing of the fleet (mentioned by 15 editors) was "the one relating to friendship, alliance and succor." Bailey elaborated on this idea, writing:

"The Russian warships had come, so the theory ran, as a demonstration of friendship, with the possibility of an alliance, as a result of which the Czar would fight on the side of the North should France and Britain intervene for the South. The fight-on-our-side aspect of this assumption, though suggested in its baldest form by only a few editors, took on greater prominence in the public as the legend crystallized."

In April 1864, Alexander sent orders to the fleet to return home. The fleet had served a two-fold purpose. It helped to preserve the Union by its presence in America and it protected itself by leaving Europe.

Alexander wanted to avoid a European war, and in doing so, he indirectly aided the Union. One must remember that this "was a most extraordinary situation: Russia had not in mind to help us but did render us distinct service; the United States was not conscious that it was contributing in any way to Russia's welfare and yet seems to have saved her from humiliation and perhaps war," according to Delahaye.

And so it appears that the legend of America hiding a payment to Russia in the check paid for Alaska for services rendered during the Civil War is a myth.

U.S. shows early interest in Alaska

Historical records show that America wanted to buy Alaska well before the Civil War.

Secretary of State William Marcy and William Gwin, Democratic Congressman from Mississippi, inquired as early as 1843 whether the Russian colony was for sale. Although the Russians did not want to sell Alaska at the time, the two expansionists made their interest in the colony known.

William Gwin wanted to buy Alaska as early as 1843.

Historian Hubert Howe Bancroft, author of "History of Alaska 1730-1885," said the United States and Russia began negotiating the price of Alaska in the late 1850s.

In December 1859, during U.S. President James Buchanan's administration, then-Senator Gwin of California held several meetings with the Russian minister and told him the United States would be willing to pay $5 million for Alaska.

"The assistant secretary of state also affirmed that the president was in favor of the purchase, and that if a favorable answer were returned by the Russian government, he would lay the matter before the cabinet," Bancroft wrote. "A few months later a dispatch was received from Prince Gortschakof stating that the sum offered was entirely inadequate; but that the minister of finance was about to inquire into the condition of the territory, after which Russia would be in a condition to treat."

After officials tallied the inventory, it turned out that the Russian American Company's capital in Alaska was estimated at $4.4 million as of Jan. 1, 1860. Those assets were mostly furs, goods, real estate, improvements and sea-going vessels. Had the United States again offered the Russians $5 million, it is possible that they would have accepted the deal. However, with the outbreak of the Civil War, negotiations were put on hold for several years.

But with the value of its assets placed at more than $4 million, it is highly unlikely Russia would have accepted only $1.4 million for Alaska as suggested by Pilgrim. In her defense, however, it must be noted that she published her book in 1939 and based it on written accounts of opinions at the time – before researchers were allowed to examine Russian records and learn Alexander's true reasons for sending his fleet to America.

Once the purchase was complete in 1867, the federal government generally neglected Alaska. It was administered first by the U.S. War Department, then the Treasury Department and finally by the U.S. Navy before civil government was established by the Organic Act of 1884. The government had little control of Alaska, however, until further laws were enacted in the early 1900s.

3

AMERICANS FLOCK NORTH

A mericans eager to engage in trade and commerce flocked to Alaska before the ink was dry on the ratified treaty to purchase Russia's northern colony in July 1867. More than 30 ships sailed from San Francisco that month, with most of them heading to the Russian center at Sitka.

Alaska Natives sell baskets and crafts along Lincoln Street in Sitka in 1897. The Marine Corps Barracks, built in 1892, can be seen to the left, and the Cathedral of St. Michael sits in the background. Sitka is the oldest community in Southeast Alaska.

Others sailed to Wrangell, Kodiak, Kenai, Unalaska, the Pribilof Islands and St. Michael, where the U.S. government built Army posts.

Above: A boardwalk leads to businesses and homes in 1900 Wrangell. Wrangell is the third-oldest community in Alaska, and the second-oldest in Southeast. It is the only city in Alaska ruled by four nations: Tlingit, Russia, England and the United States.

Below: In 1793, the Russians decided to move the capital of their colony from Three Saints Bay to the northern part of Kodiak. They established a new center of government, which they named Pavlov Harbor – "Paul Harbor" – at the site of today's city of Kodiak, pictured below at the turn-of-the-last century.

Above: A traditional home of a resident living on Unalaska Island during the 1800s.

Below: The Russian Orthodox Church established its first Alaska church, pictured here, in Kodiak in 1793 and then expanded to Unalaska in 1808. More than 3,000 Unagans — known since the Russian era as Aleuts — lived in 24 settlements on Unalaska and Amaknak Islands in 1759. Unalaska became a Russian trading port for the fur seal industry in 1768. In 1787, many hunters and their families were enslaved and relocated by the Russian American Company to the Pribilof Islands to work in the fur seal harvest.

After arriving in Unalaska in 1824, Father Ivan Veniaminov helped spread the Russian Orthodox doctrine in the Aleutians. He taught Natives in their dialect, Aleutian Fox, after creating an alphabet and translating textbooks and parts of the Bible.

Veniaminov, named Bishop Innokentii in 1840, also carefully recorded tides, winds and weather at Unalaska. He traveled thousands of miles by kayak each year, writing down his observations of Aleut life and recording the Native legends and history. He later moved to Sitka and is now known in the Orthodox Church as Saint Innocent of Alaska.

Above: An Aleutian crew onboard a pelagic fur-sealing vessel heads toward the killing grounds in the Pribilof Islands in the late 1890s.

Below: Fur seals approach the seashore in St. Paul where they mate and give birth every summer. The northern fur seal rookeries are in the Pribilof and Commanders' islands. Each seal mates on the same island where it was born.

The settlement of St. Michael, seen here around 1898, is located on the east coast of St. Michael Island in Norton Sound. It lies 125 miles southeast of Nome and 48 miles southwest of Unalakleet. The Russian-American Company built a fortified trading post called Redoubt St. Michael there in 1833; it was the northernmost Russian settlement in Alaska. The Native village of Tachik lay to the northeast. St. Michael became a popular trading post for Eskimos to trade their goods for Western supplies.

When the Russians left Alaska in 1867, several of the post's traders remained. Fort St. Michael, a U.S. military post, was established during the gold rush of 1897. The town was a major gateway to the Interior via the Yukon River, and as many as 10,000 people were said to have lived in St. Michael during the Klondike Gold Rush.

The U.S. government soon realized that the Army posts it had built in Alaska communities were too expensive to maintain, and by 1870 only the Sitka post remained.

After the purchase of Alaska, the U.S. Treasury Department sent customs collectors and Revenue Marine Service – precursor to the U.S. Coast Guard – vessels to collect taxes and enforce smuggling laws. U.S. Navy ships also came to Alaska to help support the Army.

When Ivan Petroff took the first U.S. Census in 1880, he counted 33,426 people in the colony: 430 non-Native, 1,756 Creole and more than 31,000 Natives. His report provided an abundance of information about Alaska's resources and geography.

Most Alaskans lived near the ocean or along major rivers where ships and boats could deliver supplies. When the Americans arrived, they started new settlements around Alaska, such as the Southeast communities of Juneau and Douglas, which both began as gold mining camps in 1880 and 1881.

The Treadwell gold mine in Douglas, pictured above in 1899, operated along the Gastineau Channel near Juneau.

Thousands of stampeders settled near Hope during the late 1890s.

Several other settlements began as mining camps in the late 1890s, as well, including Hope, above, on the Kenai Peninsula, Circle City, below, on the middle Yukon River, and Council on the Seward Peninsula.

Circle City, built on the banks of the Yukon River, sprouted up in the wilderness as gold seekers streamed into the territory.

Fish dries on wooden racks near Sitka in the late 1800s.

Soon after Alaska became a U.S. possession, commercial fishing started growing in importance. Many towns, like Ketchikan, pictured below in 1890, started out as fishing villages.

The Tlingits used Ketchikan Creek as a fish camp, which they called "kitschk-hin," meaning creek of the "thundering wings of an eagle."

Seldovia, pictured here in 1900, developed around commercial fishing. Located on the Kenai Peninsula across from Homer on the south shore of Kachemak Bay, its name comes from "Seldevoy," a Russian word meaning "herring bay." Native residents are a mixture of Dena'ina Indian and Sugpiaq Eskimo – also known as Alutiq.

Other communities like Karluk on Kodiak Island, Seldovia and Homer on the Kenai Peninsula and Petersburg in Southeast Alaska developed as canneries.

Alaska's commercial herring industry began in 1878 when 30,000 pounds were caught and preserved with salt in wooden barrels. That same year, salmon canneries were opened in the southeastern communities of Sitka and Klawock. By the turn of the century, commercial fishing was the leading industry as the fur industry declined.

Barrels of salted herring wait for transport at Kodiak Fisheries Company dock in 1919.

Above: Known as "Little Norway," Petersburg in Southeast Alaska was named after Peter Buschmann, a Norwegian immigrant and a pioneer in the cannery business, who arrived in the late 1890s. He built the Icy Strait Packing Company cannery, a sawmill and a dock by 1900. His family's homesteads grew into this community, populated largely by people of Scandinavian origin. By 1920, 600 people lived in Petersburg year round.

Fresh salmon and halibut were packed in glacier ice for shipment. Alaska's first shrimp processor, Alaska Glacier Seafoods, was founded in 1916. A cold storage plant was built in 1926. The cannery has operated continuously and now is known as Petersburg Fisheries, a subsidiary of Icicle Seafoods Inc.

Below: The economically vital fishing fleet sits in the Petersburg harbor at the turn-of-the-last century.

Built with sturdy logs, the boarding school at the Chilkat Mission in Haines became a center of education.

Religious factions also flooded into Alaska. The Presbyterian Church established missions in places like Wrangell, in 1877, and Haines, pictured above in the late 1890s. The Moravians began their ministry in Alaska in 1885 at the invitation of the Rev. Sheldon Jackson, a Presbyterian minister famous for developing an education system in Southeast Alaska.

A group of Alaska Natives gathers around a boat at the Moravian Mission Station in Bethel on the Kuskokwim River in the late 1890s.

The Revs. J. Adolphus Hartmann and William H. Weinland accepted Jackson's invitation as a call from God to proclaim the gospel among the Yup'ik people. From 1884 to 1885 they searched for a location to establish a Moravian Church of America mission and finally settled on Bethel, along the Kuskokwim River.

At the time of the 1880 census, 41 residents and an Alaska Commercial Company trading post were in Bethel, which was first established by Yup'ik Eskimos who called the village Mamterillermiut – "Smokehouse People."

The Rev. John Kilbuck was perhaps the most influential and capable missionary during those first years. A Native American himself, Kilbuck quickly learned the Yup'ik language.

Many Moravian congregations later were established in Alaska, most of them in the Kuskokwim region. However, Moravians also organized a following in Nushagak in the Bristol Bay area.

This photograph of Nushagak was taken by the Revs. J. Adolphus Hartmann and William H. Weinland in 1884 while searching for a location to establish a Moravian Church of America mission.

Presbyterian missionaries spread farther north and built the Point Barrow Mission, pictured above, in 1898. Whalers and traders already had established a shore-based whaling station in the area.

Whalers *Newport* and *Fearless* navigate through the ice east of Point Barrow in 1898.

Alaska Children's Services began as a Methodist orphanage in Unalaska in 1890. Called the Jesse Lee Home, it served hundreds of Alaskan children, including the girls pictured above, until 1925 when it moved to larger facilities in Seward.

By 1890, the Methodist Church also had arrived, establishing a school, a clinic and an orphanage in Unalaska. And by the turn of the century, the Episcopal Church was setting up congregations in Southeast and Interior Alaska.

The Episcopal Church arrived in Alaska in the late 1890s and built St. Matthew's Church and hospital in Fairbanks in 1905.

But while many missionaries, businessmen and adventurers streamed into Russia's former colony between 1867 and 1890, it was the Klondike Gold Rush that brought thousands of people to Alaska and almost doubled its population to more than 63,300 by 1900. Supply camps sprang up along the routes people traveled to get to the gold fields, and towns like Skagway, Dyea, Circle City and Nome sprouted up.

And with gold-rush towns blossoming in Alaska's wilderness came the need to settle the border dispute between the United States and Canada.

Rich gold fields drew hopeful stampeders north at the turn-of-the-last century and made land in both Alaska and Canada quite valuable.

Thousands of determined stampeders hiked up the Chilkoot Trail in the late 1890s.

4

BORDER DISPUTE HEATS UP

Alaska's border with Canada is one of the great feats of wilderness surveying. Marked by metal cones and a clear-cut swath 20 feet wide, the boundary is 1,538 miles long.

The line is obvious in some places, such as the Yukon River valley, where crews cut a straight line through forest on the 141st Meridian. In other areas, like the summit of 18,008-foot Mount St. Elias, the boundary is invisible.

Starting in 1905, surveyors and other workers of the International Boundary Commission trekked into some of the wildest country in North America to etch a new boundary into the landscape.

But there was no border in 1867, when the U.S. purchased Alaska from Russia for 2 cents an acre. And the lack of an agreed-upon boundary caused problems from the get-go.

Maps of the time showed more land belonging to the Russians than was stipulated in an 1825 treaty between Russia and Great Britain. That treaty divided the Northwest American territories between the Hudson's Bay Company and the Russian-American Company trading areas and described the boundary as following a range of mountains in Southeast Alaska parallel to the Pacific Coast – but in some places there were no mountains.

In 1872, British Columbia petitioned for an official survey to set

The border separating Alaska and Canada stretches 1,538 miles from the tip of Southeast Alaska on the Pacific Ocean up to the Arctic Ocean and Beaufort Sea.

Mounties guard the Canada/Alaska border at the turn-of-the-last century.

the boundary, however the United States repeatedly refused, claiming it would cost too much.

Canada surveyed the boundary at the Stikine River in 1877, so it could set up a customs station to collect duty on goods headed to the Cassiar gold fields – discovered in 1872. In 1887-1888, and again in 1895, William Ogilvie surveyed the area around the Fortymile gold discoveries.

But it was the Klondike Gold Rush that brought the boundary issue to a head. When every square foot of ground could yield enormous wealth, the exact location of the border became critical. In fact, the total value of the gold mined in the Yukon was nearly $2.5 million in 1897 and almost $22.3 million in 1900.

The Canadians sent a detachment of North-West Mounted Police to the head of the Lynn Canal, a main gateway to the Yukon, in the late 1890s. Canadian officials wanted ownership of Skagway and Dyea, which would allow Canadians access to the Klondike gold fields without crossing American soil. Canada asserted that that location was more than 10 marine leagues from the sea, which was part of the 1825 boundary definition.

But prospectors flooding into Skagway didn't agree. Some say that a group of heavily armed Americans demanded the Canadian flag at the police post be taken down or the Americans would shoot it down. Americans thought that the head of Lake Bennett, another 12 miles north, should be the boundary between the two territories.

The Canadians retreated and set up posts on the summits of the Chilkoot Pass and White Pass – each post equipped with a mounted Gatling gun.

Stampeders heading toward the gold fields of the Klondike pitched tents along the shores of Lake Bennett, pictured above in 1898.

U.S. troops stationed at Dyea during the Klondike Gold Rush tried to keep peace and order among the stampeders.

Troops perform drills at Fort Selkirk, which became the headquarters of the Canadian Army's Yukon Field Force in 1898.

The Yukon Field Force, a 200-man army unit, then set up camp at Fort Selkirk. From there, soldiers could be dispatched quickly to deal with disputes at either the coastal passes or the 141st Meridian.

The provisional boundary was grudgingly accepted, but in September 1898, serious negotiations began in Quebec City between Canada and the United States to settle the issue.

While officials were mulling over what to do about the border, other people were busy building the White Pass and Yukon Railroad through the disputed territory. And they had their share of problems, too.

In 1898, the sticky issue of the boundary line arose as the railroad approached a section of country that the Canadians considered theirs. But quick thinking of a man named Stikine Bill Robinson saved the day for the Americans.

At that time, both the Canadians and the Americans claimed the land as far down as tidewater on Lynn Canal in Southeast Alaska. Relations between the two had become strained, with the North-West

EARLY ALASKA

Mounted Police stationed at Skagway and U.S. troops stationed at Camp Dyea at the head of navigation. As the tracks of the White Pass and Yukon Railroad approached the summit of the pass, the tension mounted.

A Canadian guard was pacing a beat there to stop construction, and the railroad men were told they could come no farther, since it was British territory.

Stikine Bill went to the summit as an unofficial ambassador. The story goes that he had a bottle of Scotch whisky in each coat pocket and a box of cigars under each arm. When the guard woke up many hours later, the construction gang was working a mile down the shore of the lake.

The hardest part of the building of that railroad was over when the summit of White Pass was reached on Feb. 20, 1899, but other problems arose along the route.

Some of which were posed by Soapy Smith and his gang.

Their interference was mostly of the nuisance type, such as starting shell games along the trail and attempting to operate liquor and gambling dives near the camps.

A White Pass and Yukon Railroad train rests at the 2,900-foot level of the Alaska-Canada boundary, 13 miles northeast of Skagway in Southeast Alaska, in 1899.

Michael J. Heney, contractor of the White Pass and Yukon Railroad, had one strict and simple rule: no liquor allowed in camp.

One of Soapy's men, however, set up such a tent dive near Camp 3, Rocky Point. Heney ordered him off.

The man refused, saying he had as much right to be there as Heney. And maybe he did.

But Heney, like Stikine Bill, was never a man to split hairs over a technicality. He went to the camp foreman, a man by the name of Foy, and pointing to a big overhanging cliff just above the drinking den, told Foy to take the cliff down.

"That rock has got to be out of here by 5 a.m. tomorrow," Heney said within earshot of Soapy's cohort.

Early the next morning, Foy sent a crew to place a few sticks of dynamite in the rock cliff. The men reported all ready at 10 minutes to 5 a.m. Five minutes later, Foy sent a man to the tent to rouse the occupant, who refused – with colorful language – to get up so early.

The Alaska-Canada border, shown here in 1904 somewhere along the boundary with American and Canadian flags flying, passes through remote wilderness areas.

Klondikers, like those shown here stowing their supplies and camping just below the summit of White Pass in 1898, made easy targets for con men and bootleggers.

Foy walked into the man's tent.

"In one minute by this watch I am going to give the order to touch off the time fuse," Foy said. "It will burn for one minute, and then that rock will arrive here or hereabouts."

The man in bed told Foy where to go.

But Foy remained calm.

"I'm too busy to go there this morning," Foy told the fellow. "But you will, unless you jump lively. FIRE!"

Foy used the remaining 60 seconds to retire behind a projecting cliff, where he was joined 10 seconds later by the tent's owner. Together they witnessed the blast – and the demolition of the tent and its liquor supply.

"That rock is down, sir," Foy later reported to Heney.

"Where is the man?" Heney asked.

"The last I saw of him he was high tailing down the trail in his red flannels, cursing at every step," Foy said.

Boundary officially set

A six-man tribunal was established to finally resolve the boundary issue in 1903. Britain appointed Baron Alverstone, the Lord Chief Justice of England, Sir Louis A. Jetté, Lieutenant Governor of the Province of Quebec, and Allen B. Aylesworth to the panel.

President Theodore Roosevelt chose Secretary of War Elihu Root, Massachusetts Sen. Henry Cabot Lodge and Arthur Turner, ex-Senator from Washington, to represent America.

Roosevelt also sent word that if the panel did not settle the dispute to his liking, he would send in the U.S. Marines.

The United States claimed a continuous stretch of coastline, unbroken by the deep fiords of the region. Canada demanded control of the heads of certain fiords, especially the Lynn Canal, as it gave access to the Yukon.

Canada was confident that it would receive British support in the boundary dispute. Not only was it a British colony, it also had helped Great Britain in the Boer War. However, the British were more concerned about their relations with America than with Canada. They needed U.S. steel and support of the Americans for an arms race with Germany.

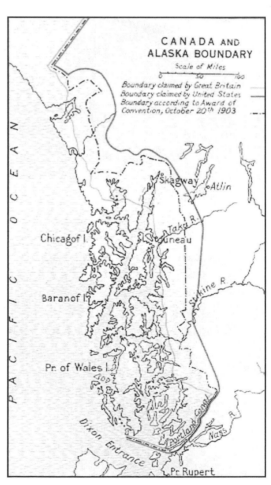

A boundary survey crew travels into Alaska's wilderness to officially mark the border between Alaska and Canada in 1904.

After three weeks of deliberations, the British representative sided with the three Americans, and the committee rejected the Canadian claims by a vote of four to two. The Alaska-Canada border was established on paper and various expeditions ordered to survey the vast area.

In 1904, crews from both Canada and the United States started work on the panhandle of Southeast Alaska. They used boats, packhorses and backpacks to reach the remote mountains.

A crew signals with heliograph near Monument 92 along the Alaska-Canada boundary.

A formal treaty was signed in 1908 between the United States and Great Britain setting up the International Boundary Commission to mark the boundary officially.

Thomas C. Riggs, who served as governor of Alaska from 1918-1921, was at this time a crew chief for the International Boundary Commission. He spent eight summers marking the border and called them the happiest time in his life. When Riggs and his crew tied in the last section of the border around McCarthy in August 1914, he sent a telegram to his supervisor that read: "Regret my work completed."

In 1925 the treaty was amended. It created a permanent International Boundary Commission to keep an accurately located and visible border. The markers are shaped like the Washington Monument and are to be placed within sight of one another.

After setting the final point on the Alaska-Canada boundary on the shore of the Arctic Ocean, Thomas C. Riggs and J.D. Craig stand in front of flags representing each country on July 15, 1912.

G L I M M E R S O F G O L D

5

GOLD-RUSH ENTERTAINERS ARRIVE

Although the frenzied gold seekers of the North lacked most of the luxuries, not to say necessities, of civilized living, they did have theaters – even opera houses. There had been entertainment in California's gold rush of 1849, but never had there been such garish and colorful entertainers as in the days of '98. And many of them went on to fame and fortune.

Sid Grauman offered vaudeville-style entertainment from tents in Nome during the gold-rush days.

Sid Grauman, later owner of Hollywood's Grauman's Chinese Theatre and high priest of Hollywood's cinematic palaces, started his career producing tent shows in Nome. Even before that he had been Dawson's foremost newsboy, and he never became so lordly that he disowned his Klondike newsboy days. In fact, he credited them as giving him the ideal background for his later career.

Another future showman early discovered that a man would spend his last dollar to be amused. Alexander Pantages concluded that supplying amusement was sounder business than supplying supposedly primary needs. Like Grauman, he started in Dawson and ended up at Nome. His Pantages Orpheum provided the best show in town. After he returned to the states, he started acquiring film palaces and ended up selling his circuit for $24 million.

Most of the actors and actresses providing gold-rush entertainment were "waitresses, box hustlers, salesmen, tinhorn gamblers and the usual hangers-on of a mining camp," sources reported. A few, however, were professionals – and some went on to stardom.

Alexander Pantages was born on the Greek island of Andros. A theatrical entrepreneur, he created a large and popular vaudeville circuit and amassed a fortune.

Marjorie Rambeau, for instance, who later became one of Broadway's leading beauties, was a child performer when she came north, traveling with her mother and missionary grandmother. The mother took no chances with her little daughter and dressed her as a boy, and it was as a street urchin Rambeau made her debut. She was a great hit singing and playing a banjo at Tex Rickard's famous Northern Saloon in Nome. Enchanted customers pelted her with gold nuggets.

Another small fry who later became famous was Hoagy Carmichael. He also entertained Tex Rickard's customers in Nome. Only 8 years old, he was billed as the "boy wonder," playing the piano in the Northern.

The entertainment business proved as profitable a gold mine as any of the rich claims on Bonanza Creek, and there were no lack of entrepreneurs to take advantage of the gold-seekers' frantic search for amusement and forgetfulness.

The theaters in boomtown Dawson were perhaps the best known, but many other communities also had their "palaces of amusement."

Some of them were quite primitive. The Wrangell Opera House was described by a traveler, Julius Price, as "a canvas-covered frame shanty ... there was no attempt at scenery and the performers were particularly feeble."

In 1897 there was an opera house in Circle City, and miners for 200 miles around would mush in to attend performances in the double-decker log building. George Snow, who once starred with Edwin Booth, put on Shakespearean plays and vaudeville acts.

A theatrical troupe marooned in Circle City one winter, when the Yukon River froze early, had to give the only play in its repertoire night after night. The play, "The Puyallup Queen," finally palled, and after seeing it nightly for seven months, the audience rebelled and howled as loudly as the malamutes outside.

Weary miners from Circle City longed for entertainment during the gold-rush days.

Dawson becomes center of entertainment

When Circle City and Fortymile were emptied as a result of the Klondike strike, Dawson became the center of entertainment.

After the historic discovery of gold on Bonanza Creek in August 1896, Dawson City grew up from a marshy swamp near the confluence of the Yukon and Klondike rivers. In two years it had become the largest city in Canada west of Winnipeg with a population that fluctuated between 30,000 and 40,000 people.

Joe Ladue, a former prospector-turned-outfitter, founded the settlement on the belief that merchants in gold camps prospered more than miners. The town's founder owned a sawmill at the mining camp of Sixtymile, and while miners staked their claims, Ladue staked out a town site.

He anticipated the coming building boom and rafted his sawmill to the new town site, which he named Dawson City in honor of George M. Dawson, a Canadian geologist who helped survey the boundary between Alaska and the Northwest Territories in the 1870s.

When he set up his sawmill in Dawson, there were two log cabins, a small warehouse and a few tents, with a total population of 25 men

The Orpheum Theatre, pictured here on Dawson's Front Street in the late 1890s, was a hub of vaudeville activity.

Actors perform a play on stage in gold-rush Dawson.

and one woman. Ladue sold all the rough lumber his small mill could produce, at $140 per thousand feet, to the miners working on Rabbit Creek, later renamed Bonanza.

As word of the rich discoveries spread, more and more people headed north. Before the ice had cleared from the river, the largest rush yet to be seen in the north was under way. By late July 1897, the district had 5,000 people, and Ladue raised his lot prices in Dawson to between $800 and $8,000.

Wave after wave of gold seekers arrived, and with them came many entertainers who transformed Dawson from a mining camp into one of the most interesting cities in all of North America. It didn't take long for theaters to pop up in the rough-and-tumble atmosphere.

Dawson's first theater was grandiosely called the Opera House. It was in reality a log building with a bar and gambling rooms in front and a theater in the rear. A traveler who attended its opening night described it:

"A few nights after my arrival in Dawson, I visited the theatre, which for a week or more had been advertising a grand opening by means of homemade posters made by daubing black paint on sheets of wrapping paper.

"The programme was of a Vaudeville nature and included half a dozen song-and-dance 'artists,' a clog dancer, a wrestling match between Jim Slavin, an old-time fighter, and Pat Rooney, a Canadian.

"The interior of the little theatre was crowded

Known as Black Prince, Sanko performed at the Monte Carlo Saloon and Theatre.

to the walls with an audience composed almost entirely of men dressed in gaudy-colored Mackinaw clothes and fur coats and caps. The orchestra consisted of a piano, violin and a flute, and the footlights were tallow candles, whose faint light was reinforced by oddly shaped reflectors made from stray bits of tin.

"The low ceiling was of hewn logs, and the walls on either side were lined with boxes, to which the miners could gain admission by paying double the price for liquors and cigars. The stage was a narrow affair, and very little space intervened between the blue denim drop curtain and the back wall of the building."

R.C. Kirk, author of "Twelve Months in the Klondike," went on to describe the play as beginning at the conclusion of a medley of popular airs by the orchestra, and during the ensuing performance, he said, the audience shouted and cheered the men and women on the stage, all of whom seemed to appreciate the laughable burlesqueness of the thing.

Crowds gather at the ruins of the Opera House on Front Street after a fire destroyed the building on Nov. 25, 1897. The Monte Carlo can be seen a few doors down.

A masquerade ball was given in the Opera House on the evening before Thanksgiving 1897, and during the early hours of the following morning, the building caught fire. Before it could be checked, the building was totally destroyed.

With the disappearance of the Opera House, other dancehalls and small theaters sprang up. By the middle of the following summer, more theaters were being erected. Some of the buildings were built of logs, others made of boards and several were walled in with nothing more substantial than cloth.

The price of admission to the theaters after the Opera House burned was 50 cents, which included a drink of liquor at the bar.

Theaters turn modern

By 1898, the buildings were quite elaborate; some of them even had painted scenery and dressing rooms. Theaters became increasingly sophisticated as Dawson grew from a gold camp to a thriving city.

The Pavilion was lit by gas instead of candles or coal oil, and in its dazzling light, a happy horde of gold miners from the creeks spent $12,000 on opening night.

To top that, the illumination of the Monte Carlo, which opened its theater the same year, was generated by wonders of wonders – electricity.

One of Dawson's finest theaters was built by Arizona Charlie Meadows, a former frontiersman, cowboy, gold miner, showman and crack shot. The Palace Grand theater opened in gala style July 1899.

The Palace Grand was one of Dawson's most beautiful theaters.

Structurally, the theater was a combination of a luxurious European opera house and a boomtown dancehall. It played host to a variety of entertainment, from wild-west shows to opera. When the show got slow, Arizona himself would get on stage and perform shooting tricks for the audience.

The Palace Grand was truly magnificent by gold camp standards. It could seat 2,200 and had several hundred "opera chairs" for the comfort of its more opulent patrons.

And what kind of entertainment was offered these patrons? It was a varied fare – songs and dances, comic sketches and one-act farces were popular. Also popular were local songs and sketches such as "Christmas on the Klondike," "The Klondike Millionaire" and "Star of the Yukon."

Two outstanding hits were written and produced by John Milligan. Titled "Still Water Willie," and its sequel, "Still Water Willie's Wedding Night," they were satires on Klondike millionaire Swiftwater Bill Gates, who was notorious for his matrimonial imbroglios.

Other locally written plays included a one-act "Ole Olson in the Klondike," and a full three-act comedy "Working a Lay in the Klondike." It's a shame that these dramas didn't survive in print or manuscript.

A crowd gathers in the bar of the Monte Carlo in 1898 Dawson.

Victorian drama and melodrama were presented, as well. "A Father's Curse," "Sentenced to Death" and "Jack the Ripper" to name a few. Later came such serious productions as "Faust," "Camille," "The Count of Monte Cristo" and "East Lynn."

Miners liked Little Egypt.

"Uncle Tom's Cabin" went over well, too. Eliza's crossing of the ice was especially realistic and well received, even though the ice was represented by crumpled newspapers. Eliza had actually seen people crossing the ice on the frozen Yukon River, so she knew just how to do it.

However, the bloodhounds were a big disappointment, wrote A.T. Walden in his book, "A Dog Puncher on the Yukon."

"The bloodhounds were represented by one malamute puppy drawn across the stage in a sitting position by an invisible wire and yelling his displeasure to the gods," according to Walden.

There were specialty acts, as well – knife throwers, trained dogs, dancing bears, magicians, tumblers, Lady Godiva and Little Egypt.

Multitude of musicians perform

There were so many musicians wandering around Dawson it was said they outnumbered the gambling house dealers.

They sang the popular songs of the period – "There'll be a Hot Time in the Old Town Tonight," "Put Your Arms Around Me, Honey," "Bird in a Gilded Cage," "After the Ball," "Ta-ra-ra Bomder-e" and "Somebody Loves Me."

But Tappan Adney, who wrote "The Klondike Stampede of 1897-1899," said he wasn't impressed by the female vocalists.

"The less said the better," he wrote, "with a few exceptions."

People flank the entrance to The Peoples' burlesque theater in Skagway awaiting entry into a "Big Show." Also advertised are fights for the Black Prince, Kid Gallagher and Dick Agnew of California. One could "buy a drink at the bar and walk in."

The Black Prince, a prize fighter connected with the Monte Carlo, serves drinks while a man called Jack, Gertie Lovejoy, also known as Diamond Tooth Gertie, Cad Wilson – the toast of Dawson – and Tommy Dolan, brother of comedian Eddie Dolan, play cards.

One exception was Cad Wilson, whose lively personality and theme song, "Such a Nice Girl, Too," made her the toast of Dawson. When she left after one season, it was reported that she took with her $24,000.

Another favorite was "Klondike Kate" Rockwell. She received thousands of dollars a month for singing and dancing. Among the gowns in her wardrobe was a Paris import that cost her $1,500. She was reputed to have collected $100,000 in cash and $50,000 in jewels during her Dawson reign.

Pantages persuaded her to finance a new music hall on the site of the Tivoli, which had burned down. But when the news of the Nome strike came, Pantages left without Kate. In 1906 she sued him on the grounds that he had run out on their partnership and on his promise to marry her. The suit was settled out of court.

The gold-filled North Country drew entertainers like Klondike Kate Rockwell, pictured here on the left, along with an unidentified dancer, into the rugged wilderness of the Klondike and Alaska.

Above: Klondikers pushed north from Dawson when they heard the news of nuggets lacing the beaches of Nome, pictured above.

Below: When miners left Dawson for Nome, actors and actresses followed them north and continued to perform for audiences in newly established theaters.

Little 9-year-old Margie Newman sang sweet, childish and sentimental songs that brought gold out of the miners' pockets, too, and tears from their eyes. The little "Princess of the Klondike" had a childish grace, according to a Dawson newspaper reporter of the time, "that was so moving she was frequently bombarded by coins, nuggets and boxes of candy." She also left Dawson considerably richer.

But according to many reports, the most talented actor in Dawson was a donkey known as "Wise Mike." He was usually curled up sleeping around the potbellied stove in a saloon.

"One of the practical jokes in Dawson was to get a 'loaded' newcomer to kick the old donkey in the ribs," wrote Richard O'Connor in his book, "High Jinks on the Klondike."

Mike would jump up, snorting and napping his teeth, and then attempt to wrestle with his tormentor. It was all a game with Mike, but the cheechako believed himself in mortal danger.

"After scaring his opponent out of his wits and listening appreciatively to the audience's laughter, Mike would throw himself dog-like next to the stove again," O'Connor wrote.

That donkey was the greatest comedian west of Broadway, according to the Dawson wags.

Even as today, there was trouble occasionally with dancers accused of indecent exposure.

At the Novelty theater, the leading attraction was Freda Maloof, "the Turkish Whirlwind Danseuse," who performed a dance deemed so salacious that the North-West Mounted Police, established in 1873, ordered her to tone down her act. She tried to prove to the judge that there was nothing lewd in her act – that the dance she performed was an "integral part of the Turkish branch of 'Mohammedanism.'"

However, the magistrate, who fined her $25, was not in the least impressed by her argument – perhaps because she was Greek, not Turkish.

As the diggings from Dawson to Nome began to wane around 1902, gold-rush entertainers and prospectors streamed into Alaska's Interior where another bonanza tantalized those with golden dreams.

6

GOLDEN HEART CITY GROWS

During the gold-rush heyday, communities like Hope, Circle City and Nome teemed with thousands of hopeful fortune seekers. But as stampeders' desires for golden riches turned into the reality of lost dreams, most gold-rush boomtowns dwindled into little more than faded memories.

One Alaska town, however, continued to grow even after the lure of gold lost its hold on miners' imaginations. But Fairbanks, located on the Chena River in Interior Alaska, didn't begin as a well-thought-out plan for civilization. It began as a wilderness trading post set up in the wrong place at the wrong time of year.

Its roots can be traced to one merchant, Elbridge Truman Barnette, a man who wanted to position himself as a supplier of goods to those who sought their fortunes from the earth.

Elbridge Truman Barnette is credited with establishing Fairbanks in Alaska's Interior.

Fort Egbert at Eagle, pictured above in 1902, was the planned terminus for J.J. Healy's all-American route railroad at the turn-of-the-last century.

Barnette, who had stampeded to Dawson City after hearing news of the Klondike strike in 1897, had some experience with boomtowns. Born in Akron, Ohio, in 1863, he had joined several mining stampedes in the American West.

When Barnette found all the best claims already staked in Dawson, he went to work managing some mines for the North American Trading and Transportation Company. Barnette returned to the states shortly thereafter, and by late 1900, had raised enough capital to start a new venture in the North Country based on information told him by J.J. Healy of the NAT&T Company.

Prospector turns trader

Barnette learned Healy was planning to build an all-American route railroad to reach the Klondike gold fields, which would start from Valdez and travel to Fort Egbert at Eagle on the Yukon River. Barnette knew that the railroad builders would have to construct a bridge to get across the river at Tanana Crossing – Tanacross – where the Interior's main trail met the Tanana River.

The Gold Rush of '98 was still in full swing at the turn of the century, even though the original strike around Dawson had pretty much played out. Stampeders now were swarming into Eagle and Nome, where even the laziest gold seekers could pan out enough dust from the beach sand to grubstake the next bonanza.

Barnette thought a trading post sitting at a strategic spot with heavy traffic just might make him a rich man, and a trading operation at Tanacross would be accessible by river in the summer and by railroad year-round. He decided to take a stock of supplies by steamship to St. Michael, then transfer the goods onto a smaller boat and travel up the Yukon, up the Tanana and then unload his cargo at Tanacross.

Barnette steamed north out of Seattle in the summer of 1901. He arrived in St. Michael in July with 130 tons of freight and a 124-foot riverboat named *Arctic Boy* that he'd purchased along the way in Circle City.

But once he'd landed in the Far North, it didn't take long for his plans to change.

While cruising around St. Michael harbor, the *Arctic Boy* hit a rock and sank. With all his funds tied up in the trading post idea, Barnette scrambled to find alternative transportation before bad weather set in.

He asked Charles W. Adams, captain of the 150-foot steamer *Lavelle Young*, to get him as close to Tanacross as possible.

Steamboats *Lavelle Young* and *Casca* carried many stampeders as they plied the waters of Alaska during the gold-rush era.

A group of people repair a birch-bark canoe in the village of Tanacross, where E.T. Barnette thought a trading post would prosper.

Adams told Barnette he didn't know of any steamboat that had gone up the Tanana, because the river had impassable rapids. The captain eventually negotiated a contract, however, which included a clause stating that Barnette, his wife, Isabelle, four men and all their freight would be put off at the farthest point the boat could reach – wherever that point might be.

Several weeks later, low water and the Bates Rapids forced the *Lavelle Young* to halt its progress in the Tanana River – about 200 miles shy of Tanacross.

A determined Barnette told Capt. Adams he'd heard from Indians that the Chena River was really a slough that led back onto the Tanana River. He convinced the captain to swing the *Lavelle Young* around and go up the Chena. It wasn't long before shallow water stopped progress again.

A lengthy argument ensued. The 37-year-old trader wanted to be taken back to the confluence of the Tanana and the Chena. He thought he'd have a better chance to go farther up the Tanana by shallow-draft barge from that point.

But Adams said he had to drop the cargo somewhere closer, because it was too dangerous to take the heavily loaded steamer back downstream. The boat could be pushed hard and fast onto a sandbar and the current would make it tough to get the boat off.

Adams also knew that the warm summer days could turn into chilly autumn overnight and that plunging temperatures would not be far behind.

Barnettes put ashore

On Aug. 26, 1901, the captain took the ship to a point about 10 miles from the mouth of the slough where the bank was high and trees plentiful. There, the crew of the *Lavelle Young* tied the stern-wheeler to a stout spruce tree on the south bank and unloaded the Barnettes, Barnette's partner Charles Smith, and the other four men – Jim Eagle, Dan McCarthy, Ben Atwater and John Johnson.

While swarms of mosquitoes descended upon them, the ship's crew helped the men fell trees and clear a space to unload cargo. That night, prospectors – who'd seen the steamer chug up the Chena – paid the camp a visit.

"From his lookout on the dome at the head of Cleary and Pedro creeks, (Felix) Pedro first saw a smoke far across the Tanana Valley – a close examination with his field glass disclosed that it was rising from

An olive-skinned, mustached, immigrant prospector named Felix Pedro spotted the *Lavelle Young* steaming up the Chena River in the rugged wilderness of the Tanana Valley, above.

a steamer on the distant river," reported an article in the May 9, 1903, issue of The Fairbanks Miner. "He watched it descend to the mouth of the Chena and enter that river, which Pedro had fully explored the year before. Hastily informing his companion (Tom Gilmore) of the locality of the steamer, they descended from the hills, crossed the valley to the Chena and that night came to the boat tied to the bank where the town of Fairbanks now grows. The merchant and the miner – the only representatives of their classes then in the splendid Tanana Valley – passed a pleasant evening aboard the boat."

Barnette informed Pedro of his inability to get over the rapids and of his intention to establish a trading post at Tanacross.

"Pedro quietly informed the merchant that he had found 'prospects' on several nearby creeks, and then and there it was agreed to establish a post on the bank where the steamer was tied up. The next

Felix Pedro was the first customer at E.T. Barnette's trading post along the Chena River.

day, Pedro and Gilmore renewed their packs (including beans, bacon and flour) from the ample supplies on the steamer and again disappeared in the wilderness," the newspaper reported.

Using the logs felled the previous day, the crew helped Barnette and his men build a small cabin and 6-foot-high walls for a 26-by-54-foot warehouse.

Soon $20,000 worth of freight, including general supplies, windows and doors, a steam launch, tools, prospecting equipment, food, hardware, a horse and a team of dogs were lined up along the remote riverbank. The freight was loaded inside the makeshift warehouse and covered with tents. (The trading post stood on a one-acre site on the riverbank between modern-day Barnette and Cushman streets.)

When the higher and lighter *Lavelle Young* departed a few days later, it left the Barnettes stranded on a bank a couple hundred miles from where they originally wanted to be with no hope of moving for many, many months. A crying Mrs. Barnette was one of the last sights the crew saw as the boat pulled away. She was not looking forward to spending a long, cold winter in the middle of the Alaska wilderness in a camp that Barnette had christened Chenoa City.

The first year at the trading post was uneventful, according to that May issue of The Fairbanks Miner, which was the only issue ever published by its editor, Judge James Wickersham, in an effort to raise funds for a hike up Denali.

"... That winter Dan McCarty went out to Valdez and met Frank J. Cleary, Mrs. Barnette's brother, and these two young men crossed the mighty Alaskan Range in midwinter, came down the Delta River and amid hardships and suffering they reached the Post on February 20, 1902, traveling the last four days without food.

The Barnettes left their trading post and headed to Valdez via dog team in March 1902 – not a trip for the faint of heart as this photo of Tiekel River Canyon indicates.

"On March 10, Captain and Mrs. Barnette left the Post for Valdez with dog teams loaded with the rich furs purchased during the winter. They went across the Tanana Valley, up the Delta and climbed through the Alpine passes of the St. Elias range, and though often in water and snow, reached Valdez in safety and thence went to Puget Sound for the next summer's outfit for the Post."

The Barnettes returned to St. Michael a few months later with more stock and a new shallow-draft boat named *Isabelle*.

While waiting in St. Michael for the *Isabelle* to be assembled – using machinery from the wreck of the sunken *Arctic Boy* – Barnette encountered Wickersham.

After hearing about the trading post along the Chena River, Wickersham, the newly appointed U.S. district judge for the territory, suggested Barnette rename his post in honor of a man the judge mightily admired: Republican Sen. Charles W. Fairbanks of Indiana.

In September, when the *Isabelle* was seaworthy, Barnette and his entourage headed off to the Fairbanks Trading Post. The trip was uneventful until the steamer encountered extreme low water in the Chena and couldn't make it to the trading post.

Gold!

Barnette's spirits brightened, however, when he learned that Felix Pedro had discovered a large quantity of gold on a small, unnamed creek 12 miles north of Barnette's trading post. The 42-year-old prospector also had staked discovery claims on four more creeks that flowed from a hill he named Pedro Dome.

According to The Fairbanks Miner, Pedro and Gilmore had gone to the post in April and renewed their prospecting outfits. They only had $100, but Cleary, though instructed to sell only for cash, gave them a full outfit and charged the balance to his own account.

Pedro returned in early July and reported that Gilmore had gone to Circle City. He was sick and got both medicines and provisions and returned to the mountains.

"On the 28th he again came into the store, very much elated and announced very secretly to Cleary that he had 'STRUCK IT.' He had

Miners work claim No. 5 Above Discovery on Fairbanks Creek.

found rich prospects on Pedro Creek but in his nervous and weak condition had been unable to sink to the bedrock – though he had gold to show as evidence of his success," the article reported.

"Pedro was known to many to be a careful and competent miner and prospector. He had been followed so often by others who sought to get the advantage of his well-known superior information and knowledge of the creeks, that when his prospects on Pedro and Cleary grew to be a certainty, he was nervously afraid these camp followers would descend upon him and stake the creeks befo[r]e he could get his friends located.

"To avoid them, he camped over on Fish Creek and came quietly across the divide and prospected even without building fires to attract their attention. He succeeded in locating the best-known claims for himself and friends – to which he was certainly entitled by reason of his arduous labors and great success. His report at the Post was quietly made known, and (Frank) Costa, Cleary and his other friends stampeded off and staked. Pedro staked both discovery on Pedro and Cleary creeks, and the splendid dome between these golden creeks is his monument – Pedro's Dome. From its summit one overlooks the wide Tanana Valley framed on its southern limit by the giant peaks of the Alaskan Range – Mt. McKinley, at its western flank, the royalist of them all.

"Accompanied by Ed Quinn and Smallwood, Pedro set out for the creeks secretly and by night and taking with them plenty of supplies.

"They sank a hole to bedrock, and there lay the glittering gold – seven feet of pay dirt. Other holes were sunk, and pay was located on Pedro, Cleary and Gold Stream. Locations were made, notices prepared and again Cleary and McCarthy took their way through the wilderness – this time to Circle City to record a large number of claims. Pedro's claims have been carefully prospected and he now seems to be sure of Fortune's smile."

Pedro, born Felice Pedroni in Bologna, Italy, in 1860, had searched for gold in the Tanana Valley for seven years. After his rich discovery on July 22, he continued prospecting and by 1903 had interest in more than 12 claims in top-producing grounds.

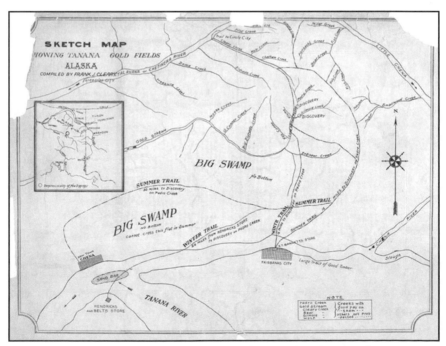

A 1904 sketch maps gold discoveries around Fairbanks and the Tanana Valley.

Stampeders flocked north to Fairbanks when they heard of rich gold fields.

In 1906, Pedro traveled to Tacoma, Washington, and married Mary Ellen Doran, whom he'd met earlier in Fairbanks. Following a honeymoon in Italy, the couple returned to the Interior via the Valdez-Fairbanks Trail in 1907.

The wiry Italian died of pneumonia in Fairbanks on July 22, 1910, exactly eight years after discovering his first rich gold claim.

Barnette's gamble pays off

Barnette knew the potential for an all-out stampede to Alaska's Interior. He vigorously promoted the Tanana gold fields and even sent his cook, a Japanese musher named Jujiro Wada, to Dawson to spread the word.

In January 1903, when the Tanana gold strike made front-page news in Dawson, even the 53-degree-below-zero temperatures couldn't slow the stampede. And although the trail to the Tanana District was in fairly good shape, many of the 1,000 or so men who darted out of Dawson took a shorter route on their way to riches and almost lost their lives. Many had to eat their pack animals when their food ran out.

Three months later, Barnette traveled to Dawson. He was quoted as saying:

"At the time of leaving Fairbanks, about 100 or 150 persons had arrived, mostly from Dawson, and a large number of others were reported within a day or two journey of the camp. Fully 200 shacks and cabins of various descriptions were in course of construction two weeks ago."

Stampeders head for the creeks

After breakup, more stampeders piled into scows, rafts, steamers and small boats and sailed down the Yukon River and the 300 miles of the Tanana to get to the new diggings. More scrambled across from the Koyukuk and Rampart regions to stake claims along creeks around Fairbanks, including Cleary, Dome, Ester, Fish, Gold Stream, Pedro and Vault. The miners and prospectors then re-supplied at Barnette's trading post.

Barnette's promotion plan worked so well that he soon ran short of supplies. During the initial days, he had to hire men with rifles to guard his stock.

His high prices were a problem, too, and the miners finally retaliated. They held a miners' meeting and forced Barnette to cut his price on flour from $12 to $6 per sack.

While Barnette was enjoying a booming business at his trading post, he also was looking to the future. He laid out a town site block down by the river, named streets and encouraged people to settle.

Town lots sold for only a $2.50 recording fee.

Fairbanks began to grow as more stampeders arrived.

Above: The steamer *Lavelle Young* lands at Fairbanks in June 1904 loaded with hopeful prospectors and businessmen.

Below: Travelers head to Fairbanks from Valdez via stagecoach in May 1907.

Upper right: By 1904, Fairbanks had grown into a substantial city.

Lower right: This commercial building in Fairbanks, photographed in 1905, housed a bank with safety deposit vaults and a drugstore.

Above: Early Fairbanks waterfront views usually included sternwheelers loading and unloading passengers and cargo. As many six or eight ships came into Fairbanks daily during the early days of the rush.

Below: Many miners who came to the Interior ended up digging underground gold mines in places like Fairbanks Creek.

Above: Three men work a windlass at a mining operation along Fairbanks Creek.

Below: Some mining operations, like the Fairbanks Gold Mining Company, used dredges to mine gold.

RESIDENCE AND GARDEN, FIRST AVENUE,
FAIRBANKS, ALASKA.

Upper left: Early residents in Fairbanks found the soil fertile enough to grow a multitude of flowers and vegetables. Gardens, like this one on First Avenue, flourished.
Lower left: Cabbages filled early settlers' gardens.
Above: This crop of celery and the surrounding greenhouses show that Fairbanks residents enjoyed fresh vegetables in the Far North.
Below: Man's best friend helps a man and a boy till land near Fairbanks.

Above: One could buy "pure milk and cream, 25 cents a quart," from Hinckley's Dairy.

Below: A horse-drawn sleigh delivers milk to the pioneers of Fairbanks. Note how the horse is draped to protect it from the severe cold.

Above: Rugged pioneers cut ice from the Chena River.

Below: A horse-drawn wagon hauls ice to customers in Fairbanks.

Above: Residents needed to have a good supply of wood cut before winter set in at Fairbanks. Note the outhouse on the left side of the photo.

Below: An early 1900 Fairbanks City Band poses for a snapshot.

Above: Two horse-drawn fire wagons carrying ladders emerge from the ground floor of the City Hall building.

Below: Fairbanks, glowing at midnight, had grown into a modern town by 1907.

Miners who didn't mind hard work had a chance to find pay dirt.

Had Barnette known back in August 1901 that Pedro would discover rich gold deposits north of Fairbanks, he would have been better off establishing his trading post on the north bank of the river. For years the residents wrestled with the problem of bridging the Chena River, and many of the first bridges were wiped out by ice during spring breakups.

A wide variety of people made their way to Fairbanks to try their hands in the rich diggings. But several accounts said that during the winter of 1902-03 the stampeders were predominately ne'er do-wells who were kicked out of Dawson.

It didn't take long for those looking for easy money, but not willing to work, to leave the area. The gold in the creeks was deeper than the gold found in the Klondike, so machinery needed to be brought in to work the claims. Most of the "get-rich-quick" miners left for easier diggings.

"Not more than 100 people who came out of the 700 or 800 that came into Fairbanks during the winter of 1902 and 1903 remained in the Fairbanks Mining District in June 1903," said Abe Spring, the first mayor of Fairbanks.

Judge comes to town

Many miners became discouraged and left the area, but more people made Fairbanks home when Wickersham decided to build a jail and government offices at Third and Cushman streets – on a lot that Barnette had cut out from his trading post site and donated to the community for that purpose.

Wickersham's decision to move his judicial headquarters from Eagle to Fairbanks helped to clean up the town and make it the center of gold mining in the Interior.

His diary notation for April 20, 1903, describes what he found upon arriving in Fairbanks.

"At this time there are three streets roughly staked out through the woods, parallel to the river. The site was covered with a fine body of spruce timber from 6 to 24 inches in diameter, which is now being cut and built up into houses. The Fairbanks hotel is a two-story log house and lodges 40 or 50 people.

"There are probably 500 people here – mostly in tents, but log houses are being constructed as rapidly as possible. Several men are sawing these logs into boards with the whipsaw, and such handmade lumber sells for $200 to $250 per thousand feet. ...

"The town is just now in its formation period – town lots are at a premium – jumping, staking, recording, building!" the judge wrote.

Several businesses, including the Arcade Café, Empire Coffee House, the Senate, Seattle, Tanana and Eagle saloons, and the O.K. Baths skirt the Chena River in early Fairbanks.

Above: Men construct a log bridge across Goldstream Creek in the Fairbanks Mining District at Mile 460.6.

Below: Other mining communities, like Ester City, also built up around Fairbanks.

The gold in the statue called "Venus the Milo in solid Gold," cast by the Washington-Alaska Bank of Fairbanks, by assayer J. Adams, was produced from 2 Below Ester. The statue was owned by H.G.C. Baldry and valued at $49,750 in the early 1900s.

"It's a motley crowd, too," Wickersham noted. "Miners, sour-doughs, cheechakos, gamblers, Indians, Negroes, Japanese, dogs, prostitutes, music, drinking! It is rough but healthy and the beginning, I hope, of an American Dawson."

Tall brass scales took the place of cash registers and gold dust the place of money. Miners tossed their pokes over the counter to the bartender to weigh out enough dust to pay the bill – $16 an ounce in trade was the current rate.

Many establishments offered to supply liquid refreshment and entertainment, including the Northern, Tanana, Senate and Washington saloons, and the Pioneer, Minook and Flora Dora Music Hall.

Fairbanks becomes civilized

The city, which was incorporated on Dec. 26, 1903, next turned its attention to laying sidewalks, digging drains and supplying the citizens with water, power and fire protection.

From 1903 to 1906, Wickersham's dream took shape. The city's population, which exploded to more than 3,000, had a post office, fire department and electric lights by yearend 1903.

Between 1904-1905, the tent and log cabin commercial district transformed into frame architecture with the advent of sawmills. Fairbanks was well on its way to becoming the center for commerce in the Interior.

Several little communities built up at diggings around Fairbanks, too, including Ester and Cleary City. It wasn't long before residents of the area saw a need for dependable, year-round means of transportation to move people and supplies to and from the mines.

The Tanana Mines Railway began after Falcon Joslin and Martin Harris of Dawson learned of the gold strikes in the Chena and Chatanika river basins. The pair traveled to the Tanana Valley, scoped out the area and laid out plans.

Construction began in late summer 1904 at Chena. The main line was completed by mid-July 1905, and then construction continued on the branch up the Goldstream valley through Fox. That branch was finished in September when it reached Gilmore.

The railroad was refinanced under a new name, Tanana Valley Railroad, in 1907 and construction began on the second phase – tracks to Chatanika.

The original route was planned to go over Cleary Summit, but mining activity in the Dome, Vault, Ridgetop and Olnes areas changed the route to go up the Fox Creek valley so it could serve the new communities.

The construction crew reached Chatanika after building an additional 19.2 miles of railroad in four months, which included more than a mile of trestles and bridges.

Railroad track gangs helped build the Tanana Valley Railroad near Fairbanks.

GLIMMERS OF GOLD

Above: Until the arrival of Engine No. 1 in Fairbanks on July 4, 1905, men and animals provided the "horsepower" for roadbed construction on the Tanana Valley Railroad. Engine No. 1, the first steam locomotive in Alaska's Interior, had been the first steam locomotive in the Yukon Territory.

Below: Businesses grew up alongside the railroad tracks in Fairbanks.

Above: Students pose in front of the Fairbanks Public School on May 26, 1908.

Below: Dressed in their Sunday best, this group of women appears to be having a garden party in early Fairbanks.

Above: Skating on the Chena River helps pass the time during long winter days in Fairbanks.

But in the springtime, the Chena can cause major damage when the ice breaks up. The first bridge, built at Cushman Street between 1904-1905, and the second bridge at Wendell Street, to the east of Barnette's Cache, both were demolished by ice and debris. A bridge at Turner Street, which had a span that could be pulled back manually, finally became the head of navigation.

Below: Flooding from the Chena River can pose threats to people and property, as in the flood of April 1929.

The newly established railroad system provided much-needed transportation to and from the small communities it served and allowed several Fairbanks businesses to branch out to these towns. Saloons and brothels sprang up, as well. Cleary City, four miles from the railroad, boasted eight saloons, two hotels, a bank, a drugstore and several smaller shops.

Fairbanks soon became the center of activity in the Interior. And during a trip to San Francisco, Barnette sold two-thirds interest in his trading post to the Northern Commercial Company. That business decision ultimately led to his and the city's success.

Northern Commercial Company soon replaced Barnette's Cache with its own complex, churches sprang up and the Episcopal mission built a hospital. By 1906, telephone service had been available for a year and the community enjoyed central water distribution, fire mains and fire pumps.

The modern firefighting conveniences couldn't stave off disaster, however, when at about 3 p.m. on May 22, 1906, a wispy curtain at an open window of a dentist's office blew across the flame of one of the dentist's tools. Within minutes, fire exploded throughout the building on the corner of First Avenue and Cushman Street.

A newspaper account stated that four hours later "the heart of town was a black and level waste."

The fire destroyed four full blocks of the Fairbanks commercial district from First to Third avenues and from Turner to Lacey streets. It incinerated two banks, two newspapers, eight saloons, four clothing stores, the federal jail and several restaurants and hotels.

The pioneer spirit of the town's residents wouldn't let the fire get them down, however. Rebuilding began immediately. And since the gold-mining operations were located in a cluster of mines more than a dozen miles from town, prospectors barely paused in their pursuit to unearth golden treasures.

And what about the man who accidentally founded the town? After selling his trading post, Barnette pursued other ventures, including the banking business. His crowning achievement was the Washington-Alaska Bank.

Above: A fire on May 22, 1906, destroyed four city blocks in the heart of Fairbanks.

Below: The elegant Arcade Café was a casualty of the fire and wasn't rebuilt.

But by the time Fairbanks residents learned that the bank had failed in 1911, and $11 million was missing, Barnette and Isabelle had skedaddled. Many years later, people learned that the Barnettes had been spotted living on a ranch in Mexico. The couple later divorced.

Indeed, many things of improper and illegal nature occurred during those gold-rush days in Wickersham's American Dawson. But while Canada had the North-West Mounted Police and courts to keep a lid on adventurers' "anything goes" mentality, the same could not be said for the American Dawson side of the border.

Anarchy reigned in many mining camps in Alaska, and without any official law enforcement officials in the vast majority of the territory, citizens relied on "miners' code" to deal with wrongdoers.

Passengers and 2,800 pounds of gold dust traveled from Fairbanks to Valdez by Kennedy's stage at the turn-of-the-last century. E.T. Barnette is standing to the far right and his wife, Isabelle, is in the center.

Nenana, as seen in 1912, is located 55 road miles southwest of Fairbanks and is in the western-most portion of Tanana Athabascan Indian territory. It was first known as Tortella, an interpretation of the Indian word "Toghotthele," which means "mountain that parallels the river."

Early explorers such as Lt. Henry Allen, Arthur Harper and Robert H. Bates, first entered the Tanana Valley in 1875-1885. However, the Tanana people were accustomed to contact with Europeans due to trading journeys to the village of Tanana, where Russians bartered Western goods for furs.

The discovery of gold in Fairbanks in 1902 brought intense activity to the region. A trading post/roadhouse was constructed by Jim Duke in 1903 to supply river travelers and trade with Indians. St. Mark's Episcopal mission and school was built upriver in 1905. Native children from other communities, such as Minto, attended school in Nenana.

A post office opened in 1908. By 1909, there were about 12,000 residents in the Nenana-Fairbanks area, most drawn by gold-mining activities.

7

TURN-OF-THE-CENTURY JUSTICE

Along with hordes of entertainers and stampeders heading north to seek their fortunes in the gold-laden territory of Alaska in the late 1890s came an abundance of gamblers, con men and thieves. And prior to the arrival of sheriffs and judges to the Last Frontier, a practical application of frontier democracy called the "miners' code" was the only law that ruled the Far North. Each camp decided matters of common concern by majority vote and meted out justice to fit the crime.

When a situation came along that necessitated a meeting, the miners came together and elected a judge and a sheriff. Defendants and plaintiffs then gave their sides of the story, and after all the evidence was weighed, the miners would render a verdict: Murder was punished by hanging; stealing meant a sound whipping or banishment. The guilty had no notice of appeal, no bill of exceptions and no stay of execution.

Miners meted out justice during the early gold-rush days in Alaska.

Miners sometimes took justice into their own hands when it came to matters of the heart, too. With no judges or preachers in the camps, they had to think up unique ways to perform nuptials, as was the case of some lovers on the Koyukuk trail.

Aggie Dalton and Frank McGillis wanted to marry, and in lieu of an official marriage contract, they created a substitute document along with one "French Joe." An account of the ceremony, which took place at a night camp with a group of stampeders en route to a Koyukuk River gold camp, was reported in the society columns of the Yukon Press on March 17, 1899:

Unique contract of marriage

"On the evening of November 10, 1898, a romantic union took place between Frank McGillis and Aggie Dalton, near the mouth of Dall River. Splicing was done by 'French Joe' (J. Durrant), and the form of the contract was as follows:

"Ten miles from the Yukon on the banks of this lake,
For a partner to Koyukuk, McGillis I take;
We have no preacher, and we have no ring,
It makes no difference, it's all the same thing."
– Aggie Dalton

"I swear by my gee-pole, under this tree,
A devoted husband to Aggie I always will be;
I'll love and protect her, this maiden so frail,
From those sourdough bums, on the Koyukuk trail."
– Frank McGillis

"For two dollars apiece, in cheechaco money,
I unite this couple in matrimony;
He be a rancher, she be a teacher,
I do the job up, just as well as a preacher."
– French Joe

8

TOMBSTONE TEMPORARILY TRANSPLANTED

Many of those hardy gunslingers and prospectors who made Tombstone a household word in the late 1800s, landed in Alaska and the Yukon after the demise of the Arizona city. Among them were Ed Schieffelin and Wyatt Earp.

Before arriving in Alaska in the 1880s, Schieffelin had searched for the mother lode of silver in the Apache country of Arizona. Day after day he rose at dawn to search the hills and desert for ore. When a soldier asked him what he was doing going out into the hills every day, he replied, "To collect rocks."

"You keep going out there among those Apaches, and the only rock you will find will be your tombstone," the soldier told him.

After searching for more than a decade, Schieffelin finally discovered the first pure vein of silver. Recalling the soldier's somber warning, he named his claim Schieffelin's Lucky Cuss and founded the Tombstone Mining District, which evolved into Tombstone, Arizona.

Ed Schieffelin briefly searched for a "highway of gold" in Alaska.

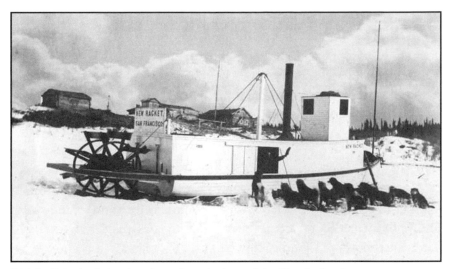
Ed Schieffelin feeds his dogs from the side door of the *New Racket* during winter.

When the silver dwindled, Schieffelin was determined to repeat his success with gold in Alaska. He had an interesting theory that somewhere in Alaska a golden highway crossed the Yukon – a continuation of a great mineral belt that girdled the world from Cape Horn to Asia.

Schieffelin searches for highway of gold

Schieffelin started from St. Michael in the spring of 1883 aboard a little steamer called *New Racket*, built especially for the trip. The Yukon River seemed to wind on endlessly, past sleeping glaciers, high clay banks, walls of granite and mountain ranges. Just a few settlements broke the monotony – old Russian villages at Holy Cross, Nulato and Andreafski.

For 1,000 miles the little vessel chugged, finally getting into the lower Ramparts. Schieffelin poked around, found some specks of gold and was encouraged to think he had found the mineral belt he thought encircled the globe. But winter was coming. Accustomed to the heat of Arizona, he became discouraged by the arctic bleakness and cold. Mining in this forbidding country would never pay, he concluded, and retraced his way without going any farther.

The gold of the Yukon had eluded him. He sold his boat to pioneer explorers and traders Arthur Harper and Jack McQuesten, and for many years it was their lifeline to the outside world.

Schieffelin, who died in 1897 at the age of 49, was buried about two miles from Tombstone. His pick, shovel and the canteen he had carried on the day he'd made his big strike of silver were buried with him.

Wyatt Earp flees to Nome

As Schieffelin was being laid to rest, Wyatt Earp was heading to Nome. He had fled Arizona under indictment for murder following the notorious 1881 massacre of the Clantons at the OK Corral and later the shooting of Frank Stillwell.

Earp, along with brothers Virgil and Morgan and friend Doc Holliday, gained immortality in the shootout with their sworn enemies. Virgil, a U.S. marshal, had deputized Wyatt, and when the bullets stopped flying, three members of the Clanton gang lay dead, and Virgil and Morgan Earp were wounded.

The surviving Clantons charged that the Earp brothers and Holliday stalked their victims, some of whom were unarmed, and shot first without provocation. But the Earps and Holliday claimed that the Clantons were waiting for them and cocked their pistols first.

Earp's 46-year companion, Josephine Marcus, later recalled that she heard the sound of guns that October evening, ran from her house and jumped on a passing wagon heading to the OK Corral. She knew the Earps and the Clantons had a showdown, but in her first moments on the scene, she couldn't tell who was left standing.

Wyatt Earp spent a few years in Alaska following the shootout at Tombstone's OK Corral.

"I didn't know at the time who was wounded and was too frightened to get closer," she later wrote about the incident. "I almost swooned when I saw Wyatt's tall figure very much alive. ... He spotted me, and came across the street. Like a feather-brained girl, my only thought was, 'My God, I haven't got a bonnet on. What will they think?'"

Although the facts of the shootout always will be disputed, the courts acquitted the Earps and Holliday and said the men shot in self-defense. The Clanton gang took revenge later and ambushed Wyatt and Morgan Earp in a saloon, killing Morgan.

Wyatt Earp and Doc Holliday took justice into their own hands by raiding various outlaw hideouts and killing individuals whom they suspected participated in Morgan's death.

Earp fled Arizona and moved to Gunnison, Colorado, where that state's governor refused to extradite Wyatt back to Arizona on the grounds that he could not get a fair trial.

He and Josie spent the next few years moving whenever a new gold-, silver- or copper-mining boomtown appeared. They invested in mines and real estate and operated saloons and gambling parlors, which eventually brought them to Alaska.

A letter found in the basement of the Juneau federal jail in the 1960s shows that Earp may have intended to settle in the Southeast area for a while but was persuaded to move on.

Written to the U.S. marshal in Sitka by the deputy marshal at Juneau, the 1901 letter said that the deputy marshal, along with a posse of local citizens deputized for the encounter, met Earp as his ship docked. In the letter, the deputy marshal called the lawman of the west "Wyatt Earp the notorious desperado."

Wyatt Earp in Nome.

The deputy disarmed Earp and told him he was not welcome in Juneau, according to Alaska State Troopers' "50 Years of History."

The former peace officer left on the next steamship. He then traveled up to Nome, where he opened the Dexter Saloon, which coincidentally bore the same name as the Dexter Corral across Allen Street from the OK Corral in Tombstone. He billed it as the only second-class saloon in Alaska.

The former deputy marshal was less than popular in the Alaska frontier town, according to some sources, although Richard O'Conner, in "High Jinks on the Klondike," wrote:

"The rowdiest sourdough in the North Country quieted down when he (Earp) flecked his eyes over anyone presuming to disturb the peace ... he could face bad luck or danger with the professional gambler's icy nerves."

However, Anton Mazzanovitch told another story.

Wyatt Earp opened a saloon in Nome to cater to hard-working miners, like those pictured above working a rocker, who wanted a drink now and then.

A large crowd stands outside Wyatt Earp's "Second Class Saloon" in 1901.

"After Wyatt struck Alaska, one night he started to show the boys up there how they used to pull a little show down Arizona way," Mazzanovitch reported. "U.S. Marshal Albert Lowe took his (Earp's) gun away, slapped his face and told him to go home and go to bed or he would run him in."

Mazzanovitch's account was corroborated by B.D. Blakeslee, a civil engineer who was mapping the Nome gold region.

"Wyatt got a drink or two too much and got the idea he was a bad man from Arizona and was going to pull some rough stuff, when U.S. Marshal Albert Lowe slapped his face and took his gun away from him," according to Blakeslee.

Earp leaves Alaska

Earp remained in Alaska for four years, running his business during the "season" for making money in mining districts in Alaska – late spring to early fall. When the ground started to freeze, he and Josie would head by steamer back to California because, as with most mining towns, Nome basically shut down.

And according to an article that appeared in the Los Angeles Times on May 1, 1900, he misbehaved in California, too.

"San Francisco, April 30 – Wyatt Earp, gunfighter and all-around 'badman,' was knocked down and out late Saturday night by Tom Mulqueen, the well-known racehorse man. The trouble occurred in a swell Market Street resort near Stockton. ..."

After leaving Alaska, Earp turned up in the boomtowns of Tonopah and Goldfield, Nevada, operating saloons, and it has been said, bunko games. He also worked mining claims in the Mojave Desert.

Wyatt and Josie finally settled in Southern California, where they owned racehorses and lived on their winnings from gambling and real estate speculation. In the 1920s, the couple invested in oil wells, worked on Wyatt's autobiography and drafted a screenplay about his career as a lawman. Earp died in Los Angeles on Jan. 13, 1929, at the age of 80.

By the late 1890s, brave lawmen began to arrive in Alaska. They attempted to stop vigilante justice in the vast, lawless territory.

LAW AND ORDER

9

ALASKA'S FIRST LAWMEN

Alaska's first law officer in the Interior knew a thing or two about the criminal element. Frank Canton, appointed deputy marshal for Circle City in February 1898, had served with distinction as a peace officer in Wyoming and Oklahoma Territory. He'd also escaped from prison while serving time for a litany of offenses.

The sketchy lawman's reputation as a range detective in Wyoming, notably as a killer who ambushed rustlers, secured his appointment in Alaska because he'd come to the attention of one very influential man, according to Gerald O. Williams in the Alaska State Troopers' "50 Years of History."

Portus B. Weare, a leading shareholder of the North American Transportation and Trading Company, which was challenging

Frank Canton found his work cut out for him when he headed to Circle City to serve as the first lawman in Interior Alaska.

the monopoly of the Alaska Commercial Company, felt his business needed the protection of a vigorous law enforcement officer. Weare agreed to supplement Canton's $750 a year salary.

On his way to his new post, weather forced Canton to spend the winter in Rampart in 1898. He tried his hand at prospecting but put his peace officer hat back on in April after passengers onboard a steamboat wintering near Rampart mutinied against their captain. They announced their intention to take the steamboat to Dawson as soon as the waterway opened.

After a two-day hike, Canton reached the vessel and arrested the leaders of the conspiracy. He then convened a meeting of the other passengers, and serving as judge, held a trial and fined the perpetrators $2,000.

Frank Canton arrived in Circle City, at one time a hub of gold-rush activity, in 1899. At the right, the sternwheeler *Yukon* is tied up to the bank of the Yukon River.

No money for law

When one of the takeover leaders attempted to kill him, Canton recognized him as a fugitive from Idaho with a $2,500 bounty on his head. Canton arrested him, and as soon as the ice went out on the Yukon River, he hauled the fellow to Circle City.

By the time he reached his new post, Canton found that most of the miners had moved on to Dawson. Their exodus meant that city coffers were limited, so the lawman had no funds with which to operate. He also found that no one in the community wanted to board federal prisoners for $3 a day, nor act as jailers.

Canton had to borrow money from the Northwest Trading Company to meet the obligations of his office. Shortly thereafter, he wrote to U.S. Marshal James Shoup in Sitka requesting money to meet daily expenses and to construct a jail.

Before he heard back from Shoup, Canton had several more suspects accused of robbery and attempted murder in custody. The small U. S. Army garrison at Circle helped him guard his prisoners while he awaited funds.

To his dismay, the reply he received in March 1899 didn't include money for running the marshal's office or any reimbursement for out-of-pocket expenses. Canton wrote an angry letter back to the U.S. marshal.

"I need some money very bad and wish you would send in some funds at once," he ranted. By that time, Canton had eight prisoners he intended to take to Sitka for trial.

Canton never did receive any funds from Shoup. Instead, he was discharged as a deputy marshal when officials learned he had resigned his Oklahoma position while being audited for fraudulent expense claims. The Justice Department hadn't been aware

Frank Canton spent his first winter in Alaska near Rampart.

Above: Early lawmen in Alaska had to cover vast amounts of territory. These prospectors are camped near the Koyukuk River in 1899.

Below: Camps popped up along creeks throughout Alaska during the gold-rush era, including at the mouth of Slate Creek, shown here, around the Koyukuk in 1898.

that Canton had been appointed a deputy marshal in Alaska until late 1898.

The discharged officer returned to Oklahoma and became deputy marshal for Judge Isaac Parker. In 1907 he became adjutant general of the Oklahoma National Guard, serving until he died in 1927. Following his death, it was revealed that his real name was Joe Horner, a wanted outlaw, murderer and bank robber who started out as a badman in Texas and later changed his name.

Harry Sinclair Drago, who wrote "The Great Range Wars: Violence on the Grasslands," summed up Canton: "Frank Canton was a merciless, congenital, emotionless killer. For pay, he murdered eight – very likely 10 men."

Trials and tribulations

Life wasn't easy for Alaska's early lawmen, which by the Klondike Gold Rush consisted of one judge, one marshal, 10 deputy marshals and 20 Native officers scattered in Southeast villages. While the lure of gold brought an abundant amount of unsavory characters north during the late 1800s, U.S. marshals didn't have budgets to pursue, capture or hold evildoers who committed crimes in the territory.

Due to the logistics of covering such a large expanse of land, suspects sometimes roamed at large for months, perhaps years, before being taken into custody.

Once lawmen did capture their quarry, there was also the problem of transporting the prisoners to Sitka for trial. More often than not, the marshals were required to pay the cost of transportation for themselves and their prisoners and then submit invoices for possible reimbursement.

This sad situation didn't escape the vigilant eye of the editor of the Sitka Alaskan in 1890:

"Under the Organic Act (of 1884) ... the judicial officers of this vast territory are a (single) United States judge, a marshal, clerk of court, and United States attorney, all stationed at Sitka; a United States commissioner at Sitka, Juneau, Wrangell and Ounalaska (Unalaska). With this vast army of officers, crime was ... to be wiped out in Alaska."

The two-story courthouse in Sitka, shown here in 1890, was the main center for trials in the territory at the turn-of-the-last century.

Vast territory proves tough to patrol

"But something seems to be lacking," the editor noted. "A murder is committed at Kodiak. A month or two later a sailing vessel arrives. The murder is reported, and on its return to San Francisco, word is sent to the deputy marshal at Ounalaska, also by sailing vessel, or possibly a revenue cutter or steamer of the Alaska Commercial Company, which makes semi-annual trips.

"He then reports to his chief in Sitka, via San Francisco, and if the vessels are not lost in the course of a year or so, he may get a warrant for the arrest of the malefactor. If he is in haste to arrest him, he will take the first vessel to San Francisco, thence to Kodiak – as this is the shortest and usually the only route between the ports.

"If he is lucky enough to find the man still alive, he will arrest him; and by this time the last vessel for the season having probably sailed, he and his prisoner will wait quietly another six months, when by schooner and steamer by way of San Francisco and Puget Sound, prisoner and marshal may arrive in Sitka to find that in the change of administration, the case (has been) forgotten, and the deputy marshal salted for all his expenses."

U.S. Revenue Marine Capt. Michael A. Healy poses with his pet parrot on the quarterdeck of his most famous command, the Revenue Cutter *Bear*, around 1895.

Healy rules Alaska waves

A "floating court" of sorts evolved when justice was meted out from the decks of revenue cutters beginning in the late 1880s.

A commander in the U.S. Revenue Marine, precursor to the U.S. Coast Guard, was the first revenue cutter commander to make regular patrols into the harsh arctic waters. Capt. Michael A. Healy was about the only source of law in a lawless land, and he transported criminals onboard the cutter *Bear* from remote Alaska communities to Sitka for trial.

Healy began his 49-year sea career in 1854 at age 15 when he signed on as a cabin boy aboard the American East Indian clipper *Jumna* bound for Asia.

The son of a Georgia plantation owner and an African slave from

Mali, Healy quickly became an expert seaman. During the Civil War, he requested and was granted a commission as a third lieutenant in the U. S. Revenue Marine from President Abraham Lincoln.

After serving successfully on several cutters in the East, Healy began his lengthy service in Alaska waters in 1875 as the second officer on the cutter *Rush*. He was given command of the revenue cutter *Chandler* in 1877. Promoted to captain in March 1883, he then assumed command of the cutter *Thomas Corwin* in 1884. Finally, in 1886, he became commanding officer of the *Bear*, taking her into Alaska waters for the first time.

He became a legend enforcing federal law along Alaska's 20,000-mile coastline. In addition to befriending missionaries and scientists, he rescued whalers, Natives, shipwrecked sailors and destitute miners, according to the U.S. Coast Guard.

The captain often drove himself and his crew beyond the call of duty, as in 1888, when the Alaska whaling fleet was anchored behind the bar at Point Barrow to ride out a southwest gale.

The *Bear* plied Arctic Ocean waters, often vying for a pathway through icebergs.

Several Eskimos lead harnessed reindeer at a camp in northern Alaska.

The wind veered to the north, and huge waves broke over the bar. Four ships broke apart and sank, tossing the ships' crews into the icy waters. Healy and the *Bear's* crew saved 160 whalers, Coast Guard records show.

Healy also assisted in serving the humanitarian needs and welfare of Native Alaskans through the introduction of reindeer to Alaska in order to replace the declining whale and seal populations, which were among the Natives' primary food sources.

While serving as second-in-command of the *Thomas Corwin* as it searched for the lost exploration ship *Jeanette* along the Siberian Coast in 1881, he noticed that the Chukchi people were able to sustain themselves by raising reindeer. In 1890, Healy used that knowledge to work with the Rev. Dr. Sheldon Jackson and famous naturalist John Muir to import reindeer to Alaska.

At his own expense, Healy transported 16 reindeer from the Natives of the Siberian Coast to the Seward Peninsula. In 1892, another 171 reindeer were added to the herd and Teller Reindeer

Station was established. More reindeer followed. These selfless acts and humanitarian efforts helped Natives continue their subsistence ways and probably saved many lives.

Coincidentally, his interpreter in the Arctic was Mary Makrikoff, who years later would become the first Native woman to own her own reindeer herd and be known as "Reindeer Mary" and "Sinrock Mary," as told in "Aunt Phil's Trunk: Volume 1." During the early 1900s, she was the richest Native woman in Alaska, selling reindeer to prospectors, the government and others.

Captain praised and denounced

An article that appeared in the New York Sun in the 1890s reported that Healy was a mighty man:

"Captain Mike Healy is a great deal more distinguished person in the waters of the far northwest than any President of the United States ... He stands for law and order in many thousands of miles of land and water, and if you should ask, 'Who is the greatest man in America?' the instant answer would be: 'Why, Mike Healy.'"

Pictured here in 1899, Ounalaska — now called Unalaska — was a port of call for the Revenue Cutter *Bear*.

Capt. Michael A. Healy takes a moment to pose with two unidentified women onboard the Revenue Cutter *Bear*.

But at the same time that Healy was being praised in some quarters, he was being denounced for his brutality in others.

Long voyages under harsh conditions often caused tempers to flare onboard vessels. And while captains had to run tight ships because breaches of discipline could mean the loss of the ship and crew, some seamen accused Healy of being downright cruel.

The San Francisco Coast Seamen's Journal, dated Feb. 21, 1894, listed two incidents involving Healy in a report on "cases of cruelty perpetrated upon American seamen. ..."

"Three seamen, Holben, Daweritz and Frandsen, of the American bark *Estrella* charged that while discharging coal into the *Bear* in the harbor of Ounalaska in June 1889, Captain Healy, without provocation, ordered them placed in irons and confined in the forepeak of the *Bear*. Then they were triced up with their hands behind them and their toes barely touching the deck. The punishment lasted 15 minutes

Capt. Michael A. Healy died at age 65.

and the pain was most excruciating. They were then tied with their backs to the stanchions and their arms around them for 42 hours. They were then put ashore and made to shift for themselves. The seamen accused both Captain Healy and Captain Avery of the *Estrella* of drunkenness and gross incapacity; ..."

The U.S. Department of the Navy exonerated Healy.

The second report came from the crew of whaling bark *Northern Light* for an incident on June 8, 1889, involving cruelty from the officers.

"Captain Healy ordered them all in irons. First Lieutenant of the *Bear* was sent aboard the *Northern Light* to execute the order. Crew triced up to the skids with arms behind their backs and toes just touching the deck. One man's hands were lashed with hambroline (small cord), as the irons were too small for his wrists; line cut into the flesh three-eights of an inch. One man fainted from pain and the *Bear's* doctor had to bring him to. Men were triced up 15 minutes, suffering untold pain."

Healy was sidelined for four years following his controversial court-martial conviction for "gross irresponsibility" and "scandalous conduct," even though "tricing" was a legal means of punishment at the time. But when the 1900 Alaska gold rush called for more cutters, Healy was given command of the cutter *McCulloch* and went north again. He spent his last two years of service on Alaska waters aboard the cutter *Thetis*. He retired in 1904 at the mandatory retirement age of 64 and died one year later.

For his service to his country, the Alaska Native people and to their way of life, Healy was honored by Congress, the whaling industry, missionary groups and civic organizations on both the Atlantic and Pacific coasts. He earned the nickname "Hell Roaring Mike" for his forceful leadership and determination to succeed in all missions, whether military or humanitarian, and some say for his actions when under the influence of alcohol.

The 420-foot U.S. Coast Guard Cutter *Healy*, the largest cutter and polar icebreaker in the Coast Guard fleet, was named in his honor and put into service in November 1999.

Another bigger-than-life member of law enforcement also made his mark on the Great Land – through wise deliberations, politics and perseverance.

The U.S. Coast Guard Cutter *Healy*, the largest cutter in the Coast Guard fleet, was named in honor of Michael A. Healy.

10

JUDGE'S LIGHT SHINES ON

While Capt. Michael A. Healy was instrumental in carrying out justice in Alaska waters and villages, Judge James Wickersham finally initiated a more formal traveling judicial system at the turn-of-the-last century.

His system evolved after he sailed to Unalaska in 1900 to preside over the first felony trial on the Aleutian Chain. Recognizing that Unalaska's small population wouldn't allow him to summon sufficient jurors, he took more than a dozen people with him to Valdez and set up court in a building housing the town's laundry. That first

Judge James Wickersham set up Alaska's first official traveling court in the laundry building in Valdez in 1900.

This photograph shows a man delivering a load of laundry to the Northern Steam Laundry via dog sled.

LAW AND ORDER

trial led to the establishment of an official traveling court.

Born in Patoka, Illinois, Wickersham emigrated west, landing in Washington Territory in 1883 where he became attorney for the city of Tacoma. While in that capacity, he won a $1 million lawsuit concerning Tacoma's water system. Tacoma acquired both the water and light systems in the settlement and thus started the first municipal light and water utilities in the West.

Judge James Wickersham, surrounded by law books, sits at his desk in the Interior.

It was said, jokingly, in the Northwest that Wickersham was sent to Alaska to get him out of Washington politics. If so, Washington tossed a whole hornet's nest into Alaska, for he was the storm center of more controversies and is credited with having written and made more history than any other of Alaska's early public figures.

Wickersham wrote in his book, "Old Yukon," that those who were active in urging his appointment to a distant post were those attorneys and representatives of certain public utilities against whom he had battled in support of the public interest. However, when he was offered a post as district judge of the newly organized Third Judicial Division of Alaska, he enthusiastically embraced the opportunity to help found "American Courts of Justice in the northern territory."

Nome judge uses bad judgment

Wickersham was called upon to travel to Nome to clear up disputed mining claims during the famous Noyes-McKenzie affair, written about in Rex Beach's "The Spoilers." It seems a federal judge and several other men worked a bit of claim jumping through the legal

Once gold was discovered on Anvil Creek in Nome in 1898, pictured above, prospectors flocked to the Seward Peninsula in hopes of striking it rich. And when they found the best claims already taken, some made plans to make those claims their own.

system, so Wickersham faced a slew of unresolved cases when he arrived during the fall of 1901.

It all started following the discovery of gold on Anvil Creek in 1898 by the "Three Lucky Swedes." When news of the strike hit the Klondikers late the next spring, 8,000 people left Dawson for the coast in a single week. But the prospectors flooding to Nome found all the best claims already staked and were unhappy that foreigners had grabbed the most valuable claims.

In an effort to drive out the Swedes and their friends, a group of prospectors gathered on July 10, 1899, for a public meeting to pass a resolution that the foreigners' claims were unlawful and that the area of Anvil Creek would be open to claims again.

It's reported that some accomplices set up large bonfires on the beach to light as soon as the resolution was passed. The fires would signal others stationed on the mountains above the beach that they could take over the Scandinavians' claims.

But before the men could carry on with their plan, a military troop from St. Michael interrupted the gathering and a Lieutenant Spaulding declared the meeting over.

That same month, gold was discovered on Nome's beaches. A judge ruled that the beach could not be staked, so more than 2,000 people camped along 30 miles of beach and mined the sand 24 hours a day with gold pans, rockers and sluice boxes.

But while the disgruntled stampeders were somewhat mollified by the gold in the sands of Nome, others in high political offices made their own plans to appropriate the gold fields staked by the Scandinavians.

Noyes-McKenzie affair

When Alexander McKenzie, an influential Republican, arranged to have President William McKinley appoint Alfred N. Noyes as judge of one of the three newly created judicial districts in Alaska, the stage was set to separate hardworking miners from their claims.

Scows brought eager prospectors from steamships to the beaches of Nome, where shady politicians and lawmen laid in wait to separate them from gold claims.

Judge James Wickersham had his work cut out for him when he arrived in Nome to clean up the mess left by Judge Alfred N. Noyes in 1901.

Pictured above is Nome's City Hall, built in 1904.

LAW AND ORDER

Noyes, along with his friend, McKenzie, arrived in Nome in July 1900 to begin their high jinks. That the judge was McKenzie's henchman would soon become apparent. The two men set up a receivership racket and hired others to jump claims.

One of the first legal proceedings the new judge enacted was to declare a row of the most valuable claims at Anvil Creek to be unlawful. The Scandinavians were not notified that their claims were the subject of a court action until McKenzie's men showed up and chased them off.

When the legitimate claim owners appeared in court to have disputes settled, Judge Noyes put the claims into receiverships to be administered by McKenzie while the judge supposedly considered the disputes. In this interim, McKenzie hired men to mine the claims and commandeer all assets, including gold already extracted.

Noyes denied the Scandinavians the right to take their cases to a higher court, but a lawyer for legitimate claim owner Charles Lane of the Wild Goose Company finally took his case to the circuit court of appeals in San Francisco and won.

When Judge Noyes said he wasn't subject to the new court and ignored the ruling, the Scandinavians lost patience. By use of force, the miners took back their claims.

Subsequently, U.S. marshals arrested McKenzie, who was sentenced to one-year imprisonment, and Noyes, who was removed from his position.

Wickersham cleans up Nome

Excerpts from Judge Wickersham's October 1901 diary entries hint at the problems he encountered when he arrived in Nome and how he meted out justice for all.

Oct. 5

"… Civil cases are crowding hard these days and I work in the office and courtroom from 9 a.m. to 10 and 11 p.m. The only way to clean up the business of this country is to push hard and I intend to clean it up before spring."

Oct. 6

"Went down to see Mrs. Noyes off today – also called at her rooms. She is greatly distressed at the conditions which compel her to leave Nome under a cloud. She could not restrain her tears, and at the beach, when about to go aboard the lighter to go out to the vessel, she all but broke down. Mrs. Frost bears up much better – but it was a distressing ordeal for each of them.

"Six insane men sent out today on the *Elihu Thomson*, prisoners go later. Working today on opinion in Butler v. Good Enough Mining Co., an important mining case.

"I am satisfied that it will go hard with Judge Noyes, Dist. Atty. Woods, Frost, and possibly (ex-Congressman Thomas J.) Geary. McKenzie got six months on each of two charges, (Dudly) Du Bose six months and the facts against the others seem stronger."

Oct. 29

"Have decided the case of Hemen v. Griffith, Rice, Wild Goose Co. and others, involving another Ophir Creek (mining) case. The attorneys now tell me that the case decided yesterday involved more than half a million dollars. I am pleased to know that mine owners now express a feeling of safety over property rights and do me the honor to say that investments can now be made here with assurance of fair protection.

"Judge Noyes seems never to have rendered even one mining opinion and but one mining case was tried by him in the more than a year that he was here. Yesterday I dismissed all the indictments in the now famous Glacier Creek riot cases.

"Judge Noyes left Nome on August 12, 1901, after signing the most contradictory and extraordinary batch of orders while out on the steamer – drunk, it is said by his enemies – certainly the orders were – and the result was a rising of people who went out to the richest mines on the Glacier Creek masked and armed and drove off all the "jumpers" and warned them to leave the country.

"They were arrested – at least half a dozen men who were supposed to be among the "rioters" were indicted and Griffin and Till

Three men, two children and a dog stand around "Wickersham Headquarters" sign displayed on the front of Lomen Brothers store in Nome.

Price have been tried. The jury in each case disagreed – so much prejudice exists against the Noyes-Stevens regime that it is impossible to convict these men for a violation of their injunctions or a contempt of their court – they ought not to be severely dealt with because the conditions were such as to drive good citizens to acts of lawlessness.

"So after the failure to convict the first two I felt justified in dismissing all the remaining indictments and did it! It is to the great advantage of this region to put that blot on the judiciary of America behind us – hide it from sight as soon as possible, and open a brighter and better page in the history of the Nome region. It has fallen to my fortune to close the unfortunate page and open the brighter and better one, and if God gives me the strength of body to do the work, I will not fail to do my best."

Wickersham heads to the Interior

Wickersham's first official judicial headquarters at the turn of the century was at Eagle, one of the largest settlements on the Yukon

These gold bars, worth $260,000, represent one week's output of the Pioneering Mining Company in Nome in July 1910.

River. Here, after building his modest log home, Wickersham began settling mining claim disputes and collecting saloon license fees for the Third Judicial District, which comprised 300,000 square miles.

He then moved when Fairbanks became the center of gold mining. Along with trading post entrepreneur Capt. E.T. Barnette and prospector Felix Pedro, who discovered gold in the region, Wickersham is credited with founding the town and naming it Fairbanks, after Sen. Charles Fairbanks of Indiana. Sen. Fairbanks was elected vice president of the United States on Theodore Roosevelt's ticket and served from 1905-1909.

During Wickersham's first term of court, more cases were tried than ever before this time in all the other places combined in Interior Alaska. He rented a room in the building that was then Carrol and Parker's Mill Office and opened the first Equity Court in town while a courthouse was being built at the corner of Second Avenue and

Judge James Wickersham delivers the Fourth of July address at the dedication of the first courthouse at Fairbanks in 1904.

Cushman Street. The Federal Building is located on the original site of that pioneer courthouse.

On July 4, 1904, when the courthouse was finished and officially dedicated, Judge Wickersham addressed a mass audience of townspeople and miners who had come in from the creeks for the holiday. In honor of the occasion, he was presented a gold spoon, the handle of which was made of four nuggets and the bowl pounded from a single gold nugget. The nuggets came from some of the original discoveries that started the young camp.

Wickersham holds many firsts

So many firsts can be attributed to Wickersham that it's difficult to know where to begin. He started the first floating court in Alaska, the first court ever held in the Aleutians. While serving as judge, he traveled thousands of miles by dogs and sled, on foot and on riverboats.

He also is credited with the first organized attempt to climb Denali, the Native name for Mount McKinley. Wickersham helped finance his 1903 expedition by publishing one issue of The Fairbanks

Judge James Wickersham lived in this frame house in Fairbanks during the early 1900s.

Miner, the first newspaper in Fairbanks and the Tanana Valley. He produced only seven copies on a typewriter, using any decent piece of paper he could find, and sold them for $5 each. He also sold 36 ads at $5 apiece and arranged to have the papers read to audiences who willingly paid $1 admission to hear news of gold discoveries about which they already knew.

In 1915, he brought together all the Native chiefs of Interior Alaska and organized the first Indian Council held in Fairbanks to discuss the effects of the railroad and homesteading on the Native way of life – one of the earliest considerations of Native land claims in Alaska.

Wickersham makes Alaska home

Wickersham resigned from the bench in 1907, practiced law in Fairbanks for a short time, and in August 1908, an overwhelming majority elected him as Alaska's third delegate to Congress. Elected for five successive terms during this turbulent time in Alaska's history, he was in the thick of struggles between conservationists, who wanted to save the resources from monopolists, and those who wanted to develop Alaska's resources. Independent by nature, Wickersham ran on nearly every political ticket in the territory. And as one source suggested, "Wickersham could have been elected Jesus Christ, had he sought the office."

While serving Alaska, Wickersham found the Library of Congress had no Alaska section. He remedied the situation by preparing a bibliography of Alaska literature, amassing 10,380 items in his tremendous undertaking – perhaps the most gigantic historical task ever attempted by a single man. Few things written about Alaska, either as a territory or as a Russian possession, escaped his attention. He collected many of the items for his own personal Alaska library, which later was acquired by the territorial library at Juneau.

Wickersham retired from politics in 1932 and lived in Juneau until his death in 1939. As his obituary aptly read:

"Alaska's wick burns out, but his light shines on ... Alaska will not forget James Wickersham. His place in our history is secure."

And Evangeline Atwood, author of "Frontier Politics," said, "... No other man has made as deep and varied imprints on Alaska's heritage, whether it be in politics, government, commerce, literature, history or philosophy. A federal judge, member of Congress, attorney and explorer, present-day Alaska is deeply in debt to him."

Grace and James Wickersham sit in front of the fireplace inside their home in Juneau, where the judge retired.

11

CITY OF SEATTLE TURNS TO PIRACY

O f the multitude of steamships that plied the waters from California to Point Barrow during the late 1890s, one has the dubious distinction of being what some may call a "pirate ship." The *City of Seattle*, which sailed from Seattle, Washington, to Skagway and points in between, played a major role in spiriting a totem pole out of Alaska.

As the story goes, the Seattle Chamber of Commerce had wanted a totem pole to erect in Pioneer Park in downtown Seattle. However, those who carved the magnificent monuments only came from the tribes of northern Vancouver Island, the Queen Charlotte Islands and the adjacent tribes in British Columbia and Alaska.

In the summer of 1899, the Seattle Post-Intelligencer put a delegation of businessmen

Three totem poles sit in a row on the edge of a forest in turn-of-the-last-century Sitka.

The steamer *City of Seattle*, seen here at the dock in Skagway in February 1900, carried a delegation onboard in 1899 that stole a totem pole from Southeast Alaska.

onboard the *City of Seattle* to sail to Sitka to see if they could find a totem pole suitable for the park. Since most of the totems by this time were stationed in Indian burial grounds, the delegation's mission was indeed delicate.

After a brief stay in Alaska's old capitol, guests returning to the ship were advised by the purser not to believe anything they heard and only half of what they saw from that time forth.

Stealing a totem

After finishing her business in the port of Sitka, the *City of Seattle* sailed out a bit and then anchored in a stream. Passengers watched as the crew lowered one of the ship's boats into the water and rowed ashore. Later, third mate R.D. McGillvery described what happened:

"The Indians were all away fishing, except for one who stayed in his house and looked scared to death. We picked out the best-looking totem pole. I took a couple of sailors ashore and we chopped it down – just like you'd chop down a tree. It was too big to roll down the beach, so we sawed it in two."

Members of the Committee of Fifteen paid McGillvery $2.50 for his effort to cut down the totem, which belonged to the Raven Clan. It was carved in 1790 to honor a woman called Chief-of-all-Women who'd drowned in the Nass River.

On Oct. 18, 1899, the 60-foot totem was unveiled in Seattle's Pioneer Square and "greeted by cheers of a multitude of people."

The Tlingits demanded $20,000 for the return of the stolen totem, but settled for $500, which the Seattle Post-Intelligencer paid.

The original totem stood proudly in Pioneer Square until a careless smoker tossed a cigarette butt against its decaying base in 1938. The city removed the original totem and replaced it in 1940 with a replica carved by the descendants of the original totem's carvers.

A 60-foot totem pole, taken by a group of Washington businessmen from a Tlingit village in Southeast Alaska in 1899, sits in Pioneer Square in Seattle at the turn-of-the-last century.

12

INMATE NO. 594

Before he became well known around the country, one of America's most famous prison inmates dug gold nuggets out of a mine in Juneau during 1908.

His employment with the gold mine didn't last long, however. After being dismissed as a troublemaker, he became a bartender and moved in with bar girl Kitty O'Brien on Gastineau Avenue. His relationship with her turned deadly the following year.

Murder rocked the gold-mining town of Juneau in 1909.

Located on the mainland of Southeast Alaska, Juneau was built at the heart of the Inside Passage along Gastineau Channel. The area was a fish camp for the indigenous Tlingit Indians. In 1880, nearly 20 years before the gold rushes to the Klondike and Nome, Joe Juneau and Richard Harris were led to Gold Creek by Chief Kowee of the Auk Tribe. They found mother lode deposits upstream, staked their mining claims and developed a 160-acre incorporated city they called Harrisburg. Miners later voted to change the name to Juneau, pictured above in 1912.

Thousands of prospectors flooded into the area. The city of Juneau was formed in 1900, and in 1906, the state capital was transferred from Sitka.

The Treadwell and Ready Bullion mines across the channel on Douglas Island became world-scale mines, operating from 1882 to 1917. In 1916, the Alaska-Juneau gold mine was built on the mainland, and it became the largest operation of its kind in the world.

In 1917, a cave-in and flood closed the Treadwell Mine on Douglas. It produced $66 million in gold in its 35 years of operation. Fishing, canneries, transportation and trading services and a sawmill contributed to Juneau's growth through the early 1900s.

While most records concerning this case have been destroyed over the years, Deputy U.S. Marshall H.L. Faulkner recalled the events, according to Alaska State Troopers' "50 Years of History."

On the evening of Jan. 18, 1909, Nels Peterson spotted Faulkner walking home from the courthouse along Fourth Street in downtown Juneau. Peterson called to the marshal and told him he'd heard a gunshot come from a small two-room cabin next to his house and had seen a man run out of the building and down Franklin Street.

Faulkner slowly approached the cabin and then noticed the door ajar. He tried to enter, but soon discovered that a man's body lay on the floor, blocking the entrance. The dead man, Charles F. Damer, had been shot through the heart.

Several hours later, the authorities identified the bartender, who would later become Inmate No. 594 at an infamous prison in California, as the prime suspect.

Faulkner and a Juneau police officer, James Mulcahey, investigated the murder. They learned that Damer and the suspect both vied for the affections of O'Brien and had had an argument earlier in the morning in one of the South Franklin Street saloons.

Some sources said O'Brien and the bartender were lovers, others suggested that she supported him and he was her pimp. Whatever

Wrongdoers were tried in the U.S. Courthouse in Juneau, pictured above behind City Hall.

the case, Faulkner and Mulcahey arrested the bartender later that evening at O'Brien's cabin. While searching the premises, they found a revolver. Faulkner later recounted that the weapon proved to be "the instrument of the murder."

Authorities questioned the bartender and O'Brien about the killing. O'Brien told the officers that Damer had struck her in the face during a quarrel, and she had told the bartender about the attack. The bartender then went looking for Damer, found him, and shot him to death. The bartender's version of events added that O'Brien had pleaded with him to kill Damer for attacking her.

Justice in Juneau proved swift and sure. A coroner's jury convened the evening of the murder, and after hearing testimony from the various parties, returned its verdict that Damer met his death at the hands of the bartender and named O'Brien as an accomplice.

Both the bartender and O'Brien were charged with murder and arraigned on Jan. 21. Authorities later dropped the charges against O'Brien, and the bartender pleaded guilty to a charge of second-degree murder. He was sentenced to serve seven years at the federal penitentiary on McNeil Island near Tacoma, Washington.

Inmate does time

While the bartender served his seven-year sentence, his mother and sister continued to work in Alaska, spending most of their earnings on attempts to have him pardoned or paroled.

Authorities transferred him to the federal penitentiary at Leavenworth, Kansas, in 1912, due to ceaseless complaints about his threats toward other prisoners and overcrowding in the prison. He kept to himself at the maximum-security facility for hard-case prisoners. Convict Morris Rudensky described him:

"Physically he was a disgrace – tall, thin and as attractive as a barracuda or a herring bone without the herring. He seldom spoke to anyone, including the cons, and vice versa. He was a ferocious misanthrope."

Just before the bartender's scheduled release on March 26, 1916, he walked into the Leavenworth mess hall and stabbed to death prison guard Andrew F. Turner in front of 1,200 convicts and prison officials. No one knows why.

"The guard (Turner) took sick of heart trouble. I guess you could call it heart puncture. I never have given them any reason for my doing it, so they won't have much to work on; only that I killed him, and that won't do much good. I admit that much," he later said to Rudensky.

Inmate turns to the birds

Convicted of Turner's murder, the bartender was sentenced to hang in April 1920. However, his mother successfully gained an audience with President Woodrow Wilson's wife. She begged her to convince her ailing husband to spare her son's life, since he was just beginning to gain a reputation as a lover of canaries and an expert on their diseases.

Elizabeth Bolling Wilson, impressed with the inmate's pioneer work with birds, convinced her husband to commute the death sentence. The same week as the bartender was scheduled for execution, the president's order arrived that changed the sentence to solitary confinement for the rest of his life.

The gold-miner-turned-bartender-turned-murderer named Robert Stroud carried on experimenting with canary diseases and ornithology while living in solitary in two adjoining cells.

Over the 30 years he was imprisoned at Leavenworth, he authored two books on canaries and their diseases, having raised nearly 300 birds in his cells, carefully studying their habits and physiology.

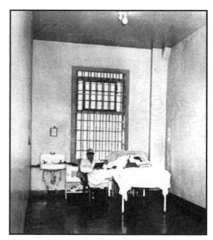

After murdering a man in Juneau in 1909, Robert Stroud was sent to McNeil Prison in Washington state, followed by time in Leavenworth Prison in Kansas. In 1942, he was transferred to a cell in Alcatraz, pictured above.

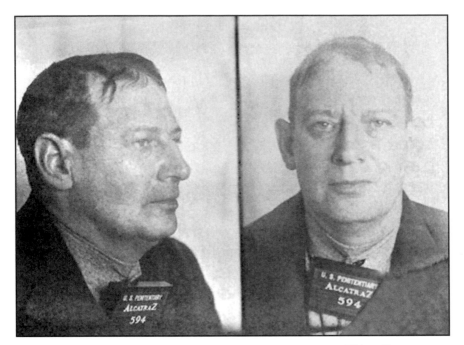

Robert Stroud, shown above in this mugshot, became prisoner No. 594 at Alcatraz maximum-security prison in 1942.

He also wrote a manuscript called "Looking Outward" about prison reform that was never published.

Stroud transferred to Alcatraz in 1942, where he became inmate No. 594 at the new maximum-security federal institution. He spent six years in segregation in D Block and 11 years in the prison hospital. In 1959 he was transferred to the Medical Center for Federal Prisoners in Springfield, Missouri, and was found dead there on Nov. 21, 1963.

His nickname, "The Birdman of Alcatraz," came from his life on the rock. And his monumental work, "Stroud's Book of Bird Diseases," published in 1942, still is regarded as an authoritative source.

13

ALASKA'S FIRST SERIAL KILLER

B etween 1912 and 1915, a number of single, unattached men mysteriously disappeared in Southeast Alaska. The few law enforcement officials in the territory were baffled, but a suspect finally emerged in the fall of 1915.

A Petersburg man named Edward Krause, who'd run for the Territorial Legislature as a Socialist Party candidate in 1912, repre-

Alaska's first-known serial killer lived in Petersburg, pictured above in 1912. Petersburg is located on the north end of Mitkof Island, where the Wrangell Narrows meet Frederick Sound. It lies midway between Juneau and Ketchikan, about 120 miles from either community in Southeast Alaska.

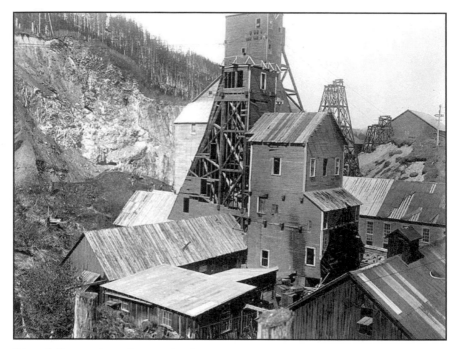

Edward Krause showed up at the Alaska Treadwell Gold Mining Company at Douglas Island, pictured above at the Glory Hole in 1911. He asked for a mine worker named James Christie, and that's the last time anyone ever saw the unfortunate miner.

sented himself as a U.S. marshal to officials at the Treadwell Mine in Douglas in mid-September. Krause told the bosses that he had a court summons for a mine worker named James Christie, according to Alaska State Troopers' "50 Years of History."

Christie departed with the bogus lawman and was never seen again.

The managers at the mine started an investigation of their own into Christie's disappearance. They suspected it was associated with labor problems between the violence-prone local Western Federation of Miners and the company union, of which Christie served as an officer. When an offer of a reward brought no information, the Treadwell Mining Company hired the Pinkerton Detective Agency.

The Pinkertons had extensive experience investigating organized labor and earlier had been retained by the Treadwell Mining

Company to infiltrate the Western Federation of Miners in Alaska. Like the managers of the company, the Pinkerton people thought Christie's disappearance was related to labor rivalries. They believed that Krause, a radical socialist, was a hired killer engaged by the violent wing of the labor union.

Catching a killer

When it was learned that Krause also was identified as the last person to see a missing charter boat operator out of Juneau, a warrant for his arrest was issued on charges of impersonating a federal officer.

Krause escaped the clutches of the law in Ketchikan and jumped onboard a steamer heading for Seattle. But a savvy passenger, who had seen posters plastered by the Treadwell Mining Company, recognized him as the man with a bounty on his head.

When the steamer docked in Puget Sound, police detectives were waiting. A search of Krause's possessions turned up incriminating evidence, including forged documents, bank accounts and real estate transactions, which tied him to not only the recent disappearances in Juneau, but to the disappearances of at least eight other men, too.

After Krause was returned to Alaska, his true identity surfaced. Krause was really Edward Slompke, who'd served with the U. S. Army at Wrangell in 1897. By using forged documents, and stealing a military payroll, he deserted from the 12th U.S. Infantry in 1902 when his regiment was sent to China to participate in the Boxer Rebellion.

A yearlong investigation, which used the services of the newly formed Federal Bureau of Investigation, as well as the U.S. State Department, revealed a series of disappearances and an intricate pattern of forged property transactions.

Alaska's first serial killer tried for murder

Authorities found that over the years Krause recovered the assets of the murdered men. They also learned that a "murder gang," run by Krause at Petersburg, was involved in additional mysterious disappearances.

Supporters of Krause, those in the radial Western Federation of Miners labor movement, thought the socialist was being framed by the capitalistic Treadwell Mining Company. Undercover government agents had to infiltrate the labor unions antagonistic to Treadwell to gain information about plans to get witnesses to change their testimony and threats to potential jurors.

Searchers combed the beaches and hillsides and divers probed the waters around Juneau throughout the spring and summer of 1916. However, none of Krause's victims were found, so authorities had to rely on strong circumstantial evidence to try him.

Krause's trials started in the spring of 1917. Among other charges, jurors found him guilty of kidnapping, robbery and forgery. His first murder trial, of Juneau charter boat operator James O. Plunkett, began in July.

THIRD ST JUNEAU, ALASKA.
NOWELL PHOTO

The U.S. Courthouse in Juneau, where Krause was tried, can be seen in the far background looking down Third and Gold with wooden streets and sidewalks.

LAW AND ORDER

Even though investigators searched far and wide, none of Krause's victims ever were found around Juneau, pictured here looking downhill toward town.

A dangerous man

To protect the jury from intimidation by Krause's still-active supporters, the judge sequestered the jury during the trial – a first in Alaska court history. Krause's trial also marked the first extensive use in Alaska of testimony from handwriting and typewriter experts.

Based on the overwhelming circumstantial evidence, the jury found Krause guilty of first-degree murder. His conviction was affirmed by the U.S. Court of Appeals in San Francisco, and Krause was sentenced to die by hanging at Juneau.

After sawing through the bars of his cell, Krause escaped from the federal jail in Juneau two days before his slated execution. That launched the most widespread manhunt in the territory's history.

A notice of a reward for his capture appeared in the April 13, 1917, Juneau Daily Empire.

Fishing fleets in every community in Southeast mobilized to block Krause's escape out of Alaska. The mines on both sides of Gastineau Channel closed down, and 1,000 miners joined in the hunt. While house-to-house searches were conducted, territorial Gov. John F.A. Strong announced his $1,000 reward, "dead or alive."

$1,000 Reward

is offered for the apprehension of Edward Krause, under sentence of death for murder, who escaped from the United States jail at Juneau, on the night of April 12, 1917.

Krause is five feet ten inches height, about forty-five years of age, heavy set, broad shoulders; walks with short quick steps; has sandy hair, curly; bald in front, blue eyes, a heavy red mustache; may now be shaved. General sandy complexion, and is pale from confinement; weight about 200 pounds; wore a dark-blue suit of heavy material. Is of very powerful build and has large muscular hands.

The above reward will be paid by the Territory of Alaska for the arrest of said Edward Krause, upon his delivery into the custody of the United States Marshal at Juneau, Alaska.

Juneau, Alaska,
April 13, 1917   **J. F. A. STRONG**, Governor

"$1,000 reward is offered for the apprehension of Edward Krause, under sentence of death for murder, who escaped from the United States jail at Juneau, on the night of April 12, 1917.

"Krause is five feet, ten inches in height, about forty-five years of age, heavy set, broad shoulders; walks with shoulders back, with short quick steps; has sandy hair, curly; bald in front, blue eyes, a heavy red mustache; may now be shaved. General sandy complexion, and is pale from confinement; weight about 200 pounds; wore a dark-blue suit of heavy material. Is of very powerful build and has large muscular hands.

"The above reward will be paid by the Territory of Alaska for the arrest of said Edward Krause, upon his delivery into the custody of the United States Marshal at Juneau, Alaska."

A few days later, a homesteader claimed the reward. He'd killed Krause after the fugitive stepped out of a stolen skiff onto the beach at Admiralty Island.

"The true story of Krause's criminal enterprises and their extent will never be known. But if the story could ever be told, it would undoubtedly be one of the most startling in the annals of American crime history," stated a letter to the Department of Justice, written by U.S. Attorney James Smiser of Juneau.

ROUTES TO RESOURCES

14

ARIZONA EDITOR MAKES MARK ON ALASKA

The colorful editor of the famous Tombstone Epitaph made his mark on Alaska in the late 1890s. But John Clum first gained fame in the 1870s as an Apache agent. He founded the Apache police force on the San Carlos reservation and was proud to proclaim himself "the only man to place Geronimo in irons."

He also became the first mayor of Tombstone, and it was during this era that the legendary gunfight at the OK Corral was fought. At least one attack was made on Clum's life, but he stayed with "the town too tough to die" until the economy of Tombstone was brought to a standstill with the flooding of the silver mines.

But it was another one of Clum's ventures that brought him to Alaska and gave him the opportunity to leave his mark on the new land. In March 1898, he was appointed post office inspector for the territory. He and his son, Woodworth, spent the next five months travel-

John Clum arrived in Alaska in the late 1890s and set up the territory's first post offices.

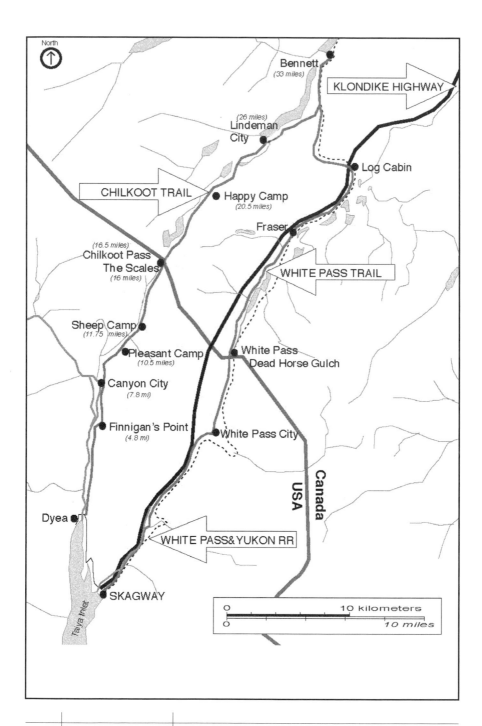

ROUTES TO RESOURCES

This log building at Eagle housed the Chamber of Commerce office in its saloon.

ing 8,000 miles around Alaska and the Yukon setting up new post offices and equipping others.

Clum travels the Yukon

It was no job for a weakling – one of his inspection trips was made on "foot and in a snowstorm" to Chilkat, and a second trip, according to his diary, was via reindeer and "lap" sled. This was during the Klondike stampede days and thousands of gold seekers were flooding the country. They wanted mail service, and Clum gave it to them as rapidly as possible.

He established post offices in Southeast Alaska at Sheep Camp, the last station before the Chilkoot Pass, Pyramid Harbor and Canyon. Clum reestablished the post office at Haines and reorganized the offices at Skagway and Dyea.

Then he started down the Yukon. Equipped with a 100-pound, 18-foot Peterborough canoe, he carried about 1,000 pounds of supplies, including mail sack keys, postal stamps and cards, and dating and canceling stamps. He found prices steep everywhere, he wrote in his diary. A bowl of soup at a restaurant cost $1, as did a one-minute dance with a dancehall girl. Eggs cost $18 a dozen, sugar $100 a sack.

Over the Yukon Trail, Clum and his son traveled to Dawson, which Clum noted was "the Coney Island of the Northwest ... wild and wooly – streets filled with surging masses from 9 a.m. until 2 a.m."

Post offices pop up in Interior

From Dawson, he traveled to Eagle via Fortymile. At Eagle, he established the first new post office of the Interior, and then traveled 18 miles down the Yukon River to set up another post office at Starr, located at the mouth of Seventymile River. His next stop was Circle, where the first post office on the Yukon River had been established in 1896. He found the post office there, under Jack McQuesten, "in good order."

On July 1, 1898, he and his son boarded the steamer *Seattle No. 1* for its maiden voyage down the Yukon to St. Michael, stopping

Sternwheelers *Seattle No. 1* and *Seattle No. 2* sit along the banks of the Yukon River in 1899.

ROUTES TO RESOURCES

People stand in front of the Nome Post Office in 1907 and watch a mail delivery dog team head back down the trail after it delivered mail.

to establish post offices at Fort Yukon, Rampart, Weare, Koyukuk, Nulato and Anvik. The boat reached St. Michael on the evening of July 9, and Clum sent 1,000 pounds of mail, the first to go back up the Yukon, on the steamer *Bella*.

Now that he had the Yukon and the Interior supplied with post offices, Clum took a ship to the Aleutians, changed the name of the post office at Ounalaska to Unalaska, then voyaged into Cook Inlet and set up post offices at Tyonek, Sunrise and Homer and arranged for one at Seldovia. He next proceeded to Prince William Sound, checking on the post offices at Nuchek and Orca.

Clum extends postal service

The postal system he set up put Alaska in touch with the United States, and when the Nome stampede occurred, Clum became a special agent in Alaska for the Post Office Department. He extended postal service to the north Bering Sea coast, and established a semi-annual monthly mail run between Nome and Point Blossom. For the next five years, he alternated between summers in Alaska and winters in New York City, but in 1906 he came back to Alaska to be the Fairbanks postmaster.

He dabbled in Alaska politics, too, as well as mining ventures, but wasn't too successful in either. His mining prospects never showed a profit, and when he ran as an Independent candidate for delegate to Congress against James Wickersham, he was soundly trounced.

But Clum successfully fulfilled his duties as the "Post Office man in Alaska," and his efforts to improve the territory's postal facilities were greatly appreciated. He resigned as the Fairbanks postmaster in 1909 and left Alaska. His daughter, Caro, after whom the settlement of Caro was named, stayed on, marrying Peter Vachon, owner of the Tanana Commercial Company.

Clum died in 1932 at the age of 81, three years after serving as a pallbearer for his lifelong friend, Wyatt Earp. As Clum's friends mourned his death, one noted that it was "a sign of the passing of the Old West."

But other rugged individuals carried on in Clum's tradition and continued to deliver mail throughout Alaska in all types of weather and travel conditions.

U. S. Postal Inspector John Clum, above, sometimes traveled by mule through parts of Alaska as he established post offices in the Last Frontier.

Above: Scores of prospectors gather their gear together in Dyea, as they prepare to head toward the Chilkoot Trail during the Klondike Gold Rush.

Below: Stampeders stand in a long line waiting for mail at the Dyea post office.

15

ALASKA'S PIONEERING POSTMEN

After the purchase of Alaska from Russia, American adventurers and entrepreneurs streamed into a territory that covered 586,412 square miles. There were no roads, only a few Native trails, and travel by water was at a minimum. To establish mail service in the Last Frontier, the territory's early postmen had to carve their routes out by hand.

Sitka has the honor of being the first post office in the territory under the U.S. government. It was established on July 23, 1867, with John. H. Kincaid (later an Alaska governor) as first postmaster three months before Alaska was formally transferred from Russia to America. The officials of both governments felt that early establishment of an American post office in the territory would be a big step toward an orderly transition from Russian to American rule. The Russians had never developed a postal system in the territory. In his book, "Philately Below Zero," James S. Couch wrote:

"The Russians maintained no postal system in Alaska. All communications between Russia and Russian America was carried on via dispatch cases transported by Russian supply ships, and Russian residents dispatched and received both business and personal mail through the Russian commanders of the community – there was no post office system as we know it."

So it was up to the Americans to establish the territory-wide postal system that Alaskans now take for granted.

Miners, hoping to hear word from the outside world, check in at the General Delivery window at the post office in Dawson.

Men and dogs establish early mail routes

The best bunk in the roadhouse, the best seat at the dinner table and the first service of pancakes in the morning was the mail driver's due, wrote Judge James Wickersham in "Old Yukon."

All other vehicles had to give way to the mail teams as they swung along the trail. There were no hardier, braver or more capable men than these pioneer mail carriers of the Yukon, Wickersham said. Sporting a striped-denim parka trimmed with wolverine fur, which does not gather frost, and wearing a gaudily beaded pair of Tena gauntlet gloves, the mail carrier would unhitch his team when he reached the station or roadhouse at the end of the day's run, turn all his dogs, except the leader, loose to rustle for themselves, and then bring his leader into the roadhouse.

"The leader slept under his bed at night – and woe unto him who complains about it!" Wickersham wrote.

Ben S. Downing developed the first mail route from Dawson to Nome.

One of the best and most widely known mail carriers was Ben S. Downing, the man who laid out the first mail route from Dawson to Nome. The tall, sinewy mail carrier from Maine, a typical frontiersman, had left his New England home as a lad, followed the sea for a while, and then turned his attention to Texas and the cattle ranges. He wound up in Montana after driving cattle herds over the Chisholm Trail, but the discovery of gold in the Black Hills lured him to South Dakota. There he pulled freight and mining supplies to the diggings, until he was injured in a fight with a band of Indians who swarmed down on his wagon train. Ben carried an Indian rifle ball in his body for the rest of his life as a token of that experience.

News of the Klondike strike in 1897 drifted down from the North and drew him to the new land of opportunity. But Downing found a claim that had few takers: to set up a mail route from Dawson to the new gold metropolis of Nome where thousands of prospectors waited anxiously for news from home.

During the gold-rush era, Dawson mail workers, pictured above, kept busy sorting thousands of pieces of mail destined for stampeders in the Klondike and points beyond.

Stampeders gather in Nome

By the fall of 1899, more than 3,000 people were in Nome, with thousands more on the way. The stampede from Dawson and other gold mining areas began after "Three Lucky Swedes" – John Byrnteson, Erik Lindblom and Jafet Lindeberg, who was actually a Norwegian – discovered bits of gold in Anvil Creek west of Cape Nome in 1898. Soon the trio had staked out 43 claims between them and, by power of attorney, 47 others for friends, relatives and backers.

When word of this leaked out, hordes of gold seekers descended on the Nome area, unaware that the Swedes had not yet found anything close to a major gold strike. The chaotic scene that unfolded involved rampant claim jumping and litigation. Adding to the confusion were the countless claims filed by power of attorney for individuals who, in many cases, didn't exist.

Confusion and unrest reigned in those early stages of the rush, and the three Scandinavians must have felt anything but lucky as the blame for the whole fiasco began to fall on them. Rumors spread that they had filed on all the productive prospects when, actually, little gold had been found by anyone.

But two men soon changed all that. A soldier, assigned to a small detachment sent up from St. Michael to guard the unruly settlement of disgruntled miners, and an old prospector from Idaho named John Hummel, found gold in the sands of Nome's beaches. Within days, gold was discovered for 40 miles along the water line in either direction from Nome.

A town exploded into life along the beaches, and almost overnight Nome turned into a bustling city filled with crowded streets, 100 saloons and dozens of stores, restaurants and "hotels" in tents and hastily constructed wooden buildings.

Frenzied digging on the beach ensued. One observer noted, "Every man in Nome, be he physician or carpenter, lawyer or bar-

Gold seekers who pitched tents and scrambled to find gold on the beaches of Nome, seen here in 1899, longed for letters from home.

keeper, dropped his usual vocation and went to work with a shovel and rocker."

During the summer of 1899, gold worth more than $2 million was taken from the beaches, and by the summer of 1900, the Nome "poor man's gold rush" reached its peak. More than 20,000 people crowded the city and beaches looking for gold – and mail.

Firsthand account 1900 Nome

Nome was the largest general delivery address in the U.S. postal system that summer. In his book, "Alaska's First Free Mail Delivery in 1900," letter carrier Fred Lockley noted that the postal clerks had to use five filing boxes just to sort letters for people named Johnson.

Lockley and fellow mailman Ben Taylor had taken leave from their mail carrier duties in Salem, Oregon, to try sifting for nuggets in Nome. Lockley described the scene that met their eyes when the two hopped off the steamer *Nome City* and onto the beaches of Nome in June 1900.

He said it was hard to convey the scene to anyone who had never witnessed a mining stampede before. Lockley and Taylor stepped from the rowboat to the lighter, from which a plank led to the shore. For about a mile, freight was piled from 10 to 20 feet high along the waterfront, and it was piled from 20 feet of the water's edge to about 50 yards back toward the tundra.

"It reminded one of some gigantic anthill, and how the human ants were swarming over the pile. Lighters were being unloaded by long lines of men wearing hip rubber boots, who waded out to the loaded barges, staggering back with heavy loads," Lockley wrote. "Others were sorting over the vast accumulation of freight of every description in search of their own belongings. The narrow strip of sand between the sea and the freight was thronged with men with stretchers or pack straps, carrying freight and baggage."

He described dog teams, consisting of 8-10 huskies and malemutes, hitched tandem, straining at their collars to drag their carts through the soft and yielding sand. Men with push carts good naturedly contended for the right of way; and here and there teams of horses and wagons earned money for their owners by carrying trunks at $2 each, or hauling freight at $10 an hour. Hoarse commands of the lighter bosses to their men added to the confusion, along with the 'Gangway there,' or 'Mush on' of the drivers of dog teams.

"Going from the turmoil of the beach up one block to Nome's principal street you found you had gotten into confusion worse confounded – a narrow street, 10 or 12 paces from store front to store front, so crowded with humanity that one could only make his way along with considerable difficulty. ..."

Within three days, Lockley and Taylor decided that they would not be able to make wages on the beach. A great many others had discovered the same fact and were applying for work unloading the lighters at $1 an hour. But since others were being refused for long-shore work by the hundreds, the men knew their chances were slim.

Lockley sees an opportunity

It was while Lockley and his friend were standing in a more than block-long line at the post office that he conceived the idea of free

A crowd gathers outside the new post office in Nome in 1900.

Men line up at the Nome Post Office in anticipation of hearing news from loved ones back home.

mail delivery to businesses in Nome. He suggested it to the postal clerk in charge and was hired on the spot. John Clum, the post office inspector, wrote up the letter authorizing the plan and sent Lockley and Taylor on their way.

"Taking our notebooks, we started down Front Street to get the names of our patrons," Lockley wrote in his book. "One of the first places I entered was a restaurant. I stated my errand. The proprietor, a woman, looked incredulous and asked, 'How much are you going to tax me to bring my mail?'

"I told her it would be a free delivery, and no charge whatever, as the government was paying me $5 a day for my services.

"'Free delivery! Now wouldn't that paralyze you!' she exclaimed incredulously. 'Going to bring us our letters around for nothing. Well, God bless Uncle Sam. That is the only thing I ever heard of in this camp that was free.'"

Almost without exception, the people offered to pay for having their mail delivered, and they could scarcely believe they were getting the service without being charged.

Improvising carriers' sacks from canvas, register-supply sacks and valise straps, and routing the mail as best they could, the two men started out the next morning on the first-ever free mail delivery in Alaska.

They were surrounded by an eager throng before they had walked a block. People gave them orders to deliver mail to this and that place. The pair knew they had to establish the rule that only those actually engaged in business, either as proprietor or as employee, could have their mail delivered, or they would have had half the population giving orders to have mail left in care of different business firms.

"I am afraid that the rule was more honored in the breach than in the observance, however, for we would deliver mail at some saloons for a score or more of persons," Lockley wrote. "When I inquired if they were all employees, the answer would be, 'Oh, yes. They are working for us, all right, but just now they are out on one of the creeks.'"

Lockley said that people often read of the postman being an ever-welcome visitor, but he never knew what that meant before.

"Welcome is a very mild term for the enthusiastic reception we

The rugged adventurers who traveled north in search of their fortunes craved letters from home. These men at Tagish Post in the Yukon Territory were no exception.

frequently received. One man on my route was so worried by not hearing from home that he was almost ready to pull up stakes and leave. He had not heard from his wife since his arrival, and he fancied someone with a similar name was receiving his mail. I took his name, and next day handed him five letters from his wife. Welcome! Well, rather."

The dedicated mailmen also had to contend with patrons' frequent relocations in the hustle and bustle of gold-rush Nome.

"I delivered the mail for a secondhand man at his tent opposite the North American Trading and Transportation Company's store," Lockley wrote. "As I passed along the street opposite the Barracks one forenoon, someone hailed me. It was my secondhand man.

"He said, 'Leave my mail here after this. I sold my business out last night.' He had put in a stock of fruits and fancy groceries, changing not only his location but his business overnight. That same afternoon I passed his way, when he again hailed me. 'Hold my mail for a few days,' he said.

"'What is up now?' I inquired.

"'I got a lease on this business site for $50,' he answered. 'This noon the Babcock Undertaking Company offered me $150, so I sold it and am $100 ahead of the game. I am going to auction my stuff off this evening, as he takes possession tomorrow morning.'

"He had owned and disposed of two business enterprises within 24 hours and made money on both transactions."

Postal Inspector's report for July 1900

• "Twenty-three clerks were employed. This number includes the day and night general delivery force at the post office proper, as well as at the paper tent. Also the register and money order department and the carrier force.

• "A trifle over $136,000 in money orders were issued during the month, the largest day's business being on July 23, when $9,252.65 represented the cash received from money orders.

• "Fifty-one pouches of letter mail, 14 pouches of registered mail and 372 sacks of papers were received during the month.

• "Dispatched 46 pouches of ordinary and registered letter mail and 18 sacks of papers.

• "1,230 registered letters were received and 1,290 registered letters dispatched.

• "$1,051.50 worth of stamps were sold and $1,293.91 represented the amount of cancellations during the month."

Downing establishes Dawson-Nome route

The mail carriers put in long hours when ships carrying mail arrived in port. Sometimes postmen spent up to 24 hours sorting, routing and delivering the massive amount of mail when several ships unloaded simultaneously. Their normal schedules involved from 10 to 12 hours per day.

But the mail didn't just arrive by ships. It also came by dog team from places like Dawson. And when the post office issued bids for the land route to Nome, P.C. Richardson – the first to get the contract – found the task too difficult. That's when Ben Downing took over.

Downing used the mail trail earlier established by John Clum, which wound from Dawson, via Eagle, Circle, Fort Yukon to Fort

Benjamin S. Downing Eagle and Dawson Stage Line horse-drawn sled crosses the Alaska-Canada boundary line on the Yukon River, Feb. 12, 1904.

Gibbon at the mouth of the Tanana River, and then to Nome.

The 1,600-mile route was largely unexplored, so Downing surveyed for cutoffs to reduce distance and danger and marked the trail with stakes or branches.

He put shelter cabins about 25 miles apart along the river, and sometimes he used wood-cutters' cabins he found near the riverbanks. He supplied them with provisions, stoves and shelters for the dogs.

Adept with handling both dogs and horses, Downing ran a four-horse bobsled stage that carried passengers and mail

A man stands in front of Northern Commercial Company mail station No. 2, Route No. 7811, somewhere along the Alaska-Canada boundary just after 1900.

from Dawson to Eagle. Below Eagle, he switched to dogs. The eight- to 10-dog mail teams were hitched tandem to sleds specially made to carry the mail. Loads averaged about 100 pounds to a dog.

The new mail carrier knew how important the dogs were in his business. He knew good ones, too, and was one of the best traders in the Yukon.

Once he got hold of a malinger, however, albeit a fine-looking dog. When Downing later came across another driver who was struck by the fine appearance of the shirker, he held his tongue about the laziness of the creature.

"Ben, you've plenty of dogs, and I need one more," the man said.

"I'm short of dogs, myself, these days," Downing countered, but the other man insisted and Downing relented. "Which one do you want?"

Benjamin S. Downing prepares to leave Circle City with U.S. mail in 1899.

Just as Downing expected, the buyer chose the fine-looking dog with the lamentable habit. When the buyer later reproached Downing for selling the dog, the mail carrier countered, "He's just homesick. I always treat my dogs well. Mush!" and he took off down the trail.

His old friend, John W. Duncan of Rampart, often told of Downing's powerful grip when he clamped down on a hand.

"The man who owned the hand was almost forced down to his knees," Duncan said. "When I shook hands with him, I usually closed the other fist ready to hit him if he squeezed too hard."

Downing seldom got angry, but the one thing that made him see red was to find a stove stolen from one of his shelter cabins. That was the unpardonable sin to an old-timer, an evil of the cheechako.

The rugged pioneer carried the mail for four years on the Dawson-to-Nome run. Then Northern Commercial Company outbid him for the contract and took over his teams and shelter cabins.

C.L. Andrews, Alaska historian and author of "Story of Alaska," said the last time he saw his old friend, Downing was standing on the bank of the Yukon with a monster of a husky, forepaws on his shoulders, trying to lick his face.

Between dodges to miss the dog's tongue, Downing managed to gasp, "I always did love my dogs."

Downing died in January 1906 while undergoing surgery in a San Francisco hospital to remove that Indian rifle ball, the souvenir from his days in Texas.

Other mail routes

Downing's route from Dawson to Nome was one of Alaska's dog trails used by many early mail carriers. All maps of the territory, prior to 1940, charted the main trails, such as the one starting at Barrow. It went west along the Arctic Coast and south down the Bering Sea coast through Wainwright, Point Lay, Point Hope, Kivalina, Kotzebue and Deering.

It wound across the Seward Peninsula to Nome; there the trail carried onto the south shore of the peninsula through White Mountain and along the Bering Coast through Unalakleet, St. Michael and on to Scammon Bay.

There was the long Kuskokwim trail, too, northeastward along that river through Bethel, Akiak, Aniok, McGrath and Nikolai, where it took off on a northerly tangent to pass through Minchumina and Nenana to Fairbanks. Besides these main trails, there were many shorter side trails serving scores of mining and trapping communities.

And it wasn't always easy to find reliable carriers. U.S. Army Lt. W.R. Abercrombie reported that the postmaster at Orca, in Prince William Sound, found it impossible early in spring 1898 to make arrangements with prospectors to pack mail from Port Valdez into the Interior – they were all too intent on searching for gold.

He eventually made arrangements with a man named Jackson, who was married to an Alaska Native. This man proved to be a very satisfactory carrier during the earlier part of the season, said Abercrombie, who explored Prince William Sound in 1884, but he couldn't stand prosperity and fell by the wayside.

After Jackson moved on to other pursuits, various carriers hauled the mail. But as they accumulated enough money to pay their passage south to the states, the mail was left abandoned along the trail.

Finally, in 1899, a mail route was started at Valdez to serve the

Horses haul mail and freight along the Valdez-Fairbanks trail in the early 1900s.

new military garrison of Fort Egbert on the Yukon River at Eagle. Richard Chilcoat packed the mail on his back for $2,839 during a single 1,200-mile roundtrip, which took him about a month. After the first winter, he gave up.

Then the Fish brothers took over the chore, hiring carriers to split up the route. Two years later, the mail service proved it could keep pace with the gold rush then going full tilt.

Once a week carriers delivered the precious mail to Eagle by horse and stagecoach, as well as sled and dog team. This service, along the Yukon winter trail by way of Rampart and Fort Gibbons, was first under military supervision. In 1908, the post office took over. By that time, there were seven post offices north of the Arctic Circle.

Dogs give way to airplanes

With the gold rushes came the first attempt to introduce horses as beasts of burden in the new land of ice and snow, but deep snow proved too much of a handicap. Next, reindeer and dogs were tried. The reindeer proved intractable and impossible to harness break, so it was up to the dogs. In Interior Alaska, the dog team was the first to prove successful in carrying the mail – until the airplane came along.

Col. Carl Ben Eielson, seen above by his open-cockpit biplane mounted on skis, made the first experimental mail flight from Fairbanks to McGrath in February 1923.

Feb. 21, 1923, showed the writing on the wall. Fred Milligan was driving his dog team with the U.S. mail on a bitterly cold day through the deep snow on the trail between Nenana and McGrath, a 20-day run, when the dogs first heard a sound from the sky.

The team stopped suddenly, looked around and then gazed skyward. Then Fred heard the noise. It got louder. He looked up as a plane passed overhead, and the pilot waved from the open cockpit. It was Col. Carl Ben Eielson in his small, single-engine plane. That event was a milestone in Alaska history.

As Fred and his dogs plodded wearily on to the end of the day's run, the plane passed again on its return trip from McGrath. Eielson had proven that flying the mail was practical, safe, economical and fast.

Last mail run with dogs

The last official dog team mail contract expired in 1949 – the mail run between Rampart and Fairbanks – but dogs continued to carry mail between Central and Miller House on the Steese Highway in emergencies. And airplane competition didn't stop Chester Noongwook of St. Lawrence Island from continuing his sled dog mail run until 1963, the last mail delivery of its kind in the country.

That year, Wien Airlines established the first commercial airplane base on St. Lawrence Island at Gambell and a landing strip at Savoonga. But Chester was retained on a supplemental basis whenever the planes couldn't get through. For six years, Chester had never once let bad weather keep him from carrying the mail between Gambell and Savoonga.

However, he had the last laugh on the planes that superseded him. A modern airplane, delayed by bad weather, caused the young Eskimo to be tardy for a very important occasion in his life – receiving an award from the post office upon his retirement.

Noongwook, who made his weekly 100-mile runs sometimes in blinding snow storms where visibility was about 10 feet and tempera-

Chester Noongwook made the last dog team mail run between Gambell and Savoonga in 1963, which ended an era of Alaska's mail delivery history.

tures ranged to minus 40 degrees Fahrenheit, was four hours late for a special ceremony in Fairbanks when fog prevented his plane from departing Nome. He didn't know why he was to report to Fairbanks, and when he finally arrived at that city, he was overwhelmed at being presented with a large, framed certificate as movie cameras rolled and flashbulbs clicked. After the presentation of the special award, the first of its kind, for outstanding service as the last dog and sled mail carrier, Noongwook was the dinner guest of the post office and high-ranking government officials.

And so the curtain was finally drawn on that exciting, dramatic era when dogs carried the mail in Alaska. It seems fitting to close the story of the early postmen with this poem by "Alaska Nellie" Lawing. Nellie came to Alaska in 1915 at the age of 42 and was the first person to get a railroad contract for a roadhouse on the way to Seward. She and her dogs hauled the mail and knew from firsthand experience that:

The Mail Goes Through
It matters not how rough the trail,
You must fight it through when you take the mail.
It matters not how the north wind blows
How bitter cold or how hard it snows.
Remember, it's not how or what you do
The important thing is – the mail must go through
Do your best to succeed – you dare not fail
For you must mush on when you take the mail.

Another rugged breed of adventurers established trails in the Alaska wilderness, too. Trappers, who followed their traplines from fall through spring, forged many routes through rugged country.

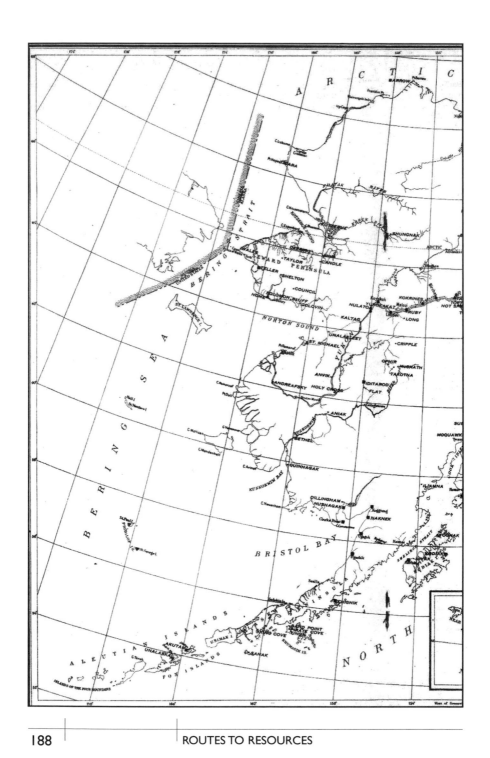

ROUTES TO RESOURCES

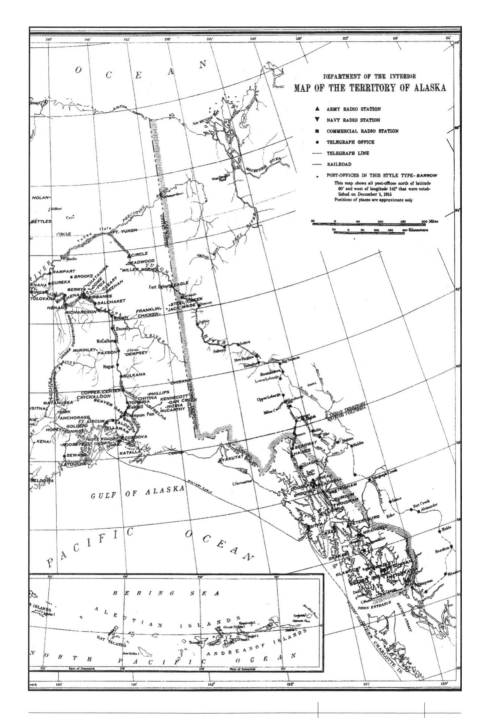

16

THE TRAPPING LIFE

Although some gold prospecting occurred during the years immediately following Alaska's purchase, the fur trade drove economic activity. The Pioneer Company entered the Yukon River fur trade in 1868 at Nuklukayet, but Parrot and Company bought out the firm. That company operated the *Yukon*, which dropped traders and supplies at Anvik, Nulato and Nuklukayet on its trip upriver in 1869. Parrot and Company then merged with the Alaska Commercial Company in 1870.

Natives arrive by canoe at Nuklukayet to trade in the late 1880s.

Arthur Harper, Alaska Commercial Company trader, and the Rev. Dr. Sims visit with Natives near the remains of Hudson's Bay Company buildings in Fort Yukon in 1883.

After also taking over the former Hudson's Bay Company post at Fort Yukon, the Alaska Commercial Company started other posts along the Yukon River. By 1880 there were additional company stations at Anvik, Russian Mission, Andreafsky, Kotlik, Shageluk and Nulato. That year, Interior Athabascans sold 75,000 pelts to the traders.

Three men who first came to Alaska searching for gold were among those who helped extend the Alaska Commercial Company's influence. Arthur Harper, Jack McQuesten and Al Mayo had already trapped and prospected their way through Canada. By 1873, when they pushed on to Alaska, Harper was convinced that the gold-bearing mountains of the Canadian Yukon extended into the new possession (more about these men in Chapter 25).

The three men soon ran out of supplies. Harper continued prospecting for gold, while McQuesten and May agreed to act as traders for the Alaska Commercial Company.

Following the Yukon upriver from Fort Yukon, the two men took a ton of supplies to establish a new outpost, Fort Reliance, south of present-day Dawson in Canada, and started trading goods for furs.

They found that the Athabascans preferred to use traditional spruce snares instead of the steel traps and wire snares that arrived through Native trade channels. The Natives took the metal traps apart and used the iron and steel to make tools.

Dog teams were an important part of the trapping process, too, because they meant that trapping could be extended over more territory, thus more furs could be collected.

Fierce competition among buyers meant higher prices for furs. But as fur prices increased, traders often raised prices on their goods.

Nastasia Deacon, a woman trapper who was quite successful in her trapping life, trapped along the Kuskokwim River.

The Athabascan people came to depend on many items brought north by the white men, including cotton fabric, gunpowder and shot, tea and sugar, combs, soap, flour, tobacco, butcher knives and pocket knives. Tobacco, which cost the trader 30 cents, might be exchanged for a marten fur valued at $5.

By the early 1880s, the Alaska Commercial Company had a monopoly and lowered the price paid for furs.

A Russian Church, an Alaska Commercial Company store and a cottage grace the tundra at St. Michael.

Alaska Commercial Company

Alaska Commercial Company can trace its roots to 1776. Catherine the Great granted trading rights to the Russian-American Trading Company, which operated trading posts throughout Alaska and traded goods and services for furs, gold and other tradable goods.

After America purchased Alaska from Russia in 1867, the company was sold to San Francisco merchants Lewis Gerstle and Louis Sloss. They renamed it the Alaska Commercial Company.

From 1868 through the gold-rush era of the early 1900s, Alaska Commercial Company provided groceries and general merchandise for trappers, explorers and stampeders. Established throughout Alaska, these village stores became the center of all community activities. They served as the post office, community hall, courtroom, marriage parlor, funeral home and a safe haven for travelers.

The company also served as the bank by extending credit to trappers, miners and fishermen. Little cash was used to purchase

A moose head stands guard among clothing, pots, pans and other wares at the Northern Commercial Company store in Rampart.

merchandise. Customers traded with pelts, gold, artifacts, fish or anything else valued by other customers.

As the gold rush wound down, many people left the territory and the number of Alaska Commercial stores shrank. The company reorganized into fewer stores, a navigation company and river barge lines.

A group of employees purchased the company in 1922 and renamed it the Northern Commercial Company. The new owners moved the corporate headquarters to Seattle and the company became a major supplier of heavy equipment and machinery, which contributed to the development of rural Alaska.

Trapping important to Natives

Jobs and cash were plentiful during the gold-rush era for Alaska Natives, with as many as 100 wood-burning steamers plying the Yukon River annually. Not only did many Native people work in wood yards or on river boats, they also sold smoke-tanned moccasins, shoepacs, hide gloves and fur caps to the stampeders.

But as the rush ended and overland routes developed, the river trade declined. The Natives needed to find alternative means to support their families in Alaska's cash economy.

Trapping worked out well for many families because they could live their subsistence lifestyles in the summer months and then in the fall, before freezeup, take a winter's grubstake and move to cabins on rivers or streams.

After the first hard freeze, they set traps and snares. The winter routine meant checking the trapline, returning to the cabin to skin the animals, stretch the fur and then head out again to check and reset traps.

A good team of sled dogs was worth its weight in gold to trappers in the Last Frontier.

A trapper scrapes a fresh skin as a beaver hide stretches on a frame nearby.

Most families traveled by dog team back to their villages to spend the Christmas holidays, trade their furs and purchase more supplies for the rest of the winter. Most traded their furs at Alaska/Northern Commercial Company stores, where they exchanged their pelts for credit, cash or merchandise.

Sometimes furs were sent to dealers, like the Seattle Fur Exchange, for auctioning. And although fur prices varied from year to year, trapping generally provided a consistent income.

Trapping season ended with the spring breakup. Families returned home via boat and prepared for a summer spent at fish camps, catching and drying enough fish to use throughout the winter for themselves and as dog food.

Belle Stevens of Stevens Village returns from her trapline with a catch of rabbits on her back.

A trapper's life

From early in the fall to the close of trapping season in April, many trappers traveled miles and miles of traplines with no company except their dogs. It was no job for a cheechako. Trappers like Ed Ueeck covered around 80 miles a week, checking to see if any animals had been caught in hidden traps.

"About 14 miles a day is my average travel on the circle, although I cover considerably more than that, of course, on the side trails," Ueeck told Tom Jackson in an article for the October 1939 issue of The Alaska Sportsman. "During the trapping season there are only six hours of daylight

A trapper carries a lynx from his trapline around Stevens Village at the turn-of-the-last century.

at the most, and it is long after dark before I reach the trail cabin at the end of a day's hike complete."

Once trappers fixed something to eat and fed their dogs, they then had to skin and care for the furs they'd picked up along the line and prepare for the next day.

"Blinding storms are sometimes encountered far out on the trail between shelter cabins, and a biting wind with the thermometer at 40-below zero makes it seem twice that cold," Ueeck said. "When a trap has been sprung, it has to be reset with bare hands, and it must be done quickly and carefully ... frozen hands can easily spell disaster to a trapper who is a hundred miles from civilization."

Building the line

Although Ueeck trapped during the 1930s, his story is similar to those early trappers who turned to the Last Frontier to eek out livings in the wilderness. He started out helping colonists harvest their crops in the Matanuska Valley. But when he saw the prices paid for furs, he switched professions and turned to trapping. He chose a spot near Lake Leila, on the divide between the Nelchina and Matanuska rivers.

After unloading six months of supplies from a pontoon aircraft, he picked up an axe and began swamping a trail through a heavy growth of willows to build his headquarters cabin on higher ground. Once that cabin was finished, he spent a few years building another six cabins on the circumference of a circle, whose center was the main cabin. He stored his winter supplies in a cache, about 18 feet above ground, to prevent wild animals from helping themselves to his food.

Like Ueeck, most trappers didn't talk much about the money they made, nor the hardships they endured climbing creeks and mountain ridges as they routed out any unlucky furbearers that happened to cross their paths. But they knew that any man who could make a living from trapping in Alaska could make a success of anything.

A trapper chops wood at his cabin near Seward.

Trappers built simple cabins in the heart of Alaska's wilderness during the early 1900s.

Rampart House Trappers, Circa 1910. Left to Right: Paul George, Joe Netro, Daniel Fredson, Billy Annett, Dan Cadzow, John McNickel. (Annetts Furs)

There were only a handful of white trappers along the Yukon River following the U.S. purchase of Alaska and up to the turn-of-the-last century.

Wildman of Dry Bay

A diary lay near the body of V. Swanson at Dry Bay, between Lituya Bay and Yakutat, in 1918. Known as the "Wildman of Dry Bay," Swanson lived and died as a lonely trapper.

When winter caught him without adequate food, he eventually succumbed to the elements and left his written words as testimony to his battle to survive. Excerpts from his diary, which was found by fellow trappers Hardy Trefzger and Fred Zastrow and later published in an Alaska Sportsman magazine, follow:

Oct. 4: Getting sick packing, now looking for camping place. Cold in the lungs with a high fever.

Oct. 6: Less fever, less pain, but getting weak.

Oct. 10: Going to build a house. Will not be able to pull canoe up this fall, got to wait for the ice.

Oct. 13: Shot a glacier bear.

Oct. 14: Shot a goat.

Oct. 17: House finished.

Oct. 18: Taking out some traps.

Oct. 20: Made a smoke house.

Oct. 21: Shot one goat.

Oct. 25: Shot one lynx.

Winter sets in

Oct. 28: Winter has come. Strong wind, two feet of snow.

Nov. 6: Made one pair of bearskin pants.

Nov. 13: Made two pair of moccasins.

Nov. 18: Finished one fur coat of bear, wolf and lynx.

Nov. 21: Finished one sleeping bag of bear, goat, blankets and canvas. Rain for several days.

Nov. 22: Left eye bothers me. Shot one goat.

Dec. 1: Getting bad. Cold for several days, river still open.

Dec. 7: The wind is so strong that you can't stand upright. River froze excepting a few riffles. Too much snow and too rough for sleighing. Snow getting deeper now.

A trapper roasts his meal of wild meat along his trapline in the White Mountains.

Dec. 19: Snowing but still very cold. Riffles up in the bend still open. Can't travel. Don't believe there will be ice a man can run a sleigh over this winter. Very little grub, snow too deep and soft for hunting goats. Stomach balking at straight meat, especially lynx.

Dec. 21: Shot a goat from the river.

Dec. 25: Very cold. A good Christmas dinner. Snow getting hard. River still open in places above camp.

Dec. 26: Broke through the ice. Skin clothes saved the day.

Dec. 31: Finished new roof on the house. One month cold weather straight. Last night and today rain. Stomach getting worse.

Tragedy in Dry Bay

Jan. 8: River open as far as can be seen. Health very poor.

Jan. 15: Goats moving out of reach. Using canoe on the river.

Jan. 28: One goat, been cold for a few days, no ice on the river.

Feb. 1: Cold weather nearly all month of Jan.. Lynx robbed my meat cache up the river. Salt and tea but once a day. Gradually getting weaker.

Animal skins made toasty sleeping bags for trappers, miners and other adventurers.

Feb. 5: Colder weather, feeling very bad. Just able to take care of myself.

Feb. 24: More snow. Living on dry meat and tallow.

March 2: Shot one goat.

March 11: Starting for Dry Bay believing the river open. Out about one hour, struck ice. Can't go either way. Too weak to haul canoe. Snow soft, no game here.

March 25: Trying to get to the house. River is frozen in places and rising. The sleigh now only three miles from there, but open river and perpendicular cliffs keep me from getting any farther. At present cannot find anything to eat here. Eyes are getting bad.

April 1: Got to house with what I could carry. Wolverines been here eating my skins, robes and moccasins, old meat and also my goatskin door. They tried to run me last night, came through the stovepipe hole showing fight. Heavy fall of snow. Canoe and some traps down the river about five miles, close to Indian Grave mark. Camp about halfways.

April 3: Still snowing. Cooking my last grub, no salt, no tea.

ROUTES TO RESOURCES

April 4: Shot one goat using all but three of my shells. Can't see the sights at all.

April 10: Wolverines ate my bedding and one snowshoe. In the tent, getting shaky in the legs. A five-mile walk a big day's work.

April 15: The no-salt diet hitting me pretty hard. Eyes are getting worse, in the bunk most of the time.

April 17: Rain yesterday and today.

April 20: Finest weather continues again, cooking the last grub, got to stay in the bunk most of the time – my legs won't carry me very far. My eyes are useless for hunting, the rest of my body also useless. I believe my time has come. My belongings, everything I got I give to Jos. Pellerine of Dry Bay. If not alive, to Paul Swartzkoph, Alsek River.

– April 22, 1918, V. Swanson

Another adventurer who established a few trails to Alaska's natural wealth arrived in the Last Frontier during the rush for gold. Jack Dalton carved out a toll road for gold miners in Southeast Alaska and later explored for routes to export other abundant resources from the territory.

17

DALTON TURNS TIMBER INTO GOLD

A short, stocky and feisty frontiersman named Jack Dalton had explored much of Southeast Alaska by the late 1890s. He'd established a toll road from Pyramid Harbor on the Lynn Canal to the Yukon, on which around 2,000 cattle had traveled and made a welcome addition to many a miner's food supply during the Klondike Gold Rush. His trail would later become part of the Haines Highway.

When the entrepreneurial Dalton had an area around the Porcupine gold field surveyed – 36 miles from Haines up the Chilkat Valley – he realized that more gold lay in the forested area surrounding the town site. He built a sawmill in 1899 that produced 5,000 board feet of lumber a day.

The abundance of tall trees in Southeast Alaska kept sawmills humming.

Loggers, standing atop a pile of cut timber, show just how big trees grow in Southeast Alaska.

The sawmill also made lumber needed for large flumes for the gold-mining effort.

However, the Tlingit Indians began using the timber resources of Southeast Alaska centuries before Dalton happened upon the area. They burned wood for heat, made dugouts from cottonwood trees, carved household and ritual items, and stripped bark from cedar trees for weavers of Chilkat blankets.

When non-Natives began settling the area, bringing a cash economy with them, the Natives supplied the new settlers with firewood. Soon that became the most common service provided by the Natives for the newcomers. A cord of wood – 4 feet by 4 feet, cut and stacked – cost $2.

While small sawmills like Dalton's could accommodate the needs of most miners for building homes and businesses, as well as construction in the gold fields, the majority of the lumber for major projects was sent via steamship from Seattle or Olympia, Washington, or from Portland, Oregon.

Above: A plentiful supply of timber around Skagway helped furnish material for industry and a growing population.

Below: Four men raft several logs downriver to a sawmill in Southeast Alaska.

A small child stands near a log cutter – note the wood-cutting tools and timber in the background.

Quite a bit of lumber from outside of Alaska was used to build Haines' Fort Seward and many local canneries, although some of the early canneries had small, private mills to use in making fish traps and other small construction projects.

Other sawmills operated in various communities, as well, including Skagway, Wrangell and an operation at the village of Port Gravina, near Ketchikan, where Tsimshian Indians from Metlakatla had settled in 1892. Their sawmill was the first business built, owned and operated by Natives in Alaska, according to historian Pat Roppel.

"The company constructed a sawmill with a wharf that unfortunately went dry at low tide," Roppel wrote in "An Historical Guide to Revillagigedo and Gravina Islands" in 1995. "Powered by steam, the sawmill had a daily capacity of 15,000 board feet of sawed and planed timber."

The sawmill initially produced box shooks for salmon boxes for the canned salmon industry that just was getting started, but soon the area construction boom had the mill primarily supplying lumber for buildings in Ketchikan and Saxman.

In 1905, Congress transferred the national forests to the U.S.

Sometimes loggers used oxen as work animals, as seen here on the Stikine River near Wrangell in 1864.

Secretary of Agriculture and provided that pulpwood or wood pulp manufactured from Alaska timber could be exported. However, without a large outside market, the timber industry remained small, mainly producing firewood.

The Combs Lumber Company built a mill in Haines in 1907 that had a capacity of 25,000 board feet. Proclaimed by local newspaper advertisements as "the largest saw and planing mill on Lynn Canal," the mill burned down in 1912.

Industrial-scale logging didn't begin until the 1950s when the U.S. Forest Service signed 50-year contracts with Ketchikan Pulp Company and foreign-owned Alaska Pulp Corporation, developing a timber industry within the Tongass forest.

Following his sojourn with timber in Southeast Alaska, Dalton next tackled opening a route to other riches in Southcentral Alaska.

18

ROUTES TO GOLD, COPPER AND COAL

Back in 1891, Jack Dalton and his traveling companion, E.J. Glave of the Leslie Exploration Expedition, decided "defective transportation is the sole reason for the undeveloped state of the land." Dalton, a rugged entrepreneur, had an important role in remedying the situation. He established a route to the gold fields of the Klondike, another to the copper ore in Prince William Sound and finally blazed trail to coal in the Matanuska Valley.

Born on the Cherokee Strip of Oklahoma in 1855, Dalton spent a few years in Oregon as a logger and cowboy. Some shooting scrapes, however, made it urgent to leave that part of the country and he shipped on a sailing vessel to Alaska.

He became a member of Lt. Frederick Schwatka's exploration party to Mount St. Elias. Later he signed up with the Leslie party to explore the Interior and write reports for the Frank Leslie Illustrated Newspaper of New York.

That's when he met up with Glave, an English explorer who had been with Henry M. Stanley in Africa. He and Dalton developed mutual respect.

"Dalton," Glave wrote later, "is a most desirable partner – has excellent judgment, cool and deliberate in times of danger and possessed of great tact in dealing with the Indians ... as a camp cook, I've never seen his equal."

Dalton's ability to deal with the Indians was very helpful, for this was Indian country they were traversing. Indians had followed game trails in the vicinity, and the proud and warlike Chilkats dominated trade. They never allowed the Interior Indians direct contact with white people.

Dalton scopes out trail to Yukon

When Glave and Dalton were on their expeditions, the Indians tried to discourage them with tales of mighty glaciers and raging rivers, for success would wrest from the Chilkats control of the gate to the Interior. But Glave and Dalton were undaunted.

On their first trip, they started in the Interior and descended the turbulent Alsek River to the sea. Next time they started from the Chilkat village of Klukwan on the coast. On their first trip, they had decided that the use of horses was practical and used them the second trip, as well. They finally arrived at Lake Kluane in Canada; then returned to the coast, following the same route as that of their inward journey, riding horses most of the way.

Haines and Fort William H. Seward, in Southeast Alaska, as seen from Mount Rippinsky, with Pyramid Harbor and Davidson Glacier in the distance.

Above: The Dalton Cache, located 41 miles northwest of Haines along the Haines Highway at the Alaska-Canada border, is a pre-Klondike Gold Rush outpost built around 1895 by Jack Dalton. This is where he stored trading goods before transport over the Chilkoot Pass into the Yukon Territory. When the Klondike Gold Rush hit in 1897-98, the cache became a stopping place for miners streaming toward Dawson.

Below: Goats pull a sled loaded with supplies destined for the Klondike gold fields.

Dalton, in 1896, established a pack trail from Pyramid Harbor to the Yukon, partly following the 1891 route. The Klondike Gold Rush would find him prepared, and the Dalton Trail became an important gateway to the gold fields.

Dalton searches for railroad route

In 1904, Dalton was selected by Irish contractor Michael J. Heney to be a member of a party to explore the feasibility of building a railroad up the Copper River Valley in Southcentral Alaska. The explorers decided that it could be done. That was the birth of the Copper River and Northwestern Railway from the coast to the copper mines at Kennecott – and the birth of Cordova, as well.

Dalton got into a beef with the railroad company during this time. In her book, "The Copper Spike," Lone Janson writes that Dalton had filed on three mineral claims straddling the 1906 railroad survey that led to the railroad's proposed dock. When company men began lay-

Workers made camps along the railroad route as they constructed the Copper River and Northwestern Railway.

ROUTES TO RESOURCES

ing rails to the dock, they were met at the property line by Dalton, who carried his trusty rifle.

"Where do you think you're going?" Dalton asked.

"Right along here," the crew boss replied.

Dalton ominously suggested it wasn't a good idea. Heading for the company's office, he informed the man in charge that the minute any man crossed his property, he would come looking for the foreman and wouldn't stop until he had found him. The argument ended up in court, which found for the railroad. It decided the land was more valuable as a railroad right-of-way than as mineral land, and Dalton had to remove his trestle that joined the railroad property. It was one battle Dalton didn't win.

Gold, copper then coal challenged Dalton's trailblazing talents. Coal was being shipped from as far away as Cardiff, Wales, to the U.S. Navy's coal station at Sitka. Some thought that the coal deposits at Chickaloon in the Matanuska Valley might meet the Navy's requirements.

The Alaska Engineering Commission dug coal mines at Chickaloon, 35 miles from Matanuska.

Knik, shown above, was a growing supply center at the turn-of-the-last century.

Dalton searches for coal route

Along with federal Bureau of Mines director A.M. Holmes, Dalton went to look the mine over in 1913. When Holmes concluded the coal would suffice, he gave Dalton the task of figuring out a way to get the coal from the mine to tidewater – at a cost the agency could afford.

Dalton concluded that the Matanuska River, when frozen, could be used part of the way and that horses could do the conveying. He headed for Seattle, where he picked up supplies, men and horses. He then returned to Alaska on Nov. 5 aboard the *General Hubbard*, recruiting more men along the way.

He reached Knik anchorage at the mouth of Ship Creek on Nov. 16 and put his outfit ashore. Moving up the east bank of Knik Arm, the party reached Old Knik, above Eklutna, where Dalton established his headquarters.

Forty-five miles of road and many bridges would be required. Three miles of the route ran from the mine to the bank of the Matanuska River. Then from Eska Creek, the road traveled to a tidewater landing.

As soon as the ice was thick enough, freight began to move. Fifty-four horses pulled five bobsleds, which carried from three to seven tons of coal. By January 1914, 700 tons had been carried as far as Eska Crossing. By Feb. 1, the entire lot had left Chickaloon.

Feisty Dalton didn't get by without another confrontation, but this time his rifle didn't play a part. "Pinch Penny" Swift, a disbursing agent of the Bureau of Mines, maintained that Dalton was using more money and supplies than necessary and refused to pay some of Dalton's men. A heated argument ended with Swift on the receiving end of Dalton's fist, and then landing in a heap on a pile of coal.

The U.S. Commissioner at Knik fined Dalton $5 and the Knik Commercial Club held an indignation meeting. They condemned both Swift and the commissioner. Soon afterward Knik got a new commissioner.

Although Dalton's men didn't get paid due to Swift's arbitrary ruling, some were loyal and stayed on, continuing to drive full-speed ahead. By March 6, the men had 900 tons of coal stacked up at ice-blocked Cook Inlet. The estimated cost of freighting the coal was $65,000.

Later, after the ice went out of the Inlet, the coal was placed aboard the battleship *USS Maryland* for testing. But before anything could be done about providing a regular supply of coal, the Navy converted to oil.

Although the Navy didn't use the coal, far-reaching consequences followed Dalton's successful plan of bringing down the coal. An article in the July 1963 Alaska Sportsman said the Matanuska coal had a great deal to do with the decision to build a government railroad from Seward to Fairbanks:

"By the time Jack Dalton died in 1944, the town at the mouth of Ship Creek, created by the railroad, was well on its way to becoming the largest city in Alaska."

Dalton didn't have an opportunity to blaze a trail to the arctic oil fields, Alaska's next important resource to be developed. However, the haul road connecting Fairbanks to the northern oil supply has been given the name of his engineer son, James Dalton.

The Alaska Railroad erected a historical marker at the spot formerly known as Matanuska Landing, where the railroad track now crosses the Matanuska River. It commemorates Jack Dalton's efforts to bring the Matanuska coal to tidewater.

19

GLACIER TRAIL BIRTHS VALDEZ

"Gold in Alaska!" "Valdez Glacier – Best Trail!" rang the headlines in 1897-1898. Promoters of this route claimed that prospectors would find more gold in the American soil along the Copper River than they would in the Canadian Klondike.

And that was one of the greatest hoaxes in Alaska's history, according to Jim and Nancy Lethcoe in their book, "Valdez Gold Rush Trails of 1898-99." Those who chose to try their luck along what had been reported as a pre-exiting trail, found a glacier twice as long and steep as reported.

"With frontier grit, they set about hand sledding more than 1,000 pounds of supplies over the glacier, building boats, rafting the Klutina River's Hell's Gate rapids, and prospecting unnamed creeks," the Lethcoes wrote.

A man and two horses descend Icy Point Trail in winter during the gold rush.

Above: Prospectors seek a trail along the Valdez Glacier during the gold-rush era.

Below: Gold seekers camp along the trail outside Valdez.

Stampeders head for glacier trail

The adventurers encountered all sorts of conditions, including snow slides, snow blindness, glacial crevasses and extreme physical challenges as they pulled their supply-laden sleds. The rugged pioneers made as many as 20 trips back and forth over the steepest legs of the journey in order to transport the necessary year's worth of supplies. The following winter of 1898-99 was long and difficult and many suffered from scurvy and inadequate supplies.

But several thousand gold seekers crossed that glacial trail, and they weren't all men. Sources say 63 women made the trek. A Mrs. Dowling became a living legend when she nursed a U.S. Army man stricken with typhoid back to health at Klutina Lake. She also inspired stampeders who were ready to quit and go home.

"When these men (crossing the glacier) were about to give up, a woman by name of Mrs. Dowling shamed them into a final effort

A group of travelers and their horses sink up to their knees along the trail from Valdez to Fairbanks.

The Valdez Glacier provides an obstacle about four miles out of Valdez en route to the Interior gold fields via Klutina Lake.

and it saved them, because one among them had the nerve, though undoubtedly she was the weakest physically," recalled Charles H. Remington, known as Copper River Joe, in his account "A Golden Cross on the Trails from the Valdez Glacier."

Other women also flourished along the way. Mrs. Anne Barrett, famous for her fresh lingonberry pies, opened an eatery at Klutina Lake and also became a mine owner at Slate Creek. She later opened a restaurant in Valdez.

Lillian Moore, who was an excellent horsewoman, hired on with U.S. Army Lt. W.R. Abercrombie and guided horses over the Valdez Glacier. She and her husband later operated a transport company and took horse-drawn sleds over what became the Richardson Trail.

Copper Center emerges from the timbers

Prospectors crossing the Valdez and Klutina glaciers then had to build boats to navigate the Klutina River. Those who successfully reached the confluence of the Klutina and Copper rivers in early summer 1898 found a busy little city of rough log cabins and tents. The settlement, called Copper Center, boasted a post office, hotel, store, blacksmith shop and smokehouses.

Copper Center became a base from which prospectors ventured out to explore the surrounding country in search of their fortunes. They panned for gold for several weeks at a time and then returned to their cabins at Copper Center to re-supply. The stampeders enjoyed several social events in Copper Center that first summer, including an elaborate Fourth of July celebration, according to the Lethcoes. But many prospectors found life too difficult in the Last Frontier and returned home in the fall.

Many prospectors set up camp in Copper Center and then ventured out to search for their fortunes.

Only about 300 prospectors wintered over in Copper Center in 1898-1899, and while some had the foresight to bring limejuice or supplement their diets with wild berries and spruce needle tea, many developed scurvy because they subsisted primarily on bacon and beans. Scurvy reached epidemic proportions in Copper Center that winter, necessitating heroic rescues, emergency deliveries of food from Valdez and specialized medical care, according to the Lethcoes.

A horse peeks out of a tent along the Valdez trail. Trail horse barns or stables were improvised by digging snow down to the ground before putting up tents for the barns. Sometimes horse tents were supplied with boards laid directly on top of snow, but others were dug out if boards were not in the stampeders' outfits.

But prospectors who made it through the first winter and continued to work the rivers for gold were industrious, hardy and dedicated. They provided shelter and company in their cabins to those explorers, surveyors and prospectors who followed them.

Valdez grows
Other stampeders stayed in Port Valdez, named in 1790 by Don Salvador Fidalgo for the celebrated Spanish Admiral Antonio Valdes

y Basan who was head of the Spanish Marines and Minister of the Indies at the time. Salvador also named Cordova, Port Gravina and other spots while on his voyage to Alaska to investigate the extent of Russian involvement and to reestablish Spanish claim to the area.

Historically, the territory south of Valdez belongs to the Chugach Eskimo, a maritime hunting people, and to the north the land is of the Ahtna, an Athabascan people of the Copper River Basin. Both the Chugach and Ahtna used the area for fishing and trading copper, jade, hides and furs.

A tent city sprang up at the head of the bay, and as some stampeders stayed on shore to set up shops and businesses, Valdez grew into a supply center.

In late summer and fall 1898, Abercrombie's men started cutting a rough trail through Keystone Canyon and over Thompson Pass. The following spring, the U.S. Army approved that route as the new military trail to Eagle and built a fort to support the efforts to upgrade the road, as well as established a telegraph line to the Alaska Interior.

Named for Col. Emerson H. Liscum, who was killed while leading his regiment at the battle of Tien Tsing in China on July 13, 1900,

This view of Fort Liscum, near Valdez, was taken from a boat in the harbor in 1918.

Horses pull freight near the summit of Thompson Pass on the Valdez-Fairbanks trail in the early 1900s.

Fort Liscum was located three miles from the head of Valdez Bay on the south shore. The fort also served to maintain law and order in the growing gold-rush community.

Due to flooding summer streams, the fort was relocated to Ludington's Landing several miles south, on the shores of Port

Passengers and drivers are bundled up in winter clothing for a horse-drawn trip to deliver mail from Valdez to Fairbanks in the early 1900s.

Valdez, one year later. The new site offered a safe anchorage and an abundant supply of water and wood for the 172 men stationed there. The fort closed in 1923.

The Keystone Canyon Trail became the Richardson Highway in 1919 and served as the only viable inland route to Fairbanks until the 1920s. Valdez became the coastal port for the majority of traffic going into and out of the Interior.

As the rush for gold in the Klondike subsided, prospectors turned their attention to the gold, copper and silver deposits on the islands and shores of Prince William Sound. The Cliff Gold Mine, which produced about 51,740 ounces of gold and 8,253 ounces of silver, and the Midas Mine, the fourth-largest producer of copper in the Sound, were the most profitable mines around Valdez. But Ellamar, near Tatitlek, and the Kennecott Mines, near McCarthy, both of which were owned by the Morgan-Guggenheim Alaska Syndicate, produced far more copper than all the other mines combined. And nearly as much gold

A view of Valdez from the water in 1904 shows a growing community.

Gov. John G. Brady turns the first shovel of dirt for the construction of the Alaska Home Railway on Aug. 13, 1907, in Valdez.

came out of Ellamar as a byproduct as came out of the Cliff Mine, according to the Valdez Museum and Historical Archive.

Railroad companies were the cause for considerable turmoil in Prince William Sound as they planned to lay track to haul out some of those valuable resources. Initially, the Alaska Syndicate was leaning toward choosing Valdez as its terminus for a railway out of the Kennecott Mine, instead of Cordova or Katalla, but it later determined that Cordova was the best choice.

"When it appeared that Valdez would not be selected, H.D. Reynolds appeared on the scene touting his plan for the Alaska Home Railroad," according to the Valdez Museum and Historical Archive. "He convinced the people of Valdez that 'his railroad was their railroad.' Many Valdezans invested their entire savings or businesses into supporting his project. Reynolds bought up much of the town; he soon owned a newspaper, hotel, bank and even some of the streets.

A man walks along a snow-covered street in Valdez in 1912.

"In 1907, a shootout erupted over the right of way through Keystone Canyon between the two rival railroad companies. The Alaska Home Railroad project fell apart and the Alaska Syndicate chose Cordova as the terminus for its Copper River and Northwestern Railway. Reynolds left town in a hurry, owing a great deal of money, and was last seen in an insane asylum. Valdezans were left with no railroad, 500 unemployed workers and little money."

Valdez was not alone in its struggle with railroads. As it grew out of the wilderness, the picturesque little town of Cordova had its problems with railway people, too.

20

CORDOVA: A TOWN BORN OF STRIFE

While thousands of gold seekers flocked to Alaska in search of nugget riches during the early 1900s, one group of prospectors in the Wrangell Mountains found a mountain of copper instead – one of the richest copper mines ever discovered. That discovery led to the building of one of Alaska's most picturesque communities: Cordova.

Others had discovered coal and oil in the Prince William Sound and Bering River regions, and only transportation – a railroad – was needed to bring the newly found copper, coal and oil together to unlock the riches of Midas.

Five separate railroads were started from three different points on the coast. Then the fight was on – gun battles, political battles, court battles, fantastic rights-of-way battles – all a part of the history of Alaska's early railroad-building days.

At first, the site of what later became Cordova was not even considered in choosing a railroad terminus. And there was a good reason. Up the Copper River valley, 49 miles away, were two live mighty glaciers, the Miles and Childs, which made that route insurmountable.

However, when Irish contractor Michael J. Heney surveyed the route, he found that nature had made a slight concession. One of the glaciers was higher upstream than the other. By building a bridge, and keeping the Copper River between the glaciers and the railroad,

Miles and Childs glaciers, both of which calve icebergs into the Copper River from opposite banks, complicated building a railroad.

Heney was sure he could pass the huge ice barriers.

He was sure, too, that this route was the best way into the Interior, for there was a "water grade" all the way and no mountains to cut through or climb over.

Rex Beach's novel, "The Iron Trail," tells of Heney's struggle to build the Copper River and Northwestern Railway, and the construction of the Million Dollar Bridge at the glaciers is the high point of the story.

Before Heney could build the railroad over this route, however, he had to persuade the Guggenheim-Morgan Syndicate that the route was feasible. The Alaska Syndicate, which had bought the original copper discovers' claims, was trying to reach the Interior from Valdez. It finally gave up when it found the going was expensive and difficult with rugged mountain grades. But it wasn't convinced that Heney's choice was the right one.

Michael J. Heney and another man cart hand trucks near Cordova.

Cordova began developing in 1898.

Syndicate tries Katalla route

Instead, the syndicate tried a route from Katalla, 40 miles east of Cordova. It had the advantage of being in the heart of the oil and coalfields. But other railroads were being built from there, also, and rival railroad gangs often clashed.

At one point, the Guggenheims had to cross the right of way of the Bruner outfit, which was trying to build a road to the coalfields and then on to the Copper River. The Bruner crew had constructed an immense "go devil," a tool that punched holes in the ground for dynamite, out of railroad ties. Its cable was operated by a machine that swung it back and forth over the disputed right of way, while armed men behind barriers guarded it.

"A $1,000 reward to any of you men with nerve enough to cut that cable," the Guggenheim boss promised.

One daring workman, under cover of protective fire, succeeded, but many men were injured during the fierce gun battle.

The Katalla route was finally abandoned as the terminus of the Guggenheim railroad when an expensive breakwater failed to hold, and the lack of a harbor proved an impossible handicap. With Valdez and Katalla both scrubbed, the syndicate turned to Heney's choice.

Materials fill the railroad yards at Miles Glacier crossing during construction of the Copper River and Northwestern Railway in May 1909.

That intrepid Irishman was so sure it was the logical route that he'd already started building with his own resources. The Guggenheims bought Heney's right of way and gave him the contract to build the railroad.

And so Cordova was born – of strife and violence and stubborn faith. The ring of hammers attended the birth as frame buildings were hurriedly flung up. The throb of dancehall music played by D.C. Kippen, the piano player in Billy Little's Bar, was its lullaby.

Its childhood was boisterous and rowdy as thousands of people milled up and down Main Street, where 23 bars supplied relaxation, fellowship and liquid refreshment.

It was a typical construction town in 1908, where men worked and played hard. It had the enthusiasm and energy of youth. Optimism ran high, and Cordova businessmen were sure the region, with its resources of copper, coal and oil, had a bright future.

But two years before Cordova's birth, early conservationist Gifford Pinchot, first director of the U.S. Forest Service and close friend of Theodore Roosevelt, ordered the withdrawal of vast coal-field holdings in the territory to protect them from the Guggenheim-Morgan Syndicate.

One man who had great dreams for the future of Cordova, pictured above in 1908, was Sam Blum. When asked why he was building on Second Street instead of Main Street, he replied: "If I thought this was going to be a one-street town, I'd never have located here!"

The building he constructed in 1909 was for a long time the largest and most substantial in Alaska. The mezzanine floor held a clothing store, and the rest of the building housed a bank, a grocery store, a general merchandise store and yet another clothing store.

Later it included the town's newspaper and the old stores were turned into apartments. Called The Times Building, it was a landmark in Cordova for 54 years. But Blum's dream for being part of a great city ended when the building burned in 1963.

The Keystone Canyon Affair

Despite Pinchot's closure of coalfield holdings, the Guggenheim-Morgan Syndicate moved forward with plans to build a railway from the Kennecott copper mines and was the subject of controversy from the beginning. Tensions escalated when a rival crew working on a railroad from Valdez was confronted by a rock barricade erected by the Guggenheims when they entered the Keystone Canyon, leading to Thompson Pass. Armed with tools, Valdez railroad men marched toward the syndicate's obstruction on Sept. 25, 1907, and were met with gunfire backed by badges.

Local syndicate officials had convinced the U.S. marshal in Fairbanks to issue temporary deputy marshal commissions to syndicate employees, including a man named Edward C. Hasey. Sheltered behind the barricade, Hasey shot three marchers, killing one.

A grand jury was hastily convened. And even though Alaska's Gov. Wilford B. Hoggatt, a well-known syndicate supporter, hurried to Valdez to intervene on Hasey's behalf, the gunman was indicted for murder. His trial then was moved to Juneau, since ill sentiments against the syndicate abounded in Valdez.

Prior to the trial, however, Hoggatt was successful in convincing the Justice Department to remove the U.S. attorney who'd refused to allow Hoggatt to interfere with the Valdez Grand Jury proceedings.

Then the Guggenheims put one of the Valdez railroad workmen on its payroll and prepared him to testify in Hasey's trial to say that the Valdez workers were armed when they marched on the barricade in Keystone Canyon.

After several weeks of testimony in spring 1908, the jurors found that Hasey's fear of bodily harm by the Valdez railroad crew justified his shooting in self-defense. They acquitted him of the murder charge.

A view of the Keystone Canyon and the wagon road called the Valdez-Fairbanks trail shows some obstacles faced by those wishing to build a railroad.

Gov. Wilford B. Hoggatt, who served from 1906-1909, supported the Guggenheim-Morgan Syndicate and tried to influence the Keystone Canyon affair.

But in February 1909, Hasey was found guilty on a second charge of assault. He served 18 months at McNeil Island in Washington state, receiving full pay and benefits for his family while incarcerated.

Judge Wickersham enters the fray

Once the trial ended, syndicate officials continued with their plans for constructing the railroad until they crossed Judge James Wickersham.

After the Guggenheim-Morgan Syndicate successfully influenced the outcome of Hasey's trials in 1908-1909, it went back to work building its railroad from Cordova to what became the Kennecott Copper mines. But tranquility was short lived.

Perhaps blinded by its success at paying off a witness in the Keystone Canyon murder trial and getting the U.S. attorney removed from the territory, syndicate officials next persuaded their workers to line up against Wickersham during his campaign for the office of Territorial Delegate to Congress.

That decision caused the judge to come down hard on the syndicate.

Wickersham got evidence from a former syndicate bookkeeper that showed how a Valdez railroad worker, who was the key witness in the first Hasey trial, had carried Guggenheim money to other witnesses for the prosecution, as well as members of the trial jury.

Copper River and Northwestern Railway dock in Cordova in 1907.

Persuading President William Howard Taft to oust U.S. Marshal Dan Sutherland of Juneau, as well as the U.S. attorney, also backfired against the Guggenheims when a Senate committee convened to consider the fitness of new appointees. Wickersham argued that the real reason behind the dismissals was because the marshal and attorney were investigating the Hasey affair.

While the Senate confirmed the new officers, John Rutgard and Herbert Faulkner, the attorney general decided to reopen the investigation into the Keystone Canyon trials and other questionable activities of the syndicate in Alaska.

As a result, subsequent digging into syndicate activities found collusive bidding on contracts for coal for the U.S. Army posts in the territory, as well as 37 fraudulent claims under the title of Clarence Cunningham and Associates. Federal officials determined that the claims had been taken out with intent to consolidate and create a monopoly in the interests of the Guggenheim-Morgan Syndicate, which needed the coal for its Copper River and Northwestern Railway.

That discovery brought about the prosecution of several syndicate officials.

And so it was that the shooting of a Valdez railroad worker on a barricaded track in Keystone Canyon, which resulted in payoffs, perjury and manipulation by the Guggenheim-Morgan Syndicate, ended the syndicate's attempt to control coal resources in Alaska. The company that wanted to dominate the territory never did secure its coal lands.

Imported coal causes consternation

Many Alaskans' dreams of riches from coal and oil dried up when Pinchot ordered the withdrawal of those coalfield holdings to protect them from the Guggenheim Syndicate. Communities had to start importing coal from Canada, and many Alaskans resented being forced to purchase high-dollar coal from foreigners when Alaska had an abundance of the resource.

At Cordova, the terminus of the Guggenheims' railroad, the townspeople got quite heated after continued and futile protests against the importation of foreign coal went unheeded. They had coal in their backyard but couldn't dig enough to fill their cook stoves.

"We have to pay high prices for Canadian coal shipped in from 1,000 miles away and there's coal all around us," Cordovans protested bitterly.

Since their protests to the government went unheeded, indignation became red hot. Then someone remembered the Boston Tea Party, and Cordova residents decided their own situation called for just such drastic action.

Shovels in hand, 300 Cordovans marched down to the Alaska Steamship Company dock in 1911.

They picked a time when the U.S. deputy marshal was conveniently several miles away, and it took a little while for the chief of police to get a federal warrant. Before he could arrive on the scene, the Cordova Coal Party was in full swing – at least the shovels were swinging lustily to the shouts of "Give us Alaska coal," as several tons of Canadian coal were dumped into the bay.

The poor steamship agent, in his office at the dock, was taken by surprise – he rushed out and demanded that this unauthorized shov-

Thwaites 4477. Bridge over Copper River between Childs and Mills Glaciers, Alaska. Said to have cost $1,000,000.

Left: Erastus Hawkins, the engineer in charge of the Copper River and Northwestern Railway project, designed a 1,550-foot steel bridge to span the Copper River at a river bend between the Miles and Childs glaciers. Starting in April 1909, workers scrambled to complete the Million Dollar Bridge, spurred on by a U.S. law that gave railroad developers four years to complete a designated route. After four years, the government would tax them $100 per operating mile per year.

Contractors finished the bridge by midsummer of 1910. Soon after construction of the Million Dollar Bridge (which cost $1.4 million to build), the glaciers threatened the railroad. In August 1910, two glaciologists from the National Geographic Society studied the sudden advances of both glaciers.

A northern lobe of Childs Glacier began creeping toward the bridge in June, and by August it was moving eight feet per day. On Aug. 17, the 200-foot face of the glacier was 1,624 feet away from the bridge. Childs Glacier did not engulf the bridge, but the glacier crept to within 1,475 feet in June 1911.

Childs and Miles glaciers retreated, sparing the Million Dollar Bridge, which served the railway from 1910 until 1938, when low copper prices forced the shutdown of the Copper River and Northwestern Railway.

Cordovans held a "coal party" in 1911 and dumped foreign coal into the bay, pictured above in 1908.

eling cease, but the coal heavers again cried, "Give us Alaska coal!"

Although the agent was armed, he was persuaded not to fire. However, he sent in a hurry-up call to the railroad shops and down rushed the railroad superintendent with a crew of husky railroaders to try and protect company property. By this time, the chief of police had managed to obtain his federal warrant and he ordered the coal shovelers to shoulder their shovels.

"Shovel away, boys," said the crew's leader. "We want Alaska coal!"

"In the name of the government of the United States of America, you are ordered to disband or be subject to arrest," was the demand.

This order was heeded – perhaps the shovelers were glad for an excuse to stop, for it was hard work shoveling the coal from the car and into the bay. Anyway, the protestors shouldered their trusty shovels, the merchants went back to their stores and the other citizens went about their regular occupations – the Cordova Coal Party was over. But they had made their point – and they made headlines throughout the United States.

Next morning, under huge banner lines, the government at Washington, D.C., was informed of what had happened at Cordova and of the indignation scene enacted in the Far North. The Capitol issued stern warnings against lawlessness.

However, assurances were given that an investigation would be made. Secretary Walter L. Fisher of the Interior Department made a visit to Alaska to get firsthand information. In due time, the land laws were modified and Cordova citizens appeased.

More than 150 restrictions were lifted. The government discovered that the spirit of American independence that had fueled the Boston Tea Party was as alive and well on its last frontier as it had been on its first.

Women and children cross the dirt-covered Main Street of Cordova in 1912.

Left: The copper mine at Kennicott pokes out of a mountainside around 1910. The Bonanza-Kennecott Mines operated until 1938 and yielded more than $200 million in copper, silver and gold.

Below: A train engine chugs across the newly erected tracks built over the Copper River in front of Miles Glacier in 1909.

The Copper River and Northwestern Railway was built to carry copper ore 196 miles from Kennicott to Cordova. Along that route were some of the greatest obstacles Alaska offers - steep canyons, rivers, hurricane-force winds, mosquitoes and dozens of glaciers.

Above: Copper ore cargo sits on the dock at Cordova in 1910. The ore was valued at $46 per sack.

Cordova, built on Orca Inlet at the base of Eyak Mountain, was the railroad terminus and ocean shipping port for copper ore from the Kennecott Mine up the Copper River.

Right: A Copper River and Northwestern Railway train crosses the Kuskulana Bridge near Cordova in the early 1900s. The Kuskulana Bridge was constructed 238 feet above the Kuskulana River during winter 1910.

21

SEWARD'S RESURRECTIONS

Alaska has no Easter Island, but it does have a Resurrection Bay. As befits the name, the Easter season has been significant in the history of the area. Russian explorer Alexander Baranof named the sheltered bay, finding it a welcome refuge from Pacific storms.

Since it was the Easter season when he first saw it, he named it "Voskresenskaya Gavan," meaning "Resurrection (Sunday) Harbor." That was in 1792, 11 years before the Lewis and Clark Expedition and

Russian explorer Alexander Baranof named Resurrection Bay in 1792.

while George Washington was president of the United States.

When orders came to Baranof to build a sea-going vessel, he remembered the sheltered bay. Nearby was timber, suitable for ship-building, and the rise and fall of the tides would make ship launching possible. Otherwise, conditions were next to impossible. *Phoenix*, the name chosen for the vessel, was very appropriate.

Like the legendary bird after which it was named, the boat liter-ally rose from ashes, for tons of wood were burned to make charcoal to forge bolts and nails. Baranof had Aleuts beach comb Kodiak Island for salvage from wrecked ships. The shipbuilders had no tools – except axes – not even a handsaw. Forest moss mixed with hot pitch was used for caulking; whale oil, thickened with red ochre from iron deposits, was used for paint.

A summer, a winter, and another summer and winter went by while Baranof and shipbuilder James Shields improvised and invented ways to build the 100-ton, 79-foot-long vessel, the first to be launched on the northwestern Pacific Coast. Shipbuilding was carried on at Fort Resurrection until 1867, when Alaska was purchased.

However, the islands guarding Resurrection Bay effectively hid its entrance. There were no nearby Native settlements, so long after other ports of coastal Alaska were settled, Resurrection Bay was left to itself. It wasn't until the 1890s that Capt. Frank Lowell, scion of that famous Boston family of Cabots and Lowells, settled in the area with his family – the first white settler of the town that was to become Seward.

The first official American mention of Resurrection Bay is found in an expedition report of Lt. W.R. Abercrombie, who explored Prince William Sound in 1884. Even the prospectors streaming into the Hope and Sunrise areas during the late 1890s bypassed the future port. They either portaged at the head of the Sound at Whittier, or sailed up the Turnagain Arm.

In 1898, another official exploring party, attempting to find possi-ble railroad routes, came into the bay. They found four or five houses built along the shore and their report said that a railroad could be built from there to Sunrise, then a busy gold-mining center.

There was little interest in the route at that time, but in the early 1900s, the idea of a railroad to the Interior was conceived, which later led to the building of the Alaska Railroad. The town, named after U.S. Secretary of State William H. Seward, was on its way.

A party of surveyors and engineers came to Resurrection Bay from Valdez in 1902, planning to build a railroad and a city. Frank and John Ballaine were agents for the railroad and they, along with W.M. Whittlesey, laid out the city. Since the surveying chain for measuring had missed the boat, the links were cut from bailing wire, and using a tailor's cloth measuring tape, the city lots were laid out. When the proper equipment arrived, the measurements were off only a few inches.

Private business initiated the venture, and in 1903, the Alaska-Central Railroad started with great plans to connect the coast of Alaska to the Matanuska coalfields and the gold mines in Fairbanks.

This view of Seward's early dock and main street – Fourth Avenue – looks north during the winter of 1903-1904.

Six men and a couple of dogs pose on the steps at warehouse C of the Alaska Central Railroad in Seward during the early 1900s.

Town's name chosen

John Ballaine said he didn't decide on a name for the new town until the spring of 1903. His engineer, C.M. Anderson, had designated the place Vituska on the blueprints – a combination of Bering's first name, Vitus, and the last syllable of Alaska.

But the only names that appealed to Ballaine were Seward, McKinley and Roosevelt. The founder was convinced the new city would one day be the metropolis of a great territory and should fittingly bear the name of the man who foresaw the primacy of the Pacific Ocean in the world's future.

Workers flocked to Seward to help build a railroad north. This northward view of Seward was taken from the Fourth Avenue dock around 1905.

In March 1903, he bestowed upon the new town the name of Seward. Ballaine wrote Frederick Seward that he'd chosen his father's name and received the following reply on April 6:

"I need hardly say that the selection of the name seems to me an appropriate one and that it will be gratifying to those who knew him in life and the still greater number who hold his name in esteem and loving remembrance. Time has now shown that his prediction in regard to the future of Alaska was not at all exaggerated."

However, the postal inspector of the district embracing Alaska filed a protest against calling the embryo city on Resurrection Bay Seward, arguing that there were already several Sewards in the territory.

"I went personally to President Teddy Roosevelt, explaining to him the basis of my desire to have the new place named Seward, pointing out to him that the other Post Offices of that name were canneries or temporary camps which could easily be changed to another name," Ballaine explained in a 1906 article in the Seward Daily Gateway.

Roosevelt agreed and asked Ballaine to write him a letter embodying the reasons given verbally and have it back to him by 10 a.m. the next day. Ballaine did as requested.

Later, Ballaine recalled what Roosevelt said upon receipt of the letter.

"'You are quite right,' Roosevelt said. 'This railroad should give rise to an important city at the ocean terminus. The city deserves to be named in honor of the man who is responsible for making Alaska an American territory.'"

Roosevelt then wrote on the margin of the letter a note addressed to Fourth Assistant Postmaster General Bristow, saying that he agreed with Ballaine's views and would be glad to have Bristow give the subject his prompt attention. The marginal note was signed "T.R."

Ballaine immediately took the letter and Roosevelt's endorsement to the Fourth Assistant Postmaster General, and within 10 minutes of the time he entered the office, Bristow had issued an order establishing the new U.S. Post Office of Seward on Resurrection Bay.

A bustling commerce along Seward's Fourth Avenue developed to support the railroad and its workers. This photo is looking south toward Resurrection Bay in 1906.

Men haul supplies with a dog team down the rail tracks near Seward.

Ballaine had won his point and Seward was officially recognized and founded on Aug. 28, 1903.

Railroad town grows

Railroad workers filled the new town – at one time there were 3,500 people living there. In the early days of the railroad, men were so eager to work that they made wooden rails and dogs pulled carts carrying supplies. Seward became a roaring construction town, but the boom collapsed when the "powers that be" in Washington decided to conserve Alaska coal, and all coal lands in Alaska were withdrawn from entry.

The Alaska Central went bankrupt in 1908, but re-emerged as the Alaska Northern in 1910. Construction resumed on the single-track standard-gauge line, and another 20 miles was added to the old Alaska Central right of way, bringing it to Kern Creek at the upper end of Turnagain Arm. From this railhead, they met boats that came up the Arm. Freight also went out over the Iditarod Trail from this point, 71 miles from Seward.

At no time was the railroad even able to earn out-of-pocket expenses. Its "tracks, bridges and docks were not adequately maintained, and by 1915 it was hardly in operating condition except for

An Alaska Northern Railway train crosses a trestle with Resurrection Bay in the background.

light gasoline-driven equipment used from Seward to Mile 16 when snow slides didn't interfere," wrote Edwin M. Fitch in his book, "The Alaska Railroad."

Seward's boom collapsed. The "boomers" began leaving town. Seward soon became a town waiting for a "resurrection." And it came.

Late one afternoon in August 1914, according to an article by Clark Dinsmore in the Alaska Sportsman, a "few loafers were hanging around the half-empty saloons, housewives were shopping for their Sunday dinners, children played in the streets and on the wharves a few boatmen were idly passing their time.

"Suddenly out of the printing office of the Seward Gateway burst a group of newsboys shouting 'EXTRA! EXTRA!'

"An extra in a small town like Seward is a sensation, but more sensational was the news. The United States Government had chosen Seward as the saltwater terminus for its proposed Government Railroad!"

Alaska Northern Railroad cars sit along Bear Creek around 1910.

The boom was on again. Houses, which the owners would have practically given away, were selling at boom prices by the afternoon, and choice lots were swallowed up by speculators. New stores opened and stores already there worked feverishly to expand and enlarge. Building went on around the clock.

From the states arrived boatloads of men seeking work on the new railroad. Those hardy souls – the Scandinavians, the Russians, Greeks, Slovenians and Irish – who did the actual work of building the railroad with their hammers and drills, their axes and mattocks, their mauls and gauges found it took muscle, hardihood and endurance.

The rest of that story will unfold in the pages of "Aunt Phil's Trunk: Volume 3."

WILDERNESS TRAILS

22

SLED DOGS LEAD THE WAY

S led dogs have an illustrious history in the North Country, from the early days of Native settlements to the gold-rush booms during the 1890-1900s.

Alaska's Natives relied on pack dogs to transport fish and supplies between seasons.

Natives of Alaska, northern Canada, Greenland and Siberia used dogs as winter draft animals for centuries. Russians arriving in western Alaska during the 1700-1800s found Alaska Natives using dogs to haul sleds loaded with fish, game, wood and other items.

The Natives ran ahead of the dogs as they guided them on the yearly trips between villages and fish and hunting camps. Russians improved the sled dog system by adding handlebars to sleds and harnessing dog teams in single file or in pairs. They also trained the dogs to follow commands given by sled drivers and introduced the "lead dog" or leader.

Early Russian fur traders added handlebars to sleds and trained lead dogs in order to use dog teams as a means of transportation through Alaska's wilderness.

Russian exploration via dog teams was limited to Alaska's coasts, as well as along some rivers, and followed existing Native trails between villages. Both Natives and Russians found frozen rivers also made useful winter trails.

Extensive use of dogs for long-distance transportation developed as gold discoveries were made in the late 1890s and early 1900s. Stampeders quickly learned that dog teams were worth their weight in gold. Thousands of dogs were imported from the contiguous states to help prospectors and adventurers reach the gold fields.

By the turn of the century, dog teams were helping cheechakos blaze new trails to establish law and order, develop mail routes and transport gold-crazed prospectors to new strikes north and west of Prince William Sound.

From Valdez, a route was blazed to the Interior boomtown of

Cases of eggs depart Valdez bound for the Valdez-Fairbanks Trail.

Frank L. Tondro, also known as The Malamute Kid, and his sled dog team pull up in front of the Valdez Mercantile around 1906.

Fairbanks. It became known as the Valdez-Fairbanks Trail. Sled dog teams, freight dog teams and mail teams streamed back and forth across that trail for many years.

From Seward, winter trails developed north and west. Russians and early traders and prospectors found traces of gold along the Kenai Peninsula, but the first major find did not occur until 1891. Al King, a veteran prospector from the Interior, working with gold pan and rocker, located gold on Resurrection Creek in Southcentral Alaska.

The Turnagain Arm Mining District boomed in 1895-1896, with about 3,000 people flooding into the area and mining mostly around the log-cabin communities of Hope and Sunrise.

Roughly blazed sled dog trails connected the communities of Sunrise, Hope and scattered trading posts at Resurrection Bay, Knik Arm and the Susitna River. Miners and merchants also combined to build a wagon road from Sunrise up Six-Mile Creek along the mining claims.

When winter came, some miners hooked up their dogs and pulled Yukon sleds loaded with needed supplies up the Kenai, Susitna, Knik or other rivers and made camp at promising locations. They

A dog team rests in front of the Pioneer Roadhouse in Knik.

then spent the winter thawing ground and digging gravel. At spring breakup, the prospectors sluiced the hoped-for gold from pay dirt. At season's end they built rafts or poling boats and floated with their dogs back downstream to the trading posts or towns. This is the way the land was prospected.

The main trail from Seward to the various prospects in Southcentral Alaska traveled along the railroad right of way to Turnagain Arm, then along the north side of the Arm to Girdwood and over Crow Pass. It dropped into the Eagle River valley, to the Indian village of Eklutna and then around the upper end of Knik Arm to Knik.

By 1905, dog teams were carrying mail over 180 miles of trail between Seward and Susitna Station, a steamboat stop on the lower Susitna River that served as a supply point for dozens of mines in the foothills of the Alaska Range. The system of trails extended as gold-fields were discovered to the north in the Talkeetna Mountains and the Yentna River drainage.

And when gold was discovered along the Innoko River around 1906-1907, another trail was forged that would become one of the most famous sled dog trails in history – the Iditarod Trail.

Susitna Station was a steamboat stop along the lower Susitna River.

23

Blazing the Iditarod Trail

The Russians had used portions of what later became the Iditarod Trail as a route for supplies and provisions for their fur-trading posts. The Russian American Company sent fur-trading expeditions across the Kaltag Portage to Nulato on the Yukon River. Americans continued using the route after they took over the Russian posts following Alaska's purchase in 1867. They extended the route to the Yukon River trail, which linked them to fur-trading posts in Canada.

Nulato, seen here around 1910, was a stop on the Russians' fur trading route.

The Pioneer and the California offered miners a bit of relaxation from their toils in the gold fields near Ophir City.

A town named Ophir grew out of the wilderness when Thomas Ganes discovered gold at Ganes Creek, about halfway between Seward and Nome, in 1906. Around 1,000 people flooded the area to make their fortunes, which caused new supply centers at Takotna and McGrath to develop.

New strikes along the Innoko River called for a more direct route from Seward to Nome through the Cook Inlet country. Whereas Nome and the Cook Inlet areas were easily accessible by ocean steamers, Interior gold strikes – the Iditarod, Innoko and Ruby districts – were isolated.

Prospectors took the natural land routes or Native routes to the Innoko mines in 1906 and 1907. They were followed the next year by Walter Goodwin of the Alaska Road Commission, which was established by Congress in 1905 as part of the U.S. Army's road- and trail-building efforts connecting the military posts and the new mining camps with tidewater ports and navigable streams.

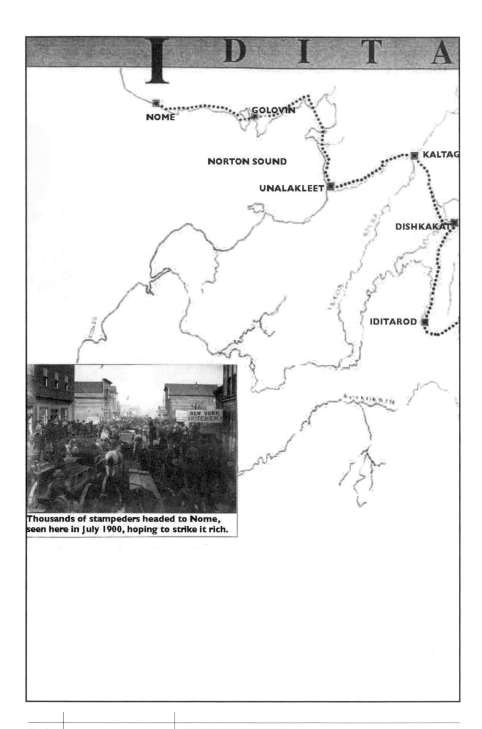

IDITA

NOME

GOLOVIN

NORTON SOUND

KALTAG

UNALAKLEET

DISHKAKAT

IDITAROD

Thousands of stampeders headed to Nome, seen here in July 1900, hoping to strike it rich.

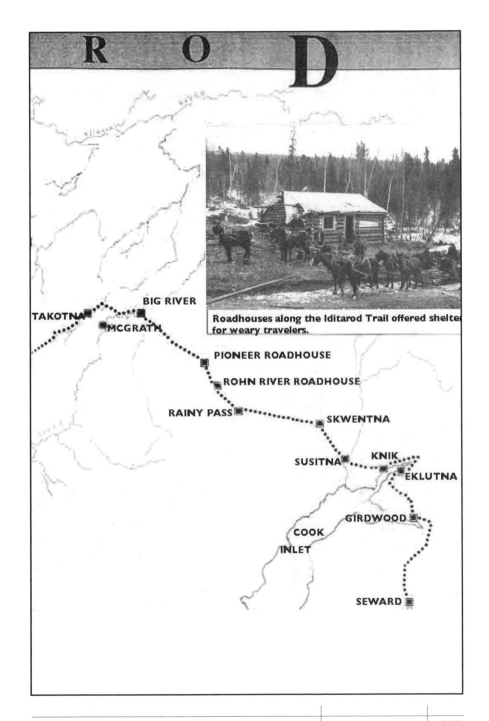

R O D

BIG RIVER

TAKOTNA

MCGRATH

Roadhouses along the Iditarod Trail offered shelter for weary travelers.

PIONEER ROADHOUSE

ROHN RIVER ROADHOUSE

RAINY PASS

SKWENTNA

SUSITNA

KNIK

EKLUTNA

GIRDWOOD

COOK INLET

SEWARD

Maj. Wilds P. Richardson headed the construction, and the Alaska Road Commission later upgraded the crude trails built by mining camp residents.

Richardson ordered Goodwin to blaze a route from Seward through the Cook Inlet country and beyond to Nome. From January to April 1908, Goodwin and a three-man crew scouted and blazed a trail from Seward to Susitna and then west through Rainy Pass, across the Kuskokwim Valley to the Innoko Mining District, which included Ophir, McGrath and Takotna.

They then angled the trail northwest across the marshy lowlands of the Innoko Valley and connected with the Yukon trail at Kaltag. This route became known as the Seward-to-Nome Mail Trail.

In his report to Richardson, Goodwin concluded that the 900-plus-mile proposed route would be feasible only if mines of value were developed that would attract additional traffic. Unknown to Goodwin, two prospectors, John Beaton and William Dikeman, had penetrated the virgin territory. On Christmas Day 1908, the pair discovered gold along the Haiditarod River, a tributary of the Innoko, in the area that soon would become the Iditarod Mining District.

It's believed that Haiditarod is what the early Athabascan Indians called their inland hunting ground. Meaning "the distant place," the miners changed the name to Iditarod when they founded the town near the gold discovery. Beaton and Dikeman told a steamboat crew about their find as they traveled to Takotna to record their claims. Word spread, and within a year the last full-scale gold rush in American history boomed in an incredibly remote section of Alaska.

The new town of Iditarod briefly became the largest town in Alaska, boasting more than 4,000 people and sporting newspapers, hotels, electricity and telephone service. Summer steamships plied their way from the Bering Sea up the Yukon, Innoko and Iditarod rivers and towns like Flat, Discovery, Otter, Willow Creek and Dikeman sprang up.

Goodwin was told to build a trail from Kaltag to Susitna Station in winter 1910. Along with a nine-man crew and several sled dog teams, Goodwin followed his 1908 Seward-Nome route and added

Jujiro Wada, pictured here after mushing from Fairbanks to Dawson to help spread word of the gold discovery in Alaska's Interior, blazed a trail to the Innoko mining area in 1909. The man in the pea coat might be his friend, Capt. H.H. Norwood with whom he had served as a cabin boy onboard the whaler *Balaena* in 1891.

Wada lived with Natives on the Arctic Coast, and along with learning about survival in Alaska's harsh conditions, he excelled at dog mushing.

He became one of Alaska's best non-Native mushers. And during the gold-rush era, when most Asians were common laborers, Wada's mushing exploits filled the northern press.

The city of Seward hired Wada to scout a 450-mile route by dog team to the gold fields of the Innoko River. His efforts later helped publicize the Iditarod Trail, and he reported that "the overland route was feasible and that Iditarod would make a good camp," according to the Dawson Daily News.

a loop from the main trail to Iditarod and Flat, which were the new district's two principal towns. He also plotted roadhouses along the route about every 20 miles.

He and his team reached Seward in February 1911, having made the first official trip along the 938-mile route that quickly became known as the Iditarod Trail.

By 1913, an alternate trail to Nome left the trunkline at Ophir and headed north to Ruby, where mushers followed the Yukon River trail east to Fairbanks or west to Nome.

The rush to Iditarod and Ruby, between 1910 and 1912, set 10,000 stampeders in motion. Within two decades, $30 million worth of gold was dug from these gold fields.

Ruby's First Avenue, pictured above, was a hub of activity during 1912.

Named after the red-colored stones found along the riverbank, Ruby developed as a supply point for gold prospectors in an area used by the Koyukon Athabascans of the Nowitna-Koyukuk band. A nomadic group, they followed game with the changing seasons. There were 12 summer fish camps located on the Yukon River between the Koyukuk River and the Nowitna River.

A gold strike at Ruby Creek in 1907, and another at Long Creek in 1911, attracted hundreds of prospectors to the area. More than 1,000 white miners lived in Ruby and nearby creeks at one time. Placerville, Poorman, Sulatna Crossing, Kokrines and Long Creek were some of the area's boom settlements.

While a post office was established in 1912, and Ruby was incorporated as a city in 1913, the population declined rapidly when the gold rush ended.

24

IDITAROD TRAIL PHOTO ESSAY

This dog team appears ready and eager to haul supplies out of Seward and tackle the Iditarod Trail.

Sled dogs have a long and illustrious past in the Great North. Natives bred dogs, which became part of Alaskan families' everyday lives, for survival in the harsh climate. Two breeds were most common: Alaska malamutes and Siberian huskies.

Alaska malamutes originated with a group of Eskimo people known as the Mahlemiut, who inhabited the upper part of the Anvik River. The large dogs mostly were used for pulling heavy loads of fish, game and supplies between camps and villages.

Siberian huskies originated with the Chuckchi people of northeastern Siberia. These people used their dogs for pulling loads and for herding reindeer. Smaller than the malamutes, these huskies were exported to Alaska during the gold-rush era and used for transportation of people and goods.

The Iditarod Trail wound north along the railroad right of way out of Seward to Turnagain Arm, and then along the north side of the arm to Girdwood and over Crow Pass.

Girdwood, originally called Glacier City, started as a trading and transportation route over the Chugach Range. It became a supply camp for placer gold miners with claims along the creeks feeding Turnagain Arm.

The settlement was renamed for Col. James Girdwood, a Belfast-born, Scottish-Irish entrepreneur and linen merchant who staked the first four gold claims along Crow Creek in 1896. The little town boomed with the prospect of gold and continued to serve as a trading route to the Ship Creek basin that later grew into the city of Anchorage. By 1906, Girdwood boasted 15 buildings, including five saloons, a bathhouse, stable, blacksmith and commissary.

The Iditarod Trail ran up the banks of Glacier Creek and over Crow Pass. The trail then traveled through Eagle River, Peters Creek and Eklutna Lake territory, which were the hunting areas of the Athabascan Natives from the Eklutna and Matanuska villages. Natives hunted sheep, goat and moose in the mountains and caught fish in late May in surrounding rivers.

As a side note, Eagle River John, a red-headed Finlander, is credited for being first non-Native settler in that area. He was a moonshiner who went back and forth to Anchorage by skiff to sell his illegal whiskey.

Above: After crossing Eagle River, the Iditarod Trail went through Knik, which sits on the west bank of the Knik Arm of Cook Inlet. Knik is a Tanaina Indian village and the name means "fire." The town grew during the 1898-1916 gold rushes.

Below: People visit in front of the Knik Trading Company on Knik's Front Street during winter.

The Iditarod Trail passed by Eklutna, a site that featured Athabascan Indian villages as long as 800 years ago. Today's residents are descendants of the Tanaina tribe.

Russian Orthodox missionaries arrived in the area in the 1840s, and graves and brightly colored "spirit houses" in the Russian Slavic style still fill the cemetery in Eklutna, which used to be called "Old Knik."

The next stop on the Iditarod Trail is Susitna Station, pictured above. Between 1903-1918, supplies and freight for gold-mining strikes in the Cache Creek Mining District were transported from tidewater at Knik to the community of Susitna Station at the conflu-ence of the Yentna and Susitna rivers. Paddle-wheel riverboats would carry freight from Susitna Station farther upriver and then horse teams would haul the load 70 miles north overland to Cache Creek.

By 1923, the community of Susitna Station was almost completely gone. The Anchorage Pioneer Press reported in 1932 that the last sternwheeler paddle boat for the Susitna and Yentna rivers was going out of business due to competition from the railroad and airplanes.

From Susitna, the next 128 miles of the route headed northwest, following the west side of the Yentna River on the north side of Beluga Mountain, then crossed the Skwentna River to follow its northern side. At the mouth of Happy River, the route turned north, following the river to Rainy Pass.

The Susitna-Rainy Pass stretch was quite suitable for dog teams during the winter. After the trail was abandoned as a mail route, the Alaska Road Commission continued to main-tain it because it provided access to potential mines.

Tent roadhouses popped up along the Iditarod Trail before more substantial structures were built.

The Iditarod Trail continued on through Skwentna, which was founded in 1923 by Max and Belle Shellabarger, who homesteaded and started a guide service. A post office was opened there in 1937.

The trail then traveled past Rohn River Roadhouse, Pioneer Roadhouse at Farewell Lake and Big River Roadhouse. The next stop was Takotna, which has been known as Berry Landing, Portage City, Takotna City, Takotna Station and Tocotna.

In 1908, Bethel merchants hired Arthur Berry to haul supplies up the Takotna River. The village, which was founded at the farthest point on the river that Berry's small sternwheeler was able to reach, grew into a supply center for miners. And when gold was discovered in the Innoko region, Takotna prospered. By 1919, there were about 50 houses, along with roadhouses, commercial companies and a post office.

Above: The John E. Baker homestead was one of several new structures in the growing community of Takotna in the early 1920s.

From Takotna, the trail went through Moose Creek and then on to Iditarod.

Below: A dog team howls as mushers rest along the trail.

A MALAMUTE CHORUS.

Above: The town of Iditarod grew out of the wilderness after prospectors John Beaton and William Dikeman discovered gold along the Haiditarod River, a tributary of the Innoko, in December 1908.

Below: A riverfront view of Iditarod in 1911 shows several businesses, including a machine shop, real estate office, public dock and several barges.

Above: The presses at Iditarod Pioneer published news of the latest gold discoveries.

Below: Oliver Johnson pours gold in the Assay Office of the American Bank of Alaska, Iditarod, on Aug. 17, 1911.

$125 000.00 in Gold Bricks

Assay Office, American Bank of Alaska,
Iditarod Alaska.

Above: A sled dog team pulls into Seward on Dec. 23, 1910, carrying one-half ton of gold dust, valued at $210,000, from the Iditarod gold fields. Consigned to Brown and Hawkins, it was the largest gold dust shipment ever carried by dog team in Alaska.

Dog teams routinely carried several hundred thousand dollars in gold on the trail, but there was only one dog team robbery, according to "Gold Fever in the North" editors Darcy Ellington and Angela Tripp. William Shermeier, owner of the Halfway Roadhouse, and a prostitute, known as the Black Bear, got driver Bill Duffy drunk one night and stole $30,000 in cash from his sled. Shermeier went to jail, and Duffy married Black Bear.

Left: Mr. and Mrs. F.W. Herms Sr. and an unidentified man stand in the Assay Office of the American Bank of Alaska in Iditarod behind $125,000 worth of gold bricks.

A group stands in front of a saloon in Dishkakat, the next stop after leaving Iditarod along the Iditarod Trail heading to Nome. The Athabascan and Euro-American boomtown thrived as a transportation depot and supply center for the gold fields in 1907.

After Dishkakat, the trail moved on to Kaltag, located in Koyukon Athabascan territory. Built on an old portage trail that led east through the mountains to Unalakleet, it was used as a cemetery for surrounding villages. The Athabascans moved as the wild game migrated. There were 12 summer fish camps located on the Yukon River between the Koyukuk River and the Nowitna River.

The village was named by Russians for a Yukon Indian named Kaltaga. By 1900, steamboats supplying gold prospectors on the Yukon peaked. Then, during 1900, food shortages and a measles epidemic struck down one-third of the Native population.

Kaltag was established shortly thereafter, when survivors from three nearby seasonal villages moved to the area.

Continuing on to Nome, the Iditarod Trail passes by the Unalakleet Range. House remnants along the beach ridge in Unalakleet date from 200 B.C. to 300 A.D. , according to archaeologists. Unalakleet, which means "place where the east wind blows," served as a major trade center.

Unalakleet was the terminus for the Kaltag Portage, an important winter travel route connecting to the Yukon River. Indians on the upper river were considered professional traders who had a monopoly on the Indian-Eskimo trade across the Kaltag Portage. The Russian-American Company built a post here in the 1830s, and in 1898 reindeer herders from Lapland came to teach herding practices to the Natives. In 1901, the U.S. Army Signal Corps built more than 605 miles of telegraph line from St. Michael to Unalakleet, over the portage to Kaltag and on to Fort Gibbon.

Golovin, originally called Chinik and settled by the Kauweramiut Eskimos – who later mixed with the Unaligmiut Eskimos – was named for Capt. Vasili Golovin of the Russian Navy. In 1887, the Mission Covenant of Sweden established a church and school south of the current site. Around 1890, John Dexter started a trading post that became the center for prospecting information for all the Seward Peninsula.

When gold was discovered in 1898 at Council, Golovin became a supply point for the gold fields. Supplies were shipped from Golovin across Golovin Lagoon and up the Fish and Niukluk rivers to Council. In 1899, a post office was opened.

Reindeer herding became an integral part of the missions in the area in the 1900s after the caribou population declined. A herd of reindeer, pictured above, are kept in check with a drift fence in Golovin.

Reindeer herding also extended to Nome, which is the end of the Iditarod Trail.

Malemiut, Kauweramiut and Unalikmiut Eskimos originally settled in the Nome area and had a well-developed culture adapted to the environment. But when the caribou became scarce, they had to change their diet.

As a result of three day's work, $36,000 worth of gold was taken during a cleanup operation on Nome's Three Star Fraction on Aug. 17, 1907.

Gold discoveries in the Nome area were reported as far back as 1865 by Western Union surveyors seeking a route across Alaska and the Bering Sea. But a $1,500-to-the-pan gold strike on Anvil Creek in 1898 by three Scandinavians – Jafet Lindeberg, Erik Lindblom and John Brynteson – brought thousands of miners to the Eldorado.

An isolated stretch of tundra fronting the beach turned into a tent and log cabin city of 20,000 prospectors, gamblers, claim jumpers, saloon keepers and prostitutes. The gold-bearing creeks were almost completely staked when others discovered the golden sands of Nome.

Thousands of gold seekers descended upon the beaches with nothing more than shovels, buckets, rockers and wheel barrows. Two months later, the beach had yielded $1 million in gold – at $16 an ounce.

A narrow-gauge railroad and telephone line from Nome to Anvil Creek was built in 1900. By 1902 the more easily reached claims were exhausted and large mining companies with better equipment took over the mining operations.

The blazing of the Iditarod Trail opened a new route to transport the precious gold to Seward.

Above: With Martin Lanning on the back of the sled, the first dog team travels down the Iditarod Trail from Nome to Seward in 1909. Since the first strike on tiny Anvil Creek, Nome's gold fields have yielded around $136 million.

Below: Express teams from Iditarod rest on Seward's main street.

A FEW TRAILBLAZERS

25

BEACONS IN THE WILDERNESS

Some courageous pioneers, with vision far beyond most, saw the possibilities of the Yukon Basin years before the Klondike Gold Rush. And a few men stand out above the rest, including Arthur Harper, Leroy Napoleon "Jack" McQuesten and Alfred Mayo. Had they not seen the need to establish supply centers in the wilderness, it is possible that gold rushes to the Yukon and Alaska would not have boomed.

In his "Recollections," the original of which is in the possession of the Yukon Order of Pioneers, McQuesten remembered that in 1871 he was wintering on the headwaters of Hay River with some companions, doing a little trapping and trading with the Indians.

"We had heard a great deal about the Yukon River from men who were in the Hudson's Bay Company employ and we concluded we would go and see for ourselves what the country was like," he wrote.

And so began a journey that would take him into the remote, unexplored territory that was the Interior of the North Country – hundreds of square miles as dark and cheerless as any place on earth. As Kentucky drew Daniel Boone, so did the great, unknown valley of the Yukon draw frontiersmen and prospectors in search of the "Run of Gold."

While on his way to the Yukon, McQuesten met up with another great early pioneer, Arthur Harper. Harper, an Ulster man, born in County Antrim, Ireland, in 1835, had come to British Columbia by way of California. His study of Arrowsmith's map of Northwest America convinced him that the mineralized zone up the Western Coast must lead into the Yukon basin. He left the Peace River country in September 1872, and with two others started to Fort Yukon by way of the Laird, McKenzie, Peel and Porcupine rivers.

Leroy Napoleon McQuesten set up supply stations in Alaska's wilderness.

It was a journey of more than 1,500 miles, taking nearly a year, and was in part through an entirely unexplored country; the rest through territory where the only white men were Hudson Bay traders, few and far between. The party lived entirely on fish and game and, said Alfred Brooks in his book "Blazing Alaska's Trails," "It was an achievement far beyond many a well-advertised and well-provisioned exploring expedition."

Harper and McQuesten ran into one another at the mouth of Nelson River. McQuesten, too, had decided to head for Fort Yukon, and after a side trip to Fort Resolution, Great Slave Lake, he followed Harper down the McKenzie to the Yukon. He arrived in the company of Al Mayo and George Nicholson at the fort on July 21, 1873, six days after the Harper party.

McQuesten, born in Litchfield, New Hampshire, in 1836, was a six-foot-tall, barrel-chested fellow with a flowing, blond mustache. He had a restless temperament that had drawn him ever onward to the Last Frontier. He had been an Indian fighter in the West and searched for gold in California. He then followed gold rushes to Canada, where he also trapped and traded. He had wanted to be a voyageur, but not being able to carry the crushing 200-pound loads his French Canadian companions so easily could, he moved on until at last he reached Fort Yukon.

There the travelers found three men employed by the Alaska Commercial Company.

"We were treated like kings," McQuesten later wrote. "We remained two days. Some of us had not had such good living in 10 years. It was there we saw the first repeating rifle. Moses Mercier (in charge of the post) had no flour to sell, but let us have 50 pounds. That was for four of us for one year."

When they attempted to obtain information about the tributaries of the Yukon River, they found little knowledge had been gleaned since Russian occupation. By 1873, less than a dozen white men inhabited the length of the Yukon, and they were concerned with furs, not gold.

White fur traders around St. Michael and the Yukon included, from back left, John Waldron; standing in front of him, John C. Smith; and sitting in front left, Moses Lorenz. From second back left are John "the engineer" R. Forbes, Arthur Harper, Al Mayo, Charles Peterson and Joseph La Due. Sitting on the cannon is A.S. Frederickson. To the right of La Due is John Franklin, Fred Mercier, W.E. Everette and Gregory Kokerine.

Furs more valuable than gold

The Russians before them had not been interested in gold, either. In fact, when a Slovenian hunter once showed up with a handful of gold in the early 1800s, and the news reached the ears of Alexander Baranof, the old Russian governor at Sitka said, "Ivan, I forbid you to go further in this undertaking," according to Jack London's "Gold Seekers of the North," an article published in The Atlantic Monthly in 1903.

"Full well did Baranof understand and fear the coming of the indomitable Anglo-Saxon gold seekers!" London wrote.

The Hudson's Bay people knew there was gold along the great waterway, too, but they did nothing about it. The Alaska Commercial Company also was uninterested. It was in the business of trading for furs, not hunting for gold, but its traders welcomed Harper, McQuesten and their companions and gave them supplies as far as their meager stores would allow.

The first winter after they arrived at Fort Yukon, Harper went prospecting along the White River. Some Indians had found native copper in that region, and Harper thought it a good field for prospecting. Meanwhile, McQuesten and his companions had gone down the Yukon to the mouth of Beaver Creek. They found some fine gold, but nothing that was worthwhile.

A steamer chugs up the Yukon River in the late 1800s.

While prospecting, the men depended on moose meat for existence. Perhaps they both came to the same conclusion about the same time – a conclusion that was to be of the utmost importance to those prospectors who came after them into the Yukon. Prospecting, Harper and McQuesten decided, was impossible in this remote area without a local base of supplies.

So, in 1875, they went down to St. Michael, the distributing point for the river. McQuesten, with two others of the group, wintered there while working for the Alaska Commercial Company. Harper, with his two companions, came back to the mouth of the

Early prospectors in Alaska's wilderness depended on wild meat to survive.

Tanana and there spent the summer prospecting, probably ascending as far as Harper's Bend, where he eventually built a cabin. He found no gold, so rejoined McQuesten who had meantime established Fort Reliance, six miles down from the present site of Dawson.

Prospecting drew Harper again, however. This time he headed to the Fortymile and Sixtymile country, but the gold there was so fine that he needed quicksilver to recover it. And until it was available, Harper joined McQuesten in the fur trade, which to him was only a means of making a living while searching for gold. Fur trading and prospecting were to be his life for the next decade.

These few prospectors and traders had the Yukon River almost as their private thoroughfare for many years. They could roam for 1,000 miles without seeing another white face. Harper and McQuesten came to have a very elastic arrangement with the Alaska Commercial Company. Sometimes they were on the company's payroll, but remained free to prospect, if they wished. Later they operated as independent contractors. Sometimes they worked together as partners, sometimes separately. And the two, with Al Mayo, were to join forces in what proved to be the opening up of the Yukon to later gold seekers.

Any systematic exploration of the country could not have been possible without their efforts. The string of posts they set up along the Yukon, their grubstaking others and providing advice where to prospect, as well as the credit they extended, helped many prospectors.

"It was Harper, Mayo and McQuesten, who far more than any others, were responsible for the mining development of the Yukon," wrote Pierre Barton in his book, "Klondike Fever."

Mayo had come into the country with McQuesten. A small man and former circus acrobat, he was lean and wiry, fond of practical jokes and had a dry wit. In later years, he claimed to have been in the country so long that when he "first arrived on the Yukon it was a small creek and the Chilkoot Pass a hole in the ground."

He was an unusually good judge of furs and preferred fur trading to gold camp trade. He spent years along the Yukon at Fort Reliance, Fort Yukon, Fort Ogilvie and Fort Selkirk. When the three partners bought Ed Schieffelin's *New Racket*, a small sternwheeler, he ran the boat while McQuesten ran the trading posts and Harper prospected.

It is known that Harper made several trips into the Tanana Valley, but of only one trip is there definite information. According to E.W. Nelson in a letter published by Alfred H. Brooks, Harper and Mayo ascended the Tanana River about 250 miles in 1878, and Harper brought back some

Al Mayo made his home in Rampart.

The *New Racket*, seen here leaving St. Michael, became a supply boat on the Yukon River.

black sand gold dust as a result of his prospecting along the river bars. This made him the discoverer of gold in the Yukon, according to Brooks, who headed the Geological Survey in Alaska in 1909.

By his arduous journeys, Brooks said, "Harper gained a general knowledge of the distribution of gold-bearing gravels in the central Yukon Valley. He was the first to find gold on the bars of the lower reaches of the Stewart and Fortymile rivers, and on the upper Sixtymile and the Tanana Valley, probably the site of Fairbanks. He was the first to appreciate the latent mineral wealth of the Yukon, and through his and McQuesten's letters to friends in the Cassair and placer camps in British Columbia, these new fields were publicized and other prospectors were induced to come to the Yukon."

An equally important role in bringing about the industrial development of the Yukon was played by his friend and business associate, McQuesten. He gave little attention to prospecting after his Beaver Creek prospecting venture in 1873, but devoted himself to trading, making many trips down the river to St. Michael to bring back supplies. This division of labor was part of the plan the men had worked out when Harper and Mayo formed a partnership. The task of looking after their business interests fell to McQuesten.

A prospector shakes his pan free of rock and silt as he looks for gold.

Once they had satisfied themselves that the Yukon was gold bearing, the men realized that their most important task was to establish a reliable source of supply. It was impossible, they had discovered, to carry on systematic prospecting without an assured source of provisions and miners' supplies. They devoted themselves to this objective, thus smoothing the paths of the prospectors who came later.

At that time, neither the Canadian nor American governments had made any surveys or investigations of the Yukon River above the Porcupine. The governments had made no attempt to open up the country or establish trails. This pioneer work was almost entirely done by Harper and McQuesten, for their faith in the country was limitless. Jack London wrote that McQuesten was well thought of in the North Country.

"In 1898, the author met Jack McQuesten at Minook on the lower Yukon. The old pioneer, though grizzled, was hale and hearty and as optimistic as when he first journeyed into the land. And no man more beloved is there in all the North."

It was said that he never turned anyone away for lack of money. He had trust in the pioneers' integrity and his trust was seldom abused. Above all he had faith in the country and was willing to stake all he had on its future.

All three of the old pioneers took Indian wives, and they and their families lived in handsome homes of square-cut logs with neat vegetable gardens in the rear. Their wives were partners in the true sense of the word. Harper, however, was determined that his children should have advantages in the outside world and sent them out to be educated. His daughter, Margaret Harper Burke, wrote to Aunt Phil in 1954.

"I am the last of Arthur Harper's children – six boys and two girls. We all, except Walter (who became the first person to summit Denali in 1913), left Alaska in 1897 on the old *Dora* and were raised in San Francisco and other peninsula towns by strangers. Father died in November of that year in Arizona and was buried in the Odd Fellows' cemetery in San Francisco. Later, when the cemetery was turned into a housing project, his bones were removed to the Odd Fellows' cemetery in Colma (not far from San Francisco).

When McQuesten retired, he took his wife to California where they had a big home in Berkeley. When he died, she managed his estate and became head of the family.

Likeable, easy-going Mayo went into partnership with the Alaska Commercial Company in 1894, at Rampart, the village with which his

A crowd gathers in front of the North American Transportation and Trading Company store in Rampart as the company steamer, *John Cudahy*, arrives around 1899.

name is associated. Later he ran the Hotel Florence, which he advertised as "the only first-class house, $1.50 a night, furnished, stables for dogs and horses." He is said to be one of the main characters in Rex Beach's book "The Barrier." The name Mayo is still prominent today along the Yukon River from Tanana to Eagle. He and his wife left many grandchildren and great-grandchildren who still live along the river.

Harper, the square-faced Irishman with shrewd eyes – and a great beard that later turned snow white, died the year after the Klondike discovery with little to show for his sacrifices and toil.

McQuesten and Mayo lived long enough to see the great developments they had prophesied and worked for come true. None of the grand old pioneers shared in the great riches that were discovered, but they were rich in respect and fellowship from their brother pioneers who realized that these men had opened up the way for the great gold stampede of 1897-1898. As Kitchener wrote in "Flag Over Alaska," "Their sign was a beacon in the wilderness."

26

VOICE OF THE YUKON

Good-bye, Little Cabin
I hear the world call and the clang of the fight
I hear the hoarse cry of my kind;
Yet, well do I know, as I quit you tonight,
It's Youth that I'm leaving behind.
And often I'll think of you, empty and black,
Moose antlers nailed over your door;
Oh, if I should perish, my ghost will come back
To dwell in you, cabin, once more!

Robert Service wrote those words in 1912. He died in September 1958, and never returned, in person, to the humble, little log cabin in Dawson. If his ghost returns, it will find the cabin has become a shrine and Mecca for thousands of visitors, and if its ghostly fingers leaf through the pages of the dog-eared guest book until it comes to the date, August 1935, it will find these words:

"To me, yours are the greatest poems ever written." — Will Rogers, Claremore, Oklahoma.

Rogers' tribute explains far better than any learned essayist can, the popularity of Robert Service. Rogers was proud to be a "common man," and Service served the common man "literary steak, well seasoned with plenty of calories and tasty trimmings!"

Prospectors, like this man with his shovel and gold pan at the edge of a creek in the Yukon Territory in 1898, inspired many poems written by Robert Service.

Service would have been the first to call what he wrote verse – and he advised young men to "write verse, not poetry – the public wants verse."

There's no question that Service discovered what the public wanted. No other works have been so parodied and anthologized as his. He stayed at the head of best-selling poetry lists for decades, and "The Shooting of Dan McGrew" and "The Cremation of Sam McGee" have become a part of American folklore.

Although his life in the New World was spent mostly in Canada, the poet of the Yukon was adopted by Alaskans, too. For surely no one before or since has better interpreted the vastness, power, beauty and cruelty of the North.

Service, born in Preston, Lancashire, England, of Scottish ancestry, proudly claimed Robert "Bobby" Burns as a distant relative. He was a worthy descendent of the Scottish bard, but his writings were more in the Rudyard Kipling style. And next to Kipling, Service made more money out of his verse than any other versifier.

His first published poem was in a boys' paper called "Chin Ching's Own." The comment by the editor was, "You've got it bad old fellow, but cheer up, you'll get over it," referring to the last line of this poem: "Alas, my love is false to me, but that was yesterday."

"I never read a poem I admired but what I tried to emulate it," Service later wrote in his autobiography, "Ploughman of the Moon." The peak of poetic taste he found in Alfred (Lord) Tennyson and Robert Browning. He aped John Keats for sonnets and Austin Dobson for ballads. He found a joy in jingles and finally tired of poetry – tired of ideals and abstractions.

"Why write about flowers, love, mythology?" he asked. "Why not write about real things – eating, drinking, lusts and common people?"

It was poetry farewell, but he stuck to verse. Although turning from nectar, he still liked beer. He practiced his versifying less and less, however, and he finally stopped. The early training wasn't wasted, though. When he began to make verse again, it came easy as "slipping off a log," he later said.

Like many young Englishmen, Service decided to seek his fortune in the New World. At the age of 20, he quit his job in a bank, withdrew his savings and bought a steerage ticket to Halifax, Nova Scotia. He kept traveling west, and by the time he reached Victoria, British Columbia, he had only a few dollars left. He worked for a while on a farm, and then he hit the road.

He traveled up and down the Pacific Coast from Canada to Mexico working as a fruit picker, field hand, dishwasher — any job that came to hand. Finally, his course in the College of Hard Knocks ended. He came full circle, and found himself again working in a bank, first in Victoria, then Kamloops, B.C., then Whitehorse – where he was to find his destiny.

From time to time he had heard exciting tales of the Klondike, but he paid little heed, because the gold fields seemed so remote and inaccessible. As he stepped off the boat at Skagway in the early 1900s, he had a premonition, he later wrote, that a new and wonderful chapter in his life was about to begin.

As Robert Service looked out the windows of the train heading to Whitehorse, he viewed the rugged trail that led to the Klondike gold fields.

Poet heads to the Yukon

He boarded a White Pass and Yukon Railroad coach. As it inched up over the narrow-gauge tracks by precipitous cliffs, he could see where so many gold seekers had fallen to their deaths. He was glad, he wrote, that he was traveling in a comfortable train. When he arrived in Whitehorse, it was 40-below zero in the dead of winter. Service found the town teeming with Klondikers loaded with gold dust and yarns on their way to and from the mines.

The sensitive young man found it a thrilling environment and began to write rhymes describing the North Country. Most of them ended up condemned to the bottom of a drawer. But some people thought his rhymes had merit, and he was asked to write a poem to recite at a church function.

Service later explained how "Dangerous Dan McGrew" began.

"Stoller White, editor of the Whitehorse Star, first suggested my writing an original poem to recite (at a church gathering). I decided to give it a try and went for a long walk to think it over. As I returned

A FEW TRAILBLAZERS

from my walk, I had nothing doped out. It was a Saturday night, and from the various bars I heard sounds of revelry. The line popped into my mind, 'A bunch of the boys were whooping it up,' and it stuck there. Good enough for a start. ..."

The rest of the stanzas came so easily he was amazed. It was as if someone was whispering in his ear. Before he crawled into bed at 5 a.m., his ballad was in the bag. However, he decided against using it for the initial purpose – the cuss words, he thought, made it impossible to recite at a church concert.

His next ballad, "The Cremation of Sam McGee," was put with his first — away in a drawer. He continued with his walks, usually carrying a book of Kipling's poetry, and he would rant poetic stanzas to chipmunks and porcupines. One early spring morning, on the heights of Miles Canyon, looking at the beauty of it, a line popped into his head:

A walk along Miles Canyon inspired Robert Service to write lines that became "The Call of the Wild." The steamboat seen in this photograph is the *Nora*, tied up at Miles Canyon Landing on the Yukon River in July 1899.

"I have gazed on naked grandeur where there's nothing else to gaze on."

So again, he hammered out a complete poem in the course of a walk. It was "The Call of the Wild," and the wild scenery and the spring in Service's blood had inspired it.

In the two months that followed, he wrote something every day on his lonely walks along the trails. He looked forward to those walks, he said, because he knew the voice would whisper in his ear, and he would bubble verse like an artesian well, composing "The Spell of the Yukon" and many other ballads.

He wrote not only of nature, but human nature as well — life in a mining camp, rough miners and dancehall girls. Vice, it seemed to him, was more vital than virtue, more colorful and dramatic, so he specialized in the Red Light atmosphere. And his piles of manuscripts grew higher. He piled his shirts on them, and forgot them, until one day he was cleaning out his bureau and came upon them.

A friend suggested he have them published and give them away for Christmas presents. He might not have taken the suggestion, but fate took a hand. He had just received a $100 bonus for Christmas and

Sam McGee, on whom Robert Service based "The Cremation of Sam McGee," lived in this cabin in Whitehorse, Yukon Territory.

Robert Service found prospectors' tough lives in the mining camps and their playgrounds of saloons mixed with dancehall girls, like Klondike Kate Rockwell shown above, ideal for inspiring verse.

It didn't take long for Whitehorse to grow into a bustling mining town as businesses like the Grand Hotel, White Horse Hotel, Arctic Restaurant and Hotel Commercial sprang up.

decided he would squander it on authorship. He would get 100 copies printed, and maybe during his lifetime, he thought, he could bestow them on kindly friends. He would finish with poetic folly for good, study finance and become a stuffy, little banker.

His plans changed, however, with the success of that first book of verse — "Songs of a Sourdough," printed in 1907, and later reprinted as "Spell of the Yukon and Other Poems." When he was transferred to Dawson, it was to find himself a celebrity, although he managed to slip into town without any great fanfare. His poems were on everyone's lips.

"The whole camp," one of Dawson's inhabitants later wrote, "was reciting 'The Shooting of Dan McGrew,' 'The Cremation of Sam McGee' and 'The Spell of the Yukon.' We knew the author of the wild ballads with the Kiplingesque lilt had never been in the Klondike, but to us the poems seemed strangely authentic and true to the country."

A FEW TRAILBLAZERS

Dawson residents made hurried excuses to get a glimpse of the poet who was weighing out gold in the teller cage of the Canadian Bank of Commerce on Front Street. They were surprised, that instead of the rip-roaring roister they expected, they saw a "shy and nondescript man in his mid-30s with a fresh complexion, clear, blue eyes and a boyish figure that made him look much younger," as Laura Berton described him in "I Married the Klondike."

The people of Dawson found that he didn't talk much, but listened intently as old timers rambled on. He could be seen strolling along the streets, looking into boarded-up saloons and shuttered dancehalls. He was a good mixer among men and spent a lot of time with the sourdoughs, but he wouldn't attend large parties or official receptions. It was easy to forget how important a literary figure he was becoming.

Dawson's Third Street bustled with activity during 1899.

There was one incident in Dawson that was typical of Service. A hanging had been scheduled on the banks of the Yukon in the yard of the Royal North-West Mounted Police barracks. Somehow, Service obtained permission to be a witness, for he felt he had to undergo every type of experience. He stayed at the scene until the black flag fluttered up the mast, and then, pale and unnerved, he moved with uncertain steps to the bank mess house where he spoke not a word but poured himself a tumbler of straight Scotch and gulped it down. That was unusual, Berton said, for all the time he was in Dawson, he very seldom drank or smoked.

His ballads had given him a reputation, however, that was hard to overcome, and it broke up a romance with a pretty young Dawson stenographer. The report was her parents did not approve of him because of his wild verses — on account of their themes, they were sure that Service was quite a rounder and drank to excess.

Antics at gold-rush era drinking establishments, like the A and A Saloon pictured here, inspired many of Robert Service's poems.

A FEW TRAILBLAZERS

A common man

And one of the men, R.J. Latshaw, who knew him in Dawson, wrote to his brother:

"… because he spent long hours alone while composing verses, some people who didn't know him very well got the impression that he was a quiet introvert, or maybe a 'High Hat.'"

That idea was certainly not true. Service was a perfectly normal, friendly type of person, who whenever he wasn't working, liked to hike, toboggan, skate, dance and occasionally participate in bull sessions. At one time he frequented a boarding house that catered to stage drivers, teamsters and laborers in order to become acquainted with their vernacular. The group's approval of him was voiced by a Cockney laborer:

"'E's no blinkin' 'igh 'at. 'E's a jolly good bloke."

Service discussed with Berton some of the new poems he was preparing for a publication called, "Ballads of a Cheechako." His soft voice, well modulated, always became strangely vibrant and emotional as he talked of the Yukon, she said. When Berton remarked that the "Ballad of Blasphemous Bill" was a near duplicate of the Sam McGee story, Service said:

"That's what I tried for. That's the stuff the public wants. That's what they pay for and I mean to give it to them."

His habits became more erratic, and he became more and more inaccessible as he plunged into writing his first novel, "The Trail of '98." He had moved into his little cabin by then, and he wrote most of this book on huge rolls of wallpaper. When he ran out, he used building paper or brown wrapping paper. The walls of his cabin were fairly covered with his writings and slogans like "Don't worry — work."

After he finished his book, he took it to New York. But he became bored with the congestion of the city and decided to walk to New Orleans. He ended up in Cuba and there he stayed in the hot, tropical sun for a while. However, he soon turned homesick for the cold quietness of the North.

Service took the long way around, traveling back by way of the McKenzie River, practically to its mouth, then crossed the mountains

Robert Service, who left Dawson when he was 36, wrote hundreds of poems during his lifetime. He died at the age of 84.

and followed the Porcupine River to where it entered the Yukon in Alaska, and then paddled upriver to Dawson. He remained in his cabin until 1912.

Probably at the request of his publishers, Service returned to writing verse (his "Trail of '98" turned out to be a lurid, heartrending opus with none of the rolling rhythm of his poetry). He composed his final book of Yukon poems, "Rhymes of a Rolling Stone," published in 1912. Again, the elements of his best poems are present in some of these — heroism, sacrifice, humor, sin, tragedy and brutal nature.

But now, as he expressed it in "Good-bye, Little Cabin," perhaps the last Yukon poem he wrote, "he heard the world call." Stuffing the manuscript of his latest book into a briefcase, he boarded the steamer for Whitehorse and departed forever from the "Arctic trails with their secret tales that would make your blood run cold." He was 36 years old.

He spent the next 48 years, until his death on Sept. 11, 1958, far from the Yukon. He had an adventurous life as a war correspondent and a Red Cross ambulance driver in World War I. He finally settled down on the Riviera with his wife and daughter, writing nonfiction, fiction and poetry. He once stated that he had written more than 800 poems and his goal was 1,000, "if the Lord of Scribes will spare me to finish the task."

He never returned to the Yukon. On leaving, he wrote in his autobiography:

Robert Service wrote much of his work in this cabin in Dawson.

"As the steamer passed the mouth of the Klondike, I was as blue as burning brimstone … it seemed to be a self I was leaving behind. As I looked my last, my eyes rested on my cabin high on the hill. The door seemed to open, and I saw a solitary figure waving his pipe in farewell — the ghost of my dead youth. No, I do not want to meet that reproachful wraith again. He might say, 'You promised to do so much, you have done so little.'

"… I felt I was not only quitting Dawson but the North itself. Nine years of my life I had given it and it was in my blood. It had inspired and sustained me, brought me fortune and a meed of fame. I thought I knew it better than most men and could express its secret spirit. Maybe I should have remained there and devoted my life to singing and writing of it. …"

27

SOURDOUGH PREACHER PAINTER

One of Alaska's early artists stepped ashore in the boom-town of Cordova in 1909. His works aptly capture the epic struggle of sourdough days, portraying that historic period when pioneer men and women conquered a rugged wilderness and opened the Alaska frontier. The hunched backs of prospectors, bowed under heavy packs; the white, desolate tundra; powerful, winding rivers; the frigid majesty of snowy mountains, and small fishing boats boldly defying the mighty oceans fill Eustace Paul Ziegler's canvases.

This scene of Cordova along Main Street in 1908 is similar to that which met artist Eustace Paul Ziegler's eyes when he stepped ashore in the Prince William Sound town a year later.

Eustace Paul Ziegler's "Native Woman," oil on masonite, is on display at the University of Alaska Fairbanks Museum of the North.

His paintings show man challenging a nature he cannot conquer, but by hope and strength can learn to live in. If now and then we lament the passing of those vivid days, we can renew our spirits before Ziegler's paintings, for he dipped his paint bush into life as it was lived in the rough and rugged days of Alaska's youth.

A FEW TRAILBLAZERS

Ziegler, himself, was just a youth when he arrived in Cordova to take charge of its Episcopal mission. It was a cold, snowy, windy day in January when Capt. "Dynamite" Johnny O'Brien tied the *Yakutan* up to the wharf, and the short, slightly built 22-year-old disembarked.

Fresh from the Yale School of Fine Arts and conventionally dressed, Ziegler must have been a shock to the thousands of roughly dressed pick-and-shovel "stiffs," lumber jacks, miners, engineers, dynamiters, surveyors, adventurers and what-not who had "floated in with the tides and the ties" to build the Copper River and Northwestern Railway from tidewater to the Kennecott copper mines in the Interior. Probably as much a shock as the sight of the rough construction town was to him.

The Rev. E.P. Newton, Episcopal minister based at Valdez, had visited the new construction camp two years before and had seen the need for a meeting place, other than saloons, for the homeless, drifting men. The Episcopal Bishop of Alaska, Peter Trimble Rowe, and Michael J. Heney, in charge of building the railroad, helped him obtain a tract of land to start a mission.

Lumber was scarce and put up for sale to the highest bidder.

There were two – a saloon keeper and Newton. The saloon keeper outbid the Episcopal minister, and he got the lumber. However, even though a saloon became the first building in the new town, the mission was the second to be started.

Newton built a bright-red building, and coupled with the name St. George Mission, it gave rise to its nickname the "Red Dragon." By 1908, the mission was ready to compete with the 26 saloons that now graced Cordova's main street.

When Ziegler arrived to take over the Red Dragon's "ecclesiastical proprietorship," it did not take him long to fit into his new life. He might have been a cheechako, but he was no tenderfoot. Although he looked deceptively slight, he'd spent summers on logging crews in the north woods of his native Michigan, and he was a dead shot and an excellent camp cook.

Soon he was friends with saloon keepers, company bosses, bar

The St. George Mission, nicknamed the Red Dragon, is arranged for service.

swampers, teachers, doctors, prospectors, trappers – he was "Zieg" to everyone, and everyone was welcome at the Red Dragon. Before its warm, friendly fireplace, wastrels and gentlemen, workers and strays gathered to sleep, wrangle, fight, read, visit, sing and play the piano. On Sundays, however, an altar was let down by block and tackle from the joists above, a screen was drawn and services were held before it by Ziegler, whose mission was to minister to men's souls as well as their bodies.

He passed a help-yourself box, which was a two-way collection plate. Hard and folding money could be taken by those in need, no receipts necessary, and repayments for years exceeded the amounts taken.

Ziegler flourishes in Cordova

The frontier mission and Ziegler supplied warmth, cheer and aid to those who came seeking. They acquired a reputation far and wide for the services they rendered – religious as well as secular.

It had been a long way for young Ziegler to travel, but a love of the outdoors and the North had always been his. He also loved art.

When he was 7, he had decided that above all he wanted to paint. He worked at many art jobs, studied at the Detroit Art School and graduated from the Yale University of Fine Arts. After graduation, he still had to realize his dream of hitting the trail north, but Bishop Rowe was a family friend, and the young artist offered to help him.

Ziegler was secular superintendent in the boomtown of Cordova from 1909 until 1916. Then, shortly after his marriage to Mary Boyle, he became ordained as an Episcopal minister as his father and brothers before him. It was said, "he married the elite of the town and buried with Christian decency the remains of murdered vagabonds."

"Zieg" was a friend of everyone and known all over the territory as he traveled up and down the coast in connection with his work. But he also painted constantly. He decorated the walls of the Red Dragon, and the church that was later built, with paintings of great beauty and deep religious feeling.

At Stephan's Church at Fort Yukon were hung canvases depicting the nativity and the crucifixion that he copied from the great masters for the Native parishioners of that village church. All the time, too, he was painting the natural beauty he saw in every direction, and the people around him went on canvas, too – the trappers, fishermen, prospectors and Natives of the Copper River Valley and all over Alaska. There was Horsecreek Mary, for instance, an old Native woman who lived in a hovel near Chitina. He painted a beautiful study of her wrinkled, brown face.

One of his most famous paintings was the "Arctic Madonna." The Eskimo mother and her placid baby won innumerable prizes and hung in many galleries. His sympathy and affection for the Native people of Alaska shines through his paintings, and the feeling was reciprocated. Chief Goodlataw of the Chitina Indians called the young preacher-painter, who brought food and clothing to his people, "George Jesus Man."

His canvases were growing in character and strength with the fundamental realism of the rough and tough mining camps and the

Ziegler painted realistic portrayals of life in gold-mining camps, like the painting above titled "Prospector's Cabin," oil on canvas board, which hangs in the Museum of the North at the University of Alaska Fairbanks.

work-a-day world around him. For years, Ziegler traveled about Alaska seeing and painting everything he could – in oils, watercolor, woodcuts and dry point – as he recorded the pioneer scenes. Tourists bought his work from the windows of local stores. And one 16-by-20-inch oil painting for sale in Fursman's drugstore in Cordova changed the direction of Ziegler's life.

Ziegler was on a dog team trip with Bishop Rowe in the Chitina region when he received a telegram saying that one of his paintings, a mountain scene, had been sold for $150 to E.T. Stannard, president of the Alaska Steamship Company. Stannard later asked Ziegler to come to Seattle and do a series of murals for the company's Seattle offices.

Bishop Rowe convinced his young friend to grasp the opportunity, and practically lifted him off his snowshoes and headed him on the new trail that was to bring him fame in the world of art.

Eustace Ziegler's friend, Bishop Peter Trimble Rowe, center, poses with Delatuck, a Kobuk Eskimo, and Maggie, an Athabascan Indian, in the Koyukuk region in 1922.

When the murals were completed, the Zieglers returned to Cordova, but new offers flooded the little Alaskan minister. He finally had to make a choice between the ministry and a career as an artist. By this time, Cordova had tamed considerably and was a respectable young city with families, a school and churches. The old, rough, frontier days were gone.

Ziegler, who fit the Red Dragon during its early mission days, no longer felt needed. As he humorously said later, "I resigned 10 minutes before Bishop Rowe fired me."

The Zieglers and their two daughters, Betty and Ann, moved to Seattle in September 1924, and from then on his art career grew. His paintings found their way into the White House, governors' mansions, art museums and collections, and he won innumerable prizes, awards and citations.

Many of his paintings hung in the Seattle museums; his religious works hung in many Pacific Northwest chapels, and many of his powerful portraits and landscapes, commissioned by wealthy patrons, now reside in the Pacific Northwest museums and universities.

His canvases also are in the homes and hearts of ordinary people. Alaskans who best know the subjects he painted in his early Alaska days like his works so much that some of them own 20 or more of his canvases. They feel that he is one of theirs, and that is how he felt to the end. Once he was asked if he could be called an "ex-sourdough," and he replied, proudly and sternly, "I'm a sourdough. There's no such thing as an ex-sourdough!"

He renewed his ties with Alaska nearly every summer, traveling to different areas to paint. Like another famous Alaska artist, Sydney Laurence, one of Ziegler's favorite subjects was Denali, which he often called "his studio." He painted the majestic mountain, first from the Denali National Park and Preserve, packing in supplies 80 miles by pack train, then later working from Talkeetna. In June 1931, he and his pupil, Ted Lambert, made a trip down the Yukon River from Fairbanks to Bethel, painting the subjects they liked as they went.

At an age when most men were forced into idleness, Ziegler in his late 70s was still painting and had no plans to retire. He was turning out one or two pictures a week, working from about 8 a.m. to midnight, five days and sometimes on Saturdays. At the time, one interviewer characterized him as a "silver-haired, peppery little artist, who at 79, enjoys good health, which bubbles to the surface of his sharp features."

In 1969, however, at the age of 87, the old sourdough came to the end of his trail. At the time of his death, the Frye Museum in Seattle was exhibiting 63 of his works. He once estimated he had painted or drawn more than 50 works a year since he began selling professionally at the age of 20. A realist, he painted what he saw, and power and meaning spoke so strongly through his paintings that they brought him prosperity as well as artistic success.

Perhaps one of his own statements explains that success: "If you don't paint for money, you'll make money."

His old friend, Bishop Rowe, once wrote of him:

"To know Eustace Ziegler was to know an unforgettable person. Few workers in the Alaska mission field were better known, or more beloved by the men who follow the frontier. He possessed a rich sense of humor, was a unique storyteller, a diligent pastor and a lover of mankind."

Although his paintings saw man stripped of stature by a wilderness he could never conquer, Ziegler believed that by hope and strength drawn from his fellow man, man can live in that wilderness. That hope and strength can be sensed in his paintings for he has expressed eloquently much that is fundamental in this business of being alive and aware. He was a fitting interpreter of the Great Land, and a fitting choice for Alaska's Hall of Fame, which inducted him in the early 1970s.

Eustace Ziegler, pictured here in May 1965, became famous for painting scenes of life in Alaska.

The "Tanana Woman and Dog" painting, oil on board, is typical of Ziegler's art that showed people living in the harsh Alaska environment.

A FEW TRAILBLAZERS

MIGHTY MOUNTAINS

28

ELIAS: TOUGH EVERY FOOT OF THE WAY

Mount St. Elias, the first point sighted by white men on the mainland of Alaska in 1741, has proved a mighty challenge to mountaineers. Only a handful of climbers have conquered it in the years since the Dane, Vitus Bering, discovered and named it for Russia.

Mount St. Elias has proved to be a difficult mountain to summit in the more than 250 years since it was first spotted by white men.

English explorers George Dixon and James Cook noted the mighty mountain, too, in their explorations, and in 1786, Comte de La Perouse's astronomer, Joseph Lepaute Dagelet, calculated its altitude at 12,672 feet. A few years later, Spanish explorer Alejandro Malaspina determined its altitude at 17,851 feet, remarkably near its true height of 18,024 feet as decided upon by Coast Survey Triangulation in 1892.

The area around Mount St. Elias contains an important grouping of Athabascan prehistoric and historic archeological sites of the Tlingit and Eyak Indians and the Chugach Eskimos, including Taral, Cross Creek and Batzulnetas.

But nearly 150 years went by after Bering's discovery before any attempt was made to ascend the vast, barren mountain, rearing

upward from the shore of the sea. Capped with snow and draped with glaciers that wind upward and back as far as the eye can see, the mountain, according to many mountaineers, presents the greatest snow climb in the world. The line of perpetual snow descends to only 400 feet above sea level.

To accept the challenge in 1886, Lt. Frederick Schwatka, accompanied by professor William Libbey and Sir Henry Seton-Karr,

Sir Henry Seton-Karr, pictured here at age 61, was a noted outdoorsman and former member of the British Parliament. His attempt to climb St. Elias failed in 1886.

led an expedition supported by the New York Times. The expedition failed, however, because so little was known of the conditions that were encountered. The party made it about 20 miles inland and obtained considerable geographical information that was valuable to subsequent explorers.

As Seton-Karr described the effort in his book, "Shores and Alps of Alaska:"

"… had the weather been clear, we might have picked out a possible way of ascent and might even have seen part of the northern face on which no white man's eye has yet rested, but compelled by all these circumstances over which we had no control, we returned to camp. I had ascended to a greater height over the summer snow level than is possible to accomplish in Europe."

Seton-Karr described Elias as forming a regular quadrilateral pyramid, the first feature as seen from Icy Bay; one also sees a detached, circular, crater-like basin nearly halfway up the central front, then one notices the regularity of three of the pyramidal side ridges and assumes that the fourth ridge must be equally regular. One notices, too, according to Seton-Karr:

"… the solitary and isolated situation of the Ice King – the termination and crowning elevation of his range, so close upon the sea, going out over the widest ocean of the world."

Two years later, in 1888, a party of three Englishmen – W.H. Topham, Edwin Topham and George Broca – and American William Williams found their way to the summit blocked by a 1,500-foot-high mound of ice at the 11,400-foot level. They decided that a temporary camp and the services of experienced packers would be needed to go any farther, so they concluded the southwestern face of Mount St. Elias would never be climbed. Williams wrote:

"It presents a mass of broken snow, beautiful, yet forbidding … the whole scene surpassed in grandeur, though not in picturesqueness, the very best that the Alps can offer. Roughly speaking, the eye encounters for miles nothing but snow and ice. I had never before thoroughly realized the vastness of the Alaskan glaciers … the groups of snow-clad peaks visible to the naked eye were countless; and to the

Israel Cook Russell was the first to explore Alaska for the U.S. Geological Survey.

northward, in which direction the view was barred, their number is doubtless quite as great."

Under the joint auspices of the National Geographic Society and the U. S. Geological Survey came the third attempt to reach St. Elias' summit. In 1890, professor Israel Cook Russell led a party composed of Mark B. Karr and six camp hands. Russell and Karr undoubtedly would have reached the top if a severe storm had not forced their retreat after a four-day wait in rude shelters, in snow banks, without fuel and almost without food. As Karr later wrote:

"I lay there in my snowy camp and began to wonder if I would be found in future ages, preserved in glacier ice like a mammoth or cave bear, as an illustration to geologists that man inhabited these regions of eternal ice, living happily on nothing, breathing the free air of prehistoric times."

He finally left his snowy shelter, but he realized that the party was too late to reach their instruments and again attempt the peak.

"If the storm had only held off for 24 hours more, the scalp of Elias would have been in our belt, and we could have finished the trip with great rejoicing. However, our attempt was bold, and our success in finding and naming new peaks, new glaciers, and studying their movements, and indeed, making a general topographical reconnaissance of this unknown region, recompensed us in part for failure in reaching the summit."

Russell tried again in 1891, and while alone, reached a height of 14,500 feet. Heavy storms again forced his retreat, but from his height, he got a glimpse of the unknown region to the north. He wrote:

"I expected to see a comparatively low, forested country, perhaps some sign of human habitation. What met my astonished gaze was a vast, snow-covered region, limitless in expanse, through which hundreds, perhaps thousands, of bare, angular mountain peaks projected.

"There was not a stream, not a lake, and not a vestige of vegetation of any kind in sight. A more desolate or utterly lifeless land one never beheld. Vast, smooth snow surfaces without crevasses, stretched away to limitless distances, broken only by jagged and angular mountain peaks."

Elias finally conquered

But the route that Russell had explored was of great assistance when, in 1897, the mountain finally was conquered by one of the world's most distinguished mountain climbers and explorers, the Italian Duke of Abruzzi. Born to King Amadeus of Spain, who was also the Duke d'Aosta in Italy, his full name was Luigi Amedeo Giuseppe Maria Ferdinando Francesco.

The duke and his party landed at Yakutat Bay, and with a large and thoroughly equipped expedition, made their way across the 40 miles of snow and ice between the coast and the base of the mountain. Crossing the Malaspina, Seward and Agassiz glaciers, the duke's party ascended the heavily crevassed Newton Glacier and climbed to Russell Col at the end of the northeast

Italian Luigi Amedeo Giuseppe Maria Ferdinando Francesco, also known as the Duke of Abruzzi, was first to summit Mount St. Elias in 1897.

ridge. From there, at about 12,300 feet, the party made the long snow ascent to the summit in a single day, July 31, five weeks after leaving tidewater, and without any technical difficulty.

The expedition occupied a 50-day roundtrip from the coast, mostly spent in bad weather, carrying or hauling loads in deep snow, across and up the glaciers. The duke's expedition was carefully planned, and he showed himself a capable leader, as well as an experienced mountaineer.

More information about the mountain became known when the matter of the International Boundary between Alaska and Canada became a question of importance after the discovery of gold in the Yukon. Twenty years of continuous survey and field work finally fixed the line.

Northwesterly, the 141st Meridian passed high on the slopes of Mount St. Elias and its survey was carried out under almost insuperable difficulties. An attempted ascent, worthy of permanent record in mountaineering annals, was that headed by Asa C. Baldwin. Unlike the other expeditions that went in from the Pacific side, the Baldwin party attacked inland, going in from McCarthy in the Copper River valley.

"We nearly conquered St. Elias," wrote a member of the party. "Our goal, the peak of St. Elias, was only 110 miles away in a direct line, but miles became a term totally without meaning. Our route was to be

Asa C. Baldwin attempted to climb Mount St. Elias from the Copper River valley side.

across indescribably rough country ... winding always upward, over and around and among vast trackless slopes that were torn and shattered by countless glaciers, which for centuries had crept relentlessly downward toward the sea.

"From McCarthy onward, we were to measure distances not by miles but by grueling hours and days and weeks of heartbreaking toil. ..."

Their aim was to reach a spot that could by celestial observations be placed on a line through the peaks of St. Elias and distant Mount Cook. There they would build a permanent monument, if possible.

When they reached the 7,000-foot divide between the Columbus and Seward glaciers, they were directly north of the peak. They struck south, then, toward the dome that still towered 11,000 feet above them. They labored up over the increasingly steep ice slope between terrifying walls, until they were about 9,000 feet above sea level. There they had to stop. The slope of ice had reached an angle of 45 degrees and was so rough they could haul the sleds no farther. A tent was pitched:

"We slept little that night. The sudden explosive crash of rupturing ice masses beneath and about us, and the slowly accumulating roar of nearby avalanches kept us constantly tense and fearful. We were pitiably tiny mites in the midst of a cauldron of titanic movement and sound."

The next morning they gladly pressed on, out of their terrifying gorge – late that afternoon they scrambled onto a shoulder of rock, 14,000 feet above sea level, and made camp. The next morning they started on what they expected to be their final climb – the scramble that would bring them out on the dome that loomed 4,000 feet above them. It was not to be.

"We had considered that we were capable mountain climbers, but we were coming to have a great deal of respect for St. Elias. It wasn't just another mountain at all. It was St. Elias and it was tough – tough every foot of the way and every second of the time."

Unnoticed as they worked across dangerous ledges, clouds had been sweeping up the gorge below and behind them. Suddenly the

Between 1912 and 1913, Asa C. Baldwin was the U. S. Chief of Party for the Mount St. Elias to Arctic Ocean 141st Meridian Boundary Demarcation Survey, which included the ascent of St. Elias in 1913. Here at the 1,000 foot level, the glacier is badly shattered.

clouds were all about, and the great dome was blotted from sight. Then, without warning, a blizzard was upon them. To stay there was simply to freeze to death in short order, so hour after hour, they worked their way back down the mountainside, half of the time without any hope at all, simply going down to meet death rather than lie down and wait for it.

"All the Gods of Luck must have been clustered about us, guiding our numbed hands and feet, our picks and spikes, for finally we staggered into camp, half frozen and exhausted but all still alive ... the lookout at the main camp sighted us as we stumbled down the seemingly endless slope of the Chitina Glacier ... a party came up to meet us and helped us into camp."

And so ended their great adventure on Mount St. Elias — a gigantic mountain, they found, locked in the heart of a vast glacial solitude. Although they had not reached the summit, their efforts had added to the knowledge of the magnificent monument that marks the southwesterly corner of the boundary between Canada and Alaska.

First successful American climb

The first American party to conquer the "Saint," the Harvard Mountaineering Club, included a woman, Betty Kauffman. The party landed at Icy Bay in 1946 and climbed the southwest ridge – more difficult than the duke's climb, but shorter and more direct.

As Maynard N. Miller, one of the successful climbers, wrote in a National Geographic article:

"The Saint was always trying to throw us off balance, it seemed to me. Across our path it threw yawning crevasses, rumbling avalanches and treacherous ice slicks."

More than three-quarters of their route was over ice and snow, over the unclimbed, broken ice of Tyndall Glacier to the 11,921-foot Mount Hayden, an unclimbed summit whose slopes formed part of their route. From the slopes of Hayden, Miller wrote that they could look across three miles of space to the appalling west face of the

The first American party to summit Mount St. Elias crossed the Tyndall Glacier, seen here, in 1946.

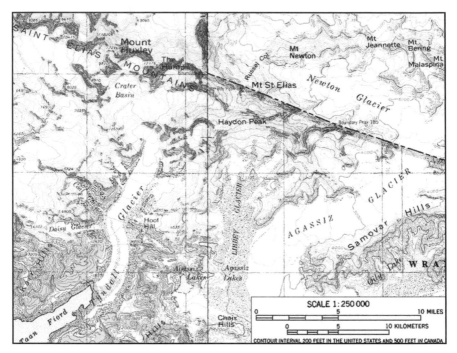

Mount St. Elias, in Southcentral Alaska, still draws bold explorers and mountaineers.

"Saint." They saw blocks of ice, some big as houses, batter into splinters as they bounced down the cliffs.

The mountain waged its war of nerves up to the bitter end, but upward they climbed, over humps, across snow faces, through gullies, from terrace to terrace, chopping, floundering and climbing. Fatigue, headaches and pounding hearts were forgotten when the summit plain – half the size of a football field – was reached.

When she finally reached the summit in 1946, Kauffman had climbed higher than any other woman up to that time in Alaska and Canada.

Dee Molenaar, photographer of the party, beat Kauffman's husband, Andrew, to the draw when he rewarded Kauffman with a big kiss on the cheek for her accomplishment.

The party unfurled American and Canadian flags over the International Boundary on July 16, which also turned out to be the 205th anniversary of the day Bering's party had first sighted the

MIGHTY MOUNTAINS

snowy peak from 140 miles out to sea and named it for the patron saint of the day, Elias.

The third successful climb added more flags to those two on top of the mountain. This climb was the first by the north route and was made in July 1964. The 20 members of the All Japan-Alaska Expedition included an Anchorage man, Scott Hamilton.

Camp Four was made at 12,800 feet, but the leader of the party was afraid the weather would change and defeat them as it had done so many others, so the two lightest men of the party, Shiro Nishimae and Tokaskio Yaname, were sent in on the final dash that took 37 hours.

"We were so tired," they said later, "we had to plant the Alaska flag twice. The first time it went in upside down."

They also planted the flags of the United States, Japan and Canada before leaving the summit on July 17 at 9 p.m.

One year later, the peak was surmounted again, and again by the Harvard Mountaineering Club. This time they climbed the northwest ridge – the first time this route had been successful. The climb took 23 days and was plagued by bad weather. The leader, Boyd N. Everett Jr., was familiar with much of the route, as he had been leader of a 1963 expedition turned back by two earthquakes and several avalanches.

"It snowed 12 of the last 13 days of the expedition," Everett said of the successful climb. "During the ascent, 57 pitons and 4,900 feet of fixed rope were used – an unusual amount of technical equipment for an Alaskan climb. But this is a very difficult mountain to climb. There's no easy way up as there is on Mount McKinley. And although it's the second-highest mountain in the United States, there's very little known about it."

Today, Mount St. Elias remains desolate and icebound. It's still a challenge to explorers and mountaineers and a vast field laboratory for students of glaciers.

Another Alaska mountain also calls climbers to pit their expertise against its treacherous weather and trails – Denali.

29

DENALI: THE HIGH ONE

Rising more than 20,000 feet above sea level, a mountain known to early Athabascan Indians of the Interior as Denali, meaning "The High One," towers over all other peaks in its mountain range.

Mount McKinley, also called Denali, in the Alaska Range is the highest peak in North America.

Generations of Athabascans hunted for caribou, moose and sheep along the lowland hills of the mountain's northern side. They also picked berries and edible plants and fished in the streams.

The first known mention of the mountain came in 1794 when English explorer Capt. George Vancouver saw what he called "a stupendous snow mountain" from Cook Inlet. Early Russian explorers and traders called the peak Bolshaia Gora, or "Big Mountain," and in 1889 prospector Frank Densmore referred to Denali as "Densmore's Mountain" after he hiked within 65 miles of its base.

William A. Dickey, a prospector, named the 20,320-foot mountain – which is said to have one of the earth's steepest vertical rises – for presidential nominee William McKinley of Ohio in 1896, even though McKinley had no ties to Alaska. Controversy surrounded that name from the get-go and continues today.

Judge James Wickersham, pictured above, failed in his attempt to climb Mount McKinley in 1903.

The history of climbs on the tallest mountain in North America is as intriguing as its names. And although it can be seen from Cook Inlet on a clear day, its base is deep in the Alaska Range. Explorers in the early 1900s used riverboats, mules and dog sleds to gain access to the mountain's glaciers in order to establish base camps.

Judge James Wickersham, who'd climbed every major peak of the Olympic Peninsula before coming to Alaska, was the first white man to tackle the mountain. He and four companions made it to about the 10,000-foot level in 1903. Later in life, while delegate to Congress, Wickersham won legislation creating Mount McKinley National Park.

Wickersham, who was the first federal district court judge in the Interior, had recently moved his headquarters from Eagle to the new boomtown of Fairbanks. However, the business of law and order was slow at that time, so "there was time to look around and consider what to do next," he later wrote in his book, "Old Yukon."

"To me the most interesting object on the horizon was the massive dome that dominates the valleys of the Tanana, the Yukon and the Kuskokwim," he said.

He and M.I. Stevens, George A. Jeffery and Johnnie McLeod left Fairbanks on May 16, 1903, heading for the Kantishna River onboard the *Tanana Chief*. The men had raised money for the adventure by issuing a newspaper and selling advertising. Lacking equipment but swamped with business, Wickersham, who was 45 at the time of the attempt, wrote that the fellows churned out an eight-page Fairbanks Miner "on the first printing press ever brought to the valley – a typewriter."

Wickersham also printed a notice in the paper that he would be conducting court in the Yukon River village of Rampart on July 27. That gave the expedition about 2-1/2 months to cover around 300 miles.

It took weeks to reach the mountain's base. The explorers rowed a boat called the *Mudlark* up the Kantishna and walked mules overland.

"All the tales the Indians told us about snow slides at this season seem to be true, for the whole western face of the mountain, above the glacier, glistens with ice sheets streaked with mineral discolorations from recent slides," Wickersham noted in his book.

The adventurers climbed the glacier's central moraine, then up a smaller glacier to the left, which soon rose into a nearly perpendicular icefall that blocked their path. The climbers sat and watched avalanches tumble down the western face, later named the Wickersham Wall.

After hiking back toward Wonder Lake, the party launched a raft in the McKinley River gorge. But it met with disaster after hitting rocks. The men rebuilt the raft, although McLeod refused to ride. He

This view of Denali from Wonder Lake may have met the eyes of Judge James Wickersham and his party in 1903 as they traveled toward the base of the mountain.

made a canoe from green spruce bark instead. After about a week, they reached Baker Creek, just upstream from Manley Hot Springs on the Tanana River, and hiked 50 miles to Rampart, reaching the Yukon River town on July 7.

While cleaning up after traveling for two months, Wickersham's clothes were thrown into the Yukon River by a friend – who also accidentally tossed one of the judge's prized possessions.

"He stepped gingerly to the bank of the Yukon and threw my cast-off clothing, with my hundred-dollar gold watch strongly attached thereto by a moose-hide string, into the river, where they took up their journey seaward!" Wickersham later wrote.

Dr. Frederick A. Cook

Dr. Cook causes controversy

That same year, Dr. Frederick A. Cook and five team members reached the 11,300-foot level. Cook's team completed the expedition by circumnavigating the mountain, a feat not duplicated until 1995. On the

Cook and his climbing team rest on the west ridge of Denali in 1903.

southeastern side, Cook named the Ruth Glacier after his daughter and the Fidele – now called Eldredge – Glacier for his wife.

Cook returned to the mountain in 1906, and on Sept. 20, reported that he and Ed Barrill, a hunting guide and blacksmith from Darby, Montana, had reached the summit on Sept. 16.

After returning from Alaska, Cook gave lectures about his achievement – including one in Seattle that started the organization of The Mountaineers. He left his 1903 and 1906 book manuscripts with a publisher in 1907 and then headed for Greenland, a trip that later evolved into an expedition to reach the North Pole.

The following year, Harper's Monthly Magazine published Cook's article, "The Conquest of Mount McKinley," about his journey to the top of the mighty mountain that included photos from the summit and a map of the route taken.

However, his vague description of his ascent route and a questionable summit photo of his guide, Barrill, shown standing on top of an outcropping of rock that was somewhat pointed in appearance, led many to doubt his claim.

Frederick Cook mounted expeditions to Alaska's Mount McKinley, being the first to circumnavigate it in 1903 and making the first claimed ascent of North America's highest peak in 1906.

At a dinner sponsored by the National Geographic Society, with a seething Admiral Robert E. Peary in attendance, President Theodore Roosevelt hailed Cook as the conqueror of McKinley and the first American to explore both polar regions.

But critics soon denounced Cook's claim and suggested his summit photo of Ed Barrill, left, was suspect.

In a speech given to Congress in 1915 by Congressman S.D. Fess of Ohio denouncing another claim by Cook – in which he said he had arrived at the North Pole in 1908, one year prior to Admiral Robert E. Peary – Fess outlined the case against Cook by the Explorers Club and professor Herschal C. Parker of Columbia University. Parker, a partner with Cook in the McKinley expedition, both physically and financially, said Cook's claim was fraudulent.

At the time of the 1906 climb, Parker said that Cook assumed the lead with a plan that proved unfeasible, and the party escaped with their lives, thanks to the local knowledge of Belmore Brown, one of its members.

"It was perfectly understood," said Parker, "that after the misadventure all further attempts were abandoned for the season."

Otherwise, Parker said, he would not have left the expedition.

Instead of this, Cook, it is charged, sidetracked all members of the expedition until there remained only himself, Barrill and one packer, John Dokkin, a gold prospector, who subsequently turned back because of a fear of glacial crevasses. These defections left Cook

Cook and his expedition work around a glacial crevasse they encountered on their way to summit Mount McKinley.

no instruments capable of measuring the altitudes he said he attained, according to Parker. Moreover, the summer's experience had shown that Cook and Barrill were the least physically fit of all the party for arduous mountain climbing.

Brown confirmed Parker's account. He also added that in Cook's book there was not one date given from the time he left the Chulitna River, which made intelligent criticism impossible. Brown asserted further that he never saw Cook make a single aneroid barometer reading during the whole trip.

And confirming a charge that had previously been made, Brown said Cook was known to be in serious financial straits and would have had great difficulty in getting out of Alaska if he had not reported that he attained the summit of Mount McKinley.

Pictures declared fake

Brown fortified his charges with the declaration that Cook and Barrill had no ice clamps, and although Cook told Parker later that he

MIGHTY MOUNTAINS

and Barrill were roped together every foot of the last stages, Parker and Brown both remembered that they had destroyed the climbing rope before they quit the expedition because it was defective.

Furthermore, no climbing rope appeared in any of the pictures published in Cook's book. Brown also reported that various photographs in Cook's book did not represent the peaks they were said to picture.

After Cook returned from the Arctic in 1909, the guide whom he alleged went to the top of Mount McKinley with him announced that they never had been to the summit and that the picture Cook took with Barrill holding a flag on the top was miles from the peak.

Cook asserted that all the allegations and Barrill's recanting the summit claim were merely part of a plot by Admiral Peary to ruin him.

Some members of Dr. Frederick Cook's 1906 expedition team carve ice steps out of a steep grade as they climb toward the summit of Mount McKinley.

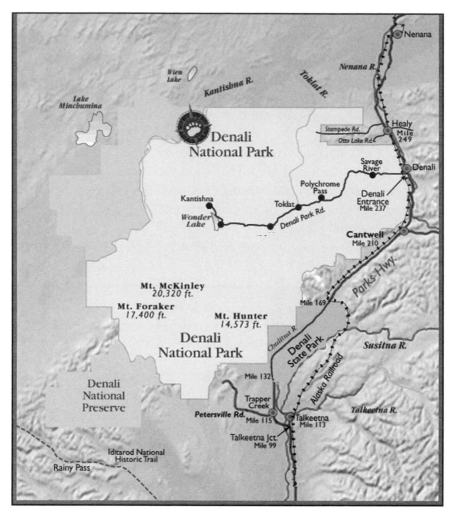

But based on its investigation into Cook's claims, the Explorers' Club ousted Cook from its membership in December 1909. The club concluded in part that:

"Dr. Cook's account of the ascent is not only such as to be unconvincing to the experienced mountaineer, but that under analysis is incredible. ... Cook's description of the ascent of Mount McKinley on the northeast ridge, which is the ridge by which he claimed to have reached the peak, is in reality, a description of the southeast ridge. The

MIGHTY MOUNTAINS

Bradford Washburn, a vocal critic of Frederick Cook, left bits of his equipment behind along McGonagall Pass as he climbed Denali. He was a member of the third expedition to successfully summit and became a well-known expert on the mountain.

former ridge was explored by him on a previous expedition and in his book he declares it impossible as a route to the peak."

Wickersham also thought Cook's claim had no merit. While serving as Alaska's delegate in Congress, he was asked his opinion of Cook's claim:

"All of us who know anything about Mount McKinley know that Cook's story of his successful ascent of that mountain is a deliberate falsehood. … His story was so fraudulent, that one does not have time to talk about it."

Others believe Cook's claim

There are others, however, who believe that Cook reached the summit, as well as reached the North Pole first, and that claims to the contrary are the result of a character assassination by Admiral Peary and his associates.

While commenting on a book written by Peter Cherici and Bradford Washburn – a noted critic of Cook – titled "The Dishonorable Dr. Cook:Debunking the Notorious McKinley Hoax," Cook supporter Ted Heckathorn wrote:

"When Dr. Cook returned from his Arctic trip in September 1909, he reported that he had reached the North Pole in April 1908. This quickly developed into a huge media controversy when Robert E. Peary, a U.S. Navy engineer, claimed to be the discoverer of the North Pole in April 1909. Peary could not prove that Cook had not been to the pole in 1908, or that he had been there in 1909, so he instigated a character assassination campaign against Cook."

Heckathorn and others present more evidence to support Cook's claim through The Frederick A. Cook Society at www.cookpolar.org.

Cook spent almost half his life surrounded by controversy associated with the Alaska climb and the North Pole expedition. His own words, written in the twilight of an amazing career, may best express the depth of his personal torment, according to the Cook Society:

"… few men in all history … have ever been made to suffer so bitterly and so inexpressibly as I because of the assertion of my achievement."

Sourdough Party takes barroom bet

A group of men called the Sourdough Party, which included Tom Lloyd, Charles McGonagall, Pete Anderson and Billy Taylor, set out to conquer the mountain in 1910. Bill Sherwonit, author of "To the Top of Denali: Climbing Adventures on North America's Highest Peak," wrote that the whole adventure began in a barroom.

"According to Lloyd's official account of the Sourdough Expedition, which appeared in The New York Times Sunday Magazine on June 5, 1910, '(bar owner) Bill McPhee and me were talking one day of the

The Sourdough Expedition to climb Denali started out as a barroom bet when Fairbanks, pictured above, was a gold-rush boomtown at the turn-of-the-last century.

possibility of getting to the summit of Mount McKinley and I said I thought if anyone could make the climb there were several pioneers of my acquaintance who could. Bill said he didn't believe that any living man could make the ascent.'

"McPhee argued that the 50-year-old Lloyd was too old and overweight for such an undertaking, to which the miner responded that 'for two cents' he'd show it could be done. To call Lloyd's bluff, McPhee offered to pay $500 to anyone who would climb McKinley and 'prove whether that fellow Cook made the climb or not.' After two other businessmen agreed to put up $500 each, Lloyd accepted the challenge.

"The proposed expedition was big news in Fairbanks, and before long it made local headlines. In his official account, Lloyd admitted, 'Of course, after the papers got hold of the story, we hated the idea of ever coming back here defeated.'"

Sourdoughs travel light

The expedition set off in February and only carried bare essentials, according to Sherwonit, including: "… snowshoes; homemade crampons, which they called creepers; and crude ice axes, which Lloyd described as 'long poles with double hooks on one end — hooks made of steel — and a sharp steel point on the other end.'

"Their high-altitude food supplies included bacon, beans, flour, sugar, dried fruits, butter, coffee, hot chocolate, and caribou meat. To endure the subzero cold, they simply wore bib overalls, long underwear, shirts, parkas, mittens, shoepacs (insulated rubber boots), and Indian moccasins. (The moccasins that the pioneer McKinley climbers wore were like Eskimo mukluks: tall, above-the-calf footwear, dry-tanned, with a moose-hide sole and caribou-skin uppers. Worn with insoles and at least three pairs of wool socks, they were reportedly very warm and provided plenty of support.)

"Even their reading material was limited. The climbers brought only one magazine, which they read from end to end. 'I don't remember the name of the magazine,' Lloyd later commented, 'but in our estimation it is the best magazine published in the world. …'"

The members of the Sourdough Expedition wore Indian moccasins, or mukluks, on their trek up Denali. Mukluks proved to be suitable gear for the U.S. Army, as well. This cart load contains 780 pairs headed to soldiers in Nome in the early 1900s.

After about two months of hiking, the men finally hauled a 14-foot spruce pole and a 6-foot by 12-foot American flag to the top of the North Peak, which people of the time thought was the highest point.

The climbers thought that the flag would be seen from Kantishna, the mining community north of the mountain, and would serve as visible proof of their conquest, according to Sherwonit.

Taylor and Anderson made their summit push from 11,000 feet, and hauling their flagpole, they climbed more than 8,000 vertical feet and then descended to camp in 18 hours' time on April 3.

"... an outstanding feat by any mountaineering standard," wrote Sherwonit, who added, that by comparison, most present-day Denali expeditions climb no more than 3,000 to 4,000 vertical feet on summit day, which typically lasts 10 to 15 hours.

However, upon reaching the North Peak, the party discovered that the South Peak is in fact higher by 850 feet. The Sourdough

Archdeacon Hudson Stuck, 1907, three years after his arrival in Alaska.

Party planted the flag, but since it could not be seen from the north, the climbers only had their word as proof of their claim.

Stuck party reaches summit

The first complete and well-documented ascent of the true summit of Denali was made on June 7, 1913, by a determined, but less than professional, party.

The Rev. Hudson Stuck, Episcopal archdeacon of the Yukon, was an experienced climber and northern traveler but had never tackled anything comparable to Denali. However, he was certain that Cook's claim of reaching the summit of the mighty mountain was false and had even made a bet with a friend that Cook's 1906 attempt would fail.

Stuck set out with Robert Tatum, his young assistant; Harry Karstens, an experienced northern outdoorsman; Johnny and Esaias, two Indian boys aged 14 and 15, and Walter Harper, a 21-year-old half-Athabascan and half-Irish fellow who was Stuck's student, guide, interpreter and dog team handler at the time. Harper became the first person to set foot on the higher South Peak.

The story of the team's achievement was recorded in Stuck's book, "The Ascent of Denali." And out of respect for the Native people among whom he lived and worked, Stuck, who was 50 at the time of the historic climb, refused to refer to the mountain as McKinley and states in the preface of his book: "Forefront in this book, because forefront in the author's heart and desire, must stand a plea for the restoration to the greatest mountain in North America of its immemorial native name."

Archdeacon Hudson Stuck's party, pictured above, included six men and two dog teams. The group started from Nenana to ascend Denali.

Stuck and his party of Alaskans struggled for three months on foot from Nenana as they forded rivers, hiked through dense forest and upland tundra and climbed up glaciers and ridges to their objective. When the group finally came upon the base of the great mountain, Stuck noted:

"On the 11th April Karstens and I wound our way up the narrow, steep defile for about three miles from the base camp and came to our first sight of the Muldrow Glacier. ... There the glacier stretched away, broad and level – the road to the heart of the mountain, and as our eyes traced its course our spirits leaped up that at last we were entered upon our real task. One of us, at least, knew something of the dangers and difficulties its apparently smooth surface concealed, yet to both of us it had an infinite attractiveness, for it was the highway of desire."

After losing their tent and many belongings in a fire at 8,000 feet, the men sewed a tent from old sled tarpaulins and continued to the summit.

"The last thing a newcomer would dream of would be danger from fire on a glacier, but we were not newcomers, and we all knew how ever-present that danger is, more imminent in Alaska in winter than in summer," Stuck wrote. "Our carelessness had brought us nigh to the ruining of the whole expedition. The loss of the films was especially unfortunate, for we were thus reduced to Walter's small camera with a common lens and the six or eight spools of film he had for it."

As they climbed higher and higher, Stuck recorded his thoughts on the sights that unfolded before him.

"Above us the sky took a blue so deep that none of us had ever gazed upon a midday sky like it before. It was a deep, rich, lustrous, transparent blue, as dark as a Prussian blue, but intensely blue; a hue so strange, so increasingly impressive, that to one at least it 'seemed like special news of God,' as a new poet sings. We first noticed the darkening tint of the upper sky in the Grand Basin (located between the North and South peaks), and it deepened as we rose. Tyndall observed and discussed this phenomenon in the Alps, but it seems scarcely to have been mentioned since."

The climbers also made a noteworthy discovery while in the Grand Basin. They spotted the Sourdough Party's flagpole.

"While we were resting ... we fell to talking about the pioneer climbers of this mountain who claimed to have set a flagstaff near the summit of the North Peak – as to which feat a great deal of incredulity existed in Alaska for several reasons – and we renewed our determination that if the weather permitted when we had reached our goal and ascended the South Peak, we would climb the North Peak also to seek for traces of this earlier exploit on Denali. ... All at once Walter (Harper) cried out: 'I see the flagstaff!'" Stuck wrote.

Athabascan Walter Harper, son of pioneer Arthur Harper, was the first person to summit Denali.

After the Stuck party successfully climbed to the summit of Denali, others attempted the feat. The photo above shows a pack train operated by Dan T. Kennedy heading into then-McKinley National Park in the 1920s.

"Eagerly pointing to the rocky prominence nearest the summit – the summit itself covered with snow – he added: 'I see it plainly!' (Harry) Karstens, looking where he pointed, saw it also and, whipping out the field glasses, one by one we all looked, and saw it distinctly standing out against the sky. With the naked eye I was never able to see it unmistakably, but through the glasses it stood out, sturdy and strong, one side covered with crusted snow. We were greatly rejoiced that we could carry down positive confirmation of this matter."

Stuck's group finally made their summit of the South Peak on June 7, 1913. The good Archdeacon wrote:

"Across the gulf, about three thousand feet beneath us and 15 or 20 miles away, sprang most splendidly into view the great mass of Denali's Wife, or Mount Foraker, as some white men misname her. Denali's Wife does not appear at all save from the actual summit of Denali, for she is completely hidden ... until the moment when (it) is surmounted. And never was (a) nobler sight displayed to man than that great, isolated mountain spread out completely ... beneath us."

The sight of Denali's Wife confirmed in Stuck's mind that Cook had never reached the summit of Denali.

"(Cook) does not mention at all the master sight that bursts upon the eye when the summit is actually gained – the great mass of

Denali's Wife ... filling the middle distance. We were all agreed that no one who had ever stood on the top of Denali ... could fail to mention the splendid sight of this great mountain."

Piloted by Joe Crosson, the first airplane landed on the mountain in 1932. Today, more than 1,000 people attempt to climb Denali each year between April and June, most flying in to base camp at 7,200 feet on Kahiltna Glacier.

Geographic features of Denali and its sister peaks bear the names of early explorers: Eldridge and Muldrow glaciers, after George Eldridge and Robert Muldrow of the U.S. Geographic Service who determined the peak's altitude in 1898; Wickersham Wall; Karsten's Ridge; Harper Icefall; and Mount Carpe and Mount Koven, named for Allen Carpe and Theodore Koven, both killed in a 1932 climb.

In 1980, the name Mount McKinley National Park was officially changed to Denali National Park and Preserve. The state of Alaska Board of Geographic Names also has officially changed the mountain's name back to Denali. Negotiations continue to officially return the original Native name to the magnificent mountain.

Two buses and one automobile drive under a sign to Mount McKinley National Park around 1925.

30

KATMAI ERUPTS

O n June 6, 1912, the earth exploded. People living within a radius of several hundred miles in Southwest Alaska were given a taste of what hellfire and brimstone of Biblical teachings might be like.

Mount Katmai erupted in Southwest Alaska during the summer of 1912.

It all began in a beautiful, broad valley about 100 miles west of Kodiak Island that was just turning green after a long winter. Dense balsam poplar, paper birch and occasional clumps of spruce covered the hills up to nearly 1,500 feet. Herds of caribou, a few moose and great, brown bears foraged for food. Packs of hungry wolves and skulking wolverine hunted for game to satisfy their hunger, and in the Ukak River, fish splashed. It was a scene of peace and tranquility.

Eskimos traveled along this route across the Alaska Peninsula, and later, Russians went through it journeying from their Kodiak Island settlement to the Bering Sea. During the gold rush at Nome, a few stampeders trudged through Katmai Pass on their way to the Seward Peninsula. There were only a few Native villages in the area, including Katmai village close by Shelikof Strait, and Savonoski, Ukak and another village near the head of Naknek Lake.

Katmai blows

It was very fortunate so few people lived there. Most authorities say no lives were lost in Katmai's eruption, although Merle Colby claims about 200 Natives in remote villages in the path of the ash fall died. If the cataclysm had occurred near a more densely populated region, a great number of lives could have been lost. A similar explosion at Mount Pelee on the Caribbean Island of Martinique killed 30,000 people on May 8, 1902.

The Natives of Savonoski and Katmai were the only eyewitnesses to the most spectacular volcanic eruption to occur in North America. In the words of American Pete, Savonoski's village chief:

"The Katmai Mountain blew up with lots of fire, and fire came down trail from Katmai, with lots of smoke. We go fast Savonoski. Everybody get in bidarka (Native boat). Helluva job. We come Naknek one day, down river, dark, no could see. Hot ash fall. Work like hell."

Of those nearest the volcano, all but six of the inhabitants of Katmai village had gone fishing at Kaflia Bay. The two families left at the village became frightened by the earthquakes that preceded the eruption and fled. They still were camped along the coast near Cape

Native residents of a Katmai village found their barabaras – Native dwellings – buried in ash from the 1912 eruption of Mount Katmai.

Kabugakli, within sight of Katmai, when the mountain blew up.

They then hurried to Cold Bay, and their accounts of the incident were transcribed in the diaries of two white men living there.

"Two families arrived from Katmai, scared and hungry, and reported the volcano blew up 15 miles from Katmai (village), to the left of the Toscar Trail and that one-half the hill blew up and covered up everything as far as they could see," wrote C.L. Boudry on June 8. "Also, that small rocks were falling for three or four miles at sea but could not see more of it as everything else closed up with smoke. ..."

The other man, Jack Lee, wrote in his diary:

"They reported the top of Katmai Mountain blun (sic) off. There was a lot of pummy stone in their dory when they got here and they say hot rocks was flying all around them."

Native fishermen tell of ordeal

The only other people anywhere near the volcano were the Natives at the fishing station at Kaflia Bay, about 30 miles from the crater and screened from the volcano by intervening mountains. Their ordeal was terrifying, nevertheless, as testified by a letter written by Ivan Orloff at the fishing camp to his wife on June 9.

"... I do not know whether we shall be either alive or well. We are awaiting death at any moment ... a mountain has burst near here so we are covered with ashes in some places 10 feet and 6 feet deep. ... We cannot see the daylight. All the rivers are covered with ashes. Here are darkness and hell, thunder and noise. I do not know whether it is day or night ... pray for us."

These fragmentary statements contain all the testimony available from points within 30 miles of the explosion, but reports came from many other places, too.

Man sees explosion

D.F. Howard, camped on the west shore of Cook Inlet, said he saw Katmai blow.

"The day was exceptionally clear, and I had a view down the Inlet for 130 miles. Early in the afternoon, I heard a series of heavy explosions ... increased until it resembled the continuous roar of a heavy canon barrage."

He said he looked toward Mount Iliamna, and to the left and far beyond, and he could see two columns of volcanic matter shooting skyward with incessant flashes of lightning darting in every direction.

View of Katmai crater during an eruption in 1913.

After passing through the largest volcanic eruption in North America in the last century, mail carrier *Dora* arrives near Kodiak Island in 1912.

Next day, he could not tell when the sun arose. Visibility was obscured beyond a distance of 150 feet. Even when the air cleared on June 9, and an unobstructed view of the Inlet was obtained, it was impossible to determine the eruption's origin.

The *Dora*, the intrepid little mail boat that had had a share in almost every adventure in Southwest Alaska, brought the first news of the eruption to the outside world. And her captain, C.B. McMullen, located the seat of the eruption.

The *Dora* brings news

On June 6, the *Dora* was sailing into Kupreanof Strait between Kodiak and Afognak islands when crewmembers noticed a huge, dense cloud rise over Mount Katmai. It spread northwestward over the sky and masses of volcanic ash settled over the sea. It became so dense the captain had to bypass Kodiak.

The clerk on the mail ship vividly described their experience as the ship crossed the area of falling ash.

"… lurid flashes of lightning glared continually around the ship while a constant boom of thunder increased the horror of the inferno raging around us … we might as well have been miles above the surface of the water ... birds floundered, crying wildly through space and fell helpless to the deck."

Before the *Dora* brought the news of the eruption to Seward, none of that town's residents knew what had happened.

"On June 7, the people of Seward heard a series of explosions that sounded like heavy blasting," Mel Horner later remembered. "High overhead a tremendous mist like a cloud formed, blotting out the brightness of the sun and turned it copper-colored. For the following three days, the cloud hung over the city, gradually settling closer and closer to the earth, and the buildings, yards and streets were covered with a fine layer of ash. Lawns were killed and the fresh shoots of trees leafing out, also."

A news dispatch from Cordova, 360 miles northeast of the eruption, reported that many people received painful burns when a heavy rain mixed with the ash in the air to form sulfuric acid. At LaTouche, also in Prince William Sound, the rain was so acidified by the fumes it caused serious burns wherever it touched flesh. The extreme limit of the fumes was much more distant for they were reported from several places in Washington state and British Columbia, about 1,500 miles from the scene of the eruption.

However, the Alaska community that underwent the most terrifying experience was much nearer — the closest sizable town, Kodiak, was 120 miles away. Terror and fear held the island's 400 inhabitants in a grip of smothering ashes and volcanic fumes for days.

None of the people who went through those days fail to mention the awful darkness, which was described as something so far beyond the darkness of the blackest night that it cannot be comprehended by those who did not experience it.

Through some freak of sound transmission, most of the people in Kodiak did not hear the explosions at all. Their first warning was a peculiar-looking, fan-shaped cloud, blacker and denser than any cloud ever seen before. Flashes of lightning flickered through the cloud, thoroughly alarming the people since electrical storms are rare at Kodiak.

By 5 p.m., a light ash began to fall and by 8 p.m. it was dark. The

Above: A person in Kodiak stands on the roof, on the right side of the photo, of a building partially buried in volcanic ash from the Katmai eruption.

Below: Ash-covered buildings around Kodiak during the eruption of Katmai in 1912 fill the landscape. About 46,000 square miles of the area surrounding Katmai was covered in more than .40 inch of ash.

Ash from the 1912 eruption of Katmai covers Kodiak.

ash fell so heavily that people were afraid they would suffocate. As it drifted through the doors and sifted through the windows, Kodiak islanders remembered the fate of the people of Pompeii, and they began to fear that they, too, would be buried alive. The ash drifted, swirled and eddied — it filled the nostrils and stung the eyes. All that first night of horror the noise, gas, earth shocks, lightning and thunder continued.

Ash continues to fall

A brief respite came on June 7, in the morning, and then it started again. The density of the ash flow was incredible. So thick was the air with ashes, that when a log building burned to the ground, people 200 feet away were unaware.

Fortunately for the people of Kodiak, the Revenue Cutter *Manning* was in the harbor at the time, and the priest of the Greek Orthodox Church told his people that if the church bells began to ring they were to go down to the dock where the *Manning* was berthed.

About 4 a.m. on the morning of June 8 the church bells began to chime and the ship's whistle blew blast after blast. People tied dampened cloths over their faces and groped their way along fences and

U.S. Revenue Cutter *Manning*, seen here in Seward between 1904-1913, carried more than 500 residents of Kodiak and Woody Island to safe waters during the eruption of Mount Katmai in 1912.

through drifted banks of ash to seek refuge. It was the longest walk they ever took, according to people who went through the experience.

The captain of the *Manning* finally decided not to stay in port, as it could mean death to all. There might be chance for life if the ship could get out to the open sea. The *Manning* first anchored off Woody Island, however, where its 103 inhabitants were brought to the boat. Many of them were nearly starving for food and water.

People flee onto cutter

More than 500 people jammed aboard the vessel, which was incapable of accommodating one-forth that number. It was standing room only on the crowded decks. During the night of June 8, ash began falling again — the fourth layer of ash. Before the air finally cleared after this last fall, Kodiak had experienced two days and three nights of practically unbroken darkness. When the morning of June 9 finally dawned, clear and bright, the people began to murmur about going home.

From the decks of the *Manning* on June 10, the Kodiak people saw their town still there, but dead. Ashes covered the town and buildings like a blanket of snow. Like snow, too, it had drifted up to the eaves in some buildings. Roofs were caved in and fences lost. Cows wandered aimlessly, or stood still with heads hunched down.

It was even more desolate in the once-beautiful valley of Katmai, however.

A year later, William Hesse, U.S. Deputy Land and Mining surveyor, and Mel Horner of Seward were the first into Katmai after the eruption. Part of their trail took them through what had once been a heavily wooded area. Nothing remained but a few dead, misshapen trunks and limbs of cottonwood and spruce. Pumice floated on the small steams up to a foot thick.

Katmai valley forever changed

When they finally arrived at the scene of the volcanic eruption, they found a huge area of mountainside blown out of Mount Martin, one of the peaks in the area. Fragments, some as large as box cars, had been hurled out, or massed on top of one another, as far as half a mile.

After two weeks, the volcanic ash from the Katmai eruption measured 10-1/2 inches deep. Note the three different layers that became settled and packed by rains.

Boulders 30-40 feet in diameter were hurled 1-1/2 miles by the explosion of Katmai volcano.

The fertile valley that once had been the home of otter, mink, ermine, fox, bear, caribou and moose, was now barren and lifeless, except for one mangy fox, thin as a pile of bones. A few bears they later found had survived, but acid had burned great holes in their fur.

Thousands of small fumaroles issued columns of steam and smoke, and the ground was a maze of wide, jagged cracks like paths of lightning. The land lay denuded of timber — only blackened stumps were left.

The man who made the Valley of 10,000 Smokes known to the world, Robert F. Griggs, arrived on the scene three years after the eruption, and to him we owe much of our knowledge of the event that produced, as he said, "... one of the great wonders of the world."

Sequence of events

Griggs' summary of events stated there were first premonitory symptoms, especially earthquakes, sufficient to warn the Natives. Early in June, rock started falling from Falling Mountain. Next, great hot sand flow came from fissures in the valley and its branches, covering 53 square miles to an estimated average depth of 100 feet. The "Smokes of the Valley" began their operation, perhaps coincident with the sand flow.

Explosive activity next began at Novarupta, when about one-half of a cubic mile of coarse pumice was thrown out over an area 10 to 15 miles in diameter, overlapping with the explosion of Katmai. Martin and Mageik may have opened next, according to Griggs, and then could have come landslides.

The first major explosions of Mount Katmai occurred on June 6 at 1 p.m., and they were responsible for the first layer of gray ash. The second major explosion came at 11 p.m., creating the second layer of ash (terracotta).

On June 7, at 10:40 p.m., the third major explosion erupted and brought a yellow layer of ash. Cap layers of fine, red mud were thrown out by Katmai, and next may have been the Katmai Mud Flow.

Then came a condition of great, but gradually subsiding, activity and the interior of the crater retained an incandescent heat manifesting red reflections on the clouds as late as July 21. The end of the

This chunk of pumice was thrown out from Novarupta. The pickaxe next to it shows the scale of the rock's size.

Above: B.B. Fulton, Robert F. Griggs and L.G. Folsom in 1915 cook over a fire at their base camp in what is now Katmai National Park and Preserve.

Below: The 1912 eruption of Mount Katmai was the largest in North America in the 20th century. It covered 46,000 square miles of area with ash. The photo below shows trees covered in ash near the Russian Orthodox Church mission house where members of the 1913 expedition stayed while in Kodiak.

Griggs' 1915 expedition saw David's Falls near a mudflow from Mount Katmai eruption.

explosive stage finally came, followed by a quiet evolution of vapor in great quantity from Katmai, Martin, Mageik, Trident and the Valley.

Novarupta may have triggered eruption

Although early National Geographic expeditions found Katmai decapitated and assumed it had blown its top, Dr. Garniss H. Curtis, professor of geology at the University of California, believed that Novarupta, a new volcano six miles away, felled its giant neighbor by siphoning off its underlying magma. Measuring each layer of ejected material, Curtis observed that all activity centered around Novarupta; the layers became thinner as they neared Katmai. Novarupta subsided after hurling more than seven cubic miles of pumice, rhyolite and dust, some soaring well into the stratosphere, according to Curtis.

Whether it was Katmai or Novarupta, the results of the cataclysm was tremendous. According to Griggs, more than 40 times the amount of material dug in the greatest excavation ever attempted by man — the Panama Canal — was thrown into the air. All the buildings of all the boroughs of greater New York City wouldn't fill Katmai's crater.

A small mud volcano bubbles near Katmai in 1915.

In fact, the buildings of 15 major U.S. cities would be less bulky than the material blown off the mountain.

Irregular temperatures recorded

No eruption since records were kept has produced so striking an irregularity in the temperature curve as this one, Griggs said. It made the summer of 1912 cooler than usual in the northern hemisphere, the haze absorbing some of the sun's heat; low temperature persisted generally in low latitudes during the remainder of 1912 and through the summer of 1913. It darkened the days and created brilliant sunsets as far away as Nova Scotia, across the North American continent.

In the summer of 1962, Ernest Gruening reported in an article in the National Geographic that he finally stood in the Valley of 10,000 Smokes.

"We go back a full half-century together. Word of the volcanic cataclysm reached the United States slowly," he wrote. "In Boston, where I was working as a newspaperman, the news was not received until three days after the event. It came from Cordova — 360 miles from the eruption — and gave few details."

Now he saw for himself the results.

"The trees were silvered skeletons, bleached sentinels in a shimmering desert of pumice. It is a pastel wasteland like no other, a vast solitude of mountains and desert and desolation; a land of snowfields and glaciers and airy pumice stones and deep crevices ... had I not known where I was, I'd have thought it was the moon."

Indeed, a few years later, some of the astronauts were taken to the region to train for their forthcoming trip to the moon.

The eruption of Katmai had created this wonderland, set aside by President Woodrow Wilson, as a great national monument to nature's awesome power ... the largest national monument in the United States.

Knife Peak rises near the Valley of 10,000 Smokes in 1917. It was later renamed Mount Griggs for Dr. Robert Fisk Griggs (1881-1962), a botanist, whose explorations of the area, after the eruption of Mount Katmai in 1912, led to the creation of Katmai National Monument by President Woodrow Wilson in 1918. The photo was taken at what was later designated as Katmai National Park and Preserve, during a National Geographic Society expedition to Katmai area.

BIBLIOGRAPHY

Adney, Tappan. The Klondike Stampede of 1897-1899. New York, NY 1900.

Alexan, Nickafor. Recorded and transcribed history of Tyonek.

Alexander, H. The Mythology of All Races. New York, NY: 1964.

Allan, A.A. Gold, Men and Dogs. New York, NY: 1931.

Allen, Lt. Henry T. Report of an Expedition to the Copper, Tanana and Koyukuk Rivers in the Territory of Alaska in the Year 1885.

Ameigh, George C. Jr. and Yule M. Chaffin, Alaska's Kodiak Island. Author: 1962.

Andrews, Clarence L. The Story of Alaska. Caldwell, ID: Caxton Printers Ltd., 1947.

Archer, S.A. A Heroine of the North. London, England: 1929.

Atwood, Evangeline. Frontier Politics. The Western Historical Quarterly, April 1980.

Bailey, Thomas A. Notes and Documents: The Russian Fleet Myth Re-examined. Mississippi Valley Historical Review, 1951.

Bancroft, Hubert Howe. The History of Alaska 1730-1885. San Francisco, CA: A.L. Bancroft & Company, 1886.

Barry, Mary J. A History of Mining on the Kenai Peninsula, Alaska. Anchorage, AK: MJP BARRY, 1997.

Beach, Rex. The Iron Trail. Hard Press, 2006.

Becker, Ethel A. Klondike '98. Portland, OR: 1949.

Berton, Laura B. I Married the Klondike. Little Brown, 1954.

Berton, Pierre. Klondike. Toronto, Canada: McClelland & Stewart Ltd., 1962.

Berton, Pierre. The Klondike Fever. Alfred A. Knopf, New York, NY: 1969.

Blower, James. Gold Rush. American Heritage Press, 1971.

Brooks, Alfred H. Blazing Alaska Trails. University of Alaska and Arctic Institute of America, 1953.

Cashen, William. Founding of Fairbanks. University of Alaska Alumni, Summer, 1968.

Chaffin, Yule M. From Koniag to King Crab. Utah: Desert News Press, 1967.

Chase, Will. Sourdough Pot. Kansas City, MO: 1923.

Chooutla Indian School. Northern Lights. Carcross, Yukon Territory, Canada: 1913.

Colby, Merle. A Guide to Alaska. New York, NY: MacMillian Company, 1954.

Couch, James S. Philately Below Zero. American Philatelic Society, State College, PA: 1853.

Dall, William H. Alaska and Its Resources. Boston, MA: Lee and Shepard, 1870.

Davis, Mary Lee. Sourdough Gold. Boston, MA: 1933.

Delahaye, Tom. The Bilateral Effect of the Visit of the Russian Fleet in 1863. Loyola University, New Orleans, LA: 1984.

Donaldson, Jordan and Edwin Pratt. Europe and the American Civil War. Boston, MA: Houghton Mifflin Company, 1931.

Drago, Harry Sinclair. The Great Range Wars: Violence on the Grasslands. University of Nebraska Press, 1985.

Farrar. Annexation of Russian America to the United States. Washington, DC: 1937.

Faulk, Odie B. Tombstone, Myth and Reality. New York, NY: 1972.

Fitch, Edwin M. The Alaska Railroad. New York, NY: Frederich A. Praeger Publishers, 1967.

Goddard. Indians of the Northwest Coast. New York, NY: 1945.

Golder, F. A. The Russian Fleet and the Civil War. American Historical Review, 1915

Griggs, Robert F. The Valley of Ten Thousand Smokes. Washington, DC: The National Geographic Society, 1935.

Hamilton, W.R. Yukon Story. Vancouver, Canada: Mitchell Press, 1964.

Harris, A.C. Alaska and the Klondike Goldfields. Chicago, IL: Monroe Book Company 1897.

Higginson, Ella. Alaska. New York, NY: MacMillan Company, 1908.

Hubbard, Father Bernard. Alaska Odyssey. Robert Hale Ltd., London, England: 1952

Hubbard, Father Bernard. Cradle of the Storms. Dodd Mead, New York, NY: 1935.

Hulley, Clarence C. Alaska 1741-1953. Binford & Morts, Portland, OR: 1953.

Huntington, James. On the Edge of Nowhere. Crown ublishers, 1966.

Ingersoll, Ernest. Gold Fields of the Klondike. New York, NY: 1897.

Janson, Lone. The Copper Spike. Alaska Northwest Books, 1975.

Kitchener, L.D. Flag Over The North. Superior Publishing Company, Seattle, WA: 1954.

Kirk, R.C. Twelve Months in the Klondike. William Hernemann, 1899.

Kushner, Howard L. The Russian Fleet and the American Civil War: Another View. Historian, 1972.

Ladue, Joseph. Klondike Facts. New York American Technical Book Co. New York, NY: 1897.

Laguna, Frederica de. Archaeology of Cook Inlet, Alaska. University of Pennsylvania Press, 1934.

Laserson, Max M. The American Impact on Russia: 1784-1917. New York, NY: Collier Books, 1950.

Lathrop, Thornton K. William Henry Seward. American Statesman Series.

Lawing, Nellie Neal. Alaska Nellie. Chieftain Press, Seattle, WA: 1940.

Leonard, John W. Gold Fields of the Klondike. Chicago, IL: A.N. Marquis and Company, 1897.

Lethcoe, Jim and Nancy. Valdez Gold Rush Trails of 1898-99. Todd Publications, 1997.

Lockley, Fred Alaska's First Free Mail Delivery in 1900.

Lung, Edward B. Black Sand and Gold. New York, NY: 1956.

Lung, Edward B. Trails to North Star Gold. Portland, OR: 1969.

Lunn, Arnold. Century of Mountaineering. George Allen and Unwin, Ltd. London, England: 1957.

Marshall, Robert. Arctic Village. University of Alaska Press, 1991.

Mathews, Richard. The Yukon. New York, NY: Holt, Rinehart and Winston, 1958.

McLain, John Scudder. Alaska and the Yukon. New York, NY: McClure, Phillips and Company, 1905.

McMorris, Ian, Noyce, Wilfred, editors. World Atlas of Mountaineering. Thomas Nelson and Son, Ltd. London, England: 1969.

McQuesten, L.N. Recollections of Leroy Napoleon McQuesten, Life on the Yukon, 1871-1885. Dawson City, Canada.

Michael, Henry. Lieutenant Zagoskin's Travels in Russian America, 1842-1844.

Morgan, Lael. Good Time Girls. Seattle, WA: Epicenter Press Inc., 1998.

Morgan, Murray. One Man's Gold Rush. Seattle, WA: 1967.

Naske, Claus M. and Slotnick, Herman E. Alaska, A History of the 49th State. Grand Rapids, MI: William E. Eerdmans Publishing Company, 1979.

O'Conner, Richard. High Jinks on the Klondike. New York, NY: Bobbs-Merrill Company, New York, NY: 1954.

Ogilvie, William. Early Days on the Yukon. New York, NY: John Lane Company, 1913.

Ogilvie, William. Klondike Official Guide. Hunter Rose Co., Toronto, Canada: 1898.

Osgood, Cornelius. Contributions to the Ethnography of the Kutchin. New Haven, CT: 1936.

Osgood, Cornelius. Ethnology of the Tanaina. New Haven, CT: Yale University Press, 1937.

Osgood, Cornelius. Ingalik Mental Culture. New Haven, CT: Yale University, Press, 1959.

Oswalt, M. Alaskan Eskimos. San Francisco, CA: 1967.

Pearson, Grant. My Life of High Adventure. Englewood Cliffs, NJ: Prentice-Hall, 1962.

Petroff, Ivan. 10th Census Report, 1880. Washington, DC.

Petroff, Ivan. Report on the Population, Industries, and Resources of Alaska. Washington, DC: U.S. Printing Office, 1884.

Pierce, Richard A. Russian America: A Biographical Dictionary. Fairbanks, AK: The Limestone Press, 1990.

Pilgrim Shaw, Mariette. Alaska, Its History, Resources, Geography, and Government. Caldwell, ID: Caxton Printers, 1939.

Remington, Charles H. A Golden Cross on the Trails from the Valdez Glacier.

Richard, T.A. Through the Yukon and Alaska. San Francisco, CA: 1909.

Roppel, Pat. An Historical Guide to Revillagigedo and Gravina Islands, 1995.

Schaller, George B. When the Earth Exploded. Alaska Book, Ferguson Press, Chicago, IL: 1960.

Schwatka, Frederick. Along Alaska's Gret River. George M. Hill Co. New York, NY: 1900.

Seton-Karr. Shores and Alps of Alaska. Samson Low, Marston, Seane and Rivington. London, England: 1887.

Service, Robert W. Harper of Heaven. Dodd, Mead, 1948.

Service, Robert W. Ploughman of the Moon. Dodd, Mead, 1945.

Seton-Watson, Hugh. The Russian Empire: 1801-1917. Oxford: The Clarendon Press, 1967.

Seward, Frederick W. Reminiscences of a War-time Statesman, Seward at Washington as Senator and Secretary of War, and William H. Seward, an Autobiography ... Selections from Letters.

Sherwonit, Bill. To the Top of Denali: Climbing Adventures on North America's Highest Peak.

Sherwood, Morgan. Alaska and Its History. Seattle, WA: University of Washington Press, 1967.

Sherwood, Morgan. Explorations of Alaska, 1865-1900. New Haven, CT: Yale University Press, 1965.

Sinclair Drago, Harry. "The Great Range Wars: Violence on the Grasslands." University of Nebraska Press, 1985.

Sovereign, A.H. In Journeyings Often.

Spencer, R. North Alaskan Eskimo. Washington, DC: Smithsonian Press, 1969.

Stauter, J.J. Genius of Seward. Chicago, IL: J.G. Ferguson Company, 1960.

Stuck, Hudson. Episcopal Missions in Alaska. New York, NY: Domestic and Foreign Missionary Society, 1920.

Stuck, Hudson. The Ascent of Denali. Brompton Book Corp., 1989.

Stuck, Hudson. Voyages on the Yukon and its Tributaries. Schribners, New York, NY: 1917.

Stumer, Harold M. This was Klondike Fever. Seattle, WA: Superior Publishing Company, 1978.

Swineford, Alfred P. Report of the Governor of Alaska. Sitka: 1886.

Tollemache, Hon. Stratford. Reminiscences of the Yukon. Toronto, Canada: 1912.

Tomkins, Stuart R. Alaska, Promyshiennik and Sourdough. University of Oklahoma, 1945.

Underhill, R. Red Man's Religion. Chicago, IL: 1965.

U.S. Department of the Interior, Bureau of Land Management. Iditarod Gold Rush Trail Seward-Nome.

U.S. Revenue Cutter Service. Report of the Operations of the U.S. Revenue Steamer Nunivak on the Yukon River Station, Alaska, 1899-1901.

U.S. War Department Adjutant Office. Reports of Exploration in Territory of Alaska. Washington, DC: 1899.

Valdez Museum and Historical Archive

Walden, Arthur T. A Dog Puncher on the Yukon. Boston, MA: 1928.

Waters, Frank. The Earp Brothers of Tombstone. New York, NY: 1960.

Wickersham, Hon. James. Old Yukon. Washington, DC: Washington Law Book Company, 1938.

Wickersham, James. Personal diaries. Alaska State Library.

Williams, Gerald O. 50 Years of History. Alaska State Troopers, 1991.

Williams, Howell. Landscapes of Alaska. University of California Press, 1958.

Williams, William. Mountain Climbing. Climbing Mt. St. Elias; Karr, Mark, Mt. St. Elias and Its Glaciers. Charles Schibners & Son, 1897.

Winslow, Kathryn. Big Pan-Out. New York, NY: 1951.

Wold, Jo Anne. Fairbanks The $200 Million Gold Rush Town. Wold Press, 1971.

Woldman, Albert A. Lincoln and the Russians. Cleveland, OH: The World Publishing Company, 1952.

Whymper, Frederick. Travels and Adventures in the Territory of Alaska. London, England: 1868.

Periodicals and Newspapers

Alaska, May 1971

Alaska Call, May 1959

Alaska Call, March 1960

Alaska Life, July 1941

Alaska Life, March 1943

Alaska Life, August 1944

Alaska Life, November 1945

Alaska Life, February 1946

Alaska Life, April 1946

Alaska Life, January 1947

Alaska Living, October 1968

Alaska Review, Fall 1965

Alaska Sportsman, July 1937

Alaska Sportsman, May 1938

Alaska Sportsman, October 1939

Alaska Sportsman, May 1942

Alaska Sportsman, May 1951

Alaska Sportsman, January 1953

Alaska Sportsman, January 1956

Alaska Sportsman, December 1958

Alaska Sportsman, February 1959

Alaska Sportsman, April 1963

Alaska Sportsman, July 1963

Alaska Sportsman, October 1965

Alaska Yukon Magazine, 1909

American Heritage, December 1960

Island Times, January 1971

Journal of the West, Vol. 5, 1966

Anchorage Daily Times, July 2, 1964

Anchorage Daily Times, July 29, 1964

Anchorage Daily Times, August 5, 1965

Anchorage Daily Times, June 15, 1967

Atlantic Monthly, July 1903

Fairbanks Daily News Miner, May 9, 1903

Heritage of Alaska (The Flying North)
Juneau Daily Empire, April 13, 1917
Klondike News, April 1898
Kodiak Daily Mirror, June 1971
Los Angeles Times, May 1, 1900
National Geographic, February 1948
National Geographic, June 1963
New York Sun, 1896
Nome News, various
Orphanage Newsletter (Wood Island), 1905
Pacific Northern Quarterly, January 1968
Pathfinder, September 1920
Pathfinder, October 1922
The San Francisco Coast Seamen's Journal, February 21, 1894
True West, December 1972
Tundra Times, June 17, 1963
Seward Daily Gateway, 1906
Sitka Alaskan, 1890
Yukon Press, March 17, 1899

Web sites:
U.S. Postal Museum at www.postalmuseum.si.edu/gold
Public Broadcasting System
The Frederick A. Cook Society at www.cookpolar.org.

Other material
Burke, Louise Harper, Letter, Los Angeles, California, 1964
Canadian Encyclopedia: Alaska Boundary Dispute
University of Alaska Fairbanks, Science Writer Ned Rozell

PHOTO CREDITS

FOREWORD
P.7, Aunt Phil's Files; P.8, top, University of Alaska Anchorage, National Geographic Society Katmai Expeditions Collection, UAA-hmc-0186-volume6-H138; P.8, bottom, University of Alaska Anchorage, Edwin Forbes Glenn Collection, UAA-hmc-0116-series3a-32-1; P.11, Seward Community Library, SCL-1-798.

CHAPTER 1: SUMMARY OF VOLUME 1
P.14, Alaska State Library, Dr. Daniel S. Neuman Collection, ASL-P307-0035; P.15, Department of the Interior, Bureau of Land Management; P.16, left, Alaska State Library, History Collection, ASL-Bering-Vitus-1; P.16, right, Anchorage Museum of History and Art, General Photograph File, AMRC-b96-10-1; P.17, University of Alaska Fairbanks, Charles S. Hamlin Collection, UAF-728-11; P.18, University of Alaska Fairbanks, Alaska and Polar Regions Collections, A0867-15; P.19, Alaska State Library, William A. Kelly Collection, ASL-P427-12; P.20, Alaska State Library, Dr. Daniel S. Neuman Collection, ASL-P307-0119; P.21, Alaska State Library, History Collection, ASM-III-R-267; P. 22, Alaska State Library, History Collection, ASM-III-R-150; P.23, Anchorage Museum of History and Art, O.D. Goetze Collection, AMRC-b01-41-259.

CHAPTER 2: MYTH SURROUNDS ALASKA'S PURCHASE
P.24, Harpers Weekly, Sonofthesouth.net, Russian Fleet; P.26, University of Texas Library; P.27, Harpers Weekly, Sonofthesouth.net, Flagship Nevski; P. 28, Library of Congress; P.29, University of Texas Library; P.31, Harpers Weekly, Sonofthesouth.net, Broadway parade; P.33, Library of Congress.

CHAPTER 3: AMERICAN'S FLOCK NORTH
P.35, University of Washington, Frank La Roche Collection, LAR110; P.36, top, University of Washington, Wilhelm Hester Collection, HES125; P.36, bottom, University of Washington, Alaska and Western Canada Collection, AWC0540; P.37, top, University of Washington, Frank H. Nowell Collection, NOW084; P.37, bottom, University of Washington, Alaska and Western Canada Collection, AWC1346; P.38, Alaska State Library, History Collection, ASL-Veniaminov-Ivan-2; P.39, top, University of Washington, Alaska and Western Canada Collection, AWC0058; P.39, bottom, University of Alaska Fairbanks, Charles S. Hamlin Collection, UAF-728-12; P.40, University of Washington, Alaska and Western Canada Collection, AWC0277; P.41, Alaska State Library, Winter and Pond Collection, ASL-P87-0333; P.42, top, Alaska State Library, William R. Norton Collection, ASL-P226-481; P.42, bottom, University of Washington, Eric A. Hegg Collection, HEG695; P.43, top, Alaska State Library, William A. Kelly Collection, ASL-P427-43; P.43, bottom, University of Alaska Anchorage, Julia Willma Weber Collection, UAA-hmc-0344-13-a; P.44, top, University of Washington, John E. Thwaites Collection, THW103; P.44, bottom, University of Alaska Anchorage, National Geographic Society Katmai Expeditions Collection, UAA-hmc-0186-volume6-H441; P.45, top, Alaska State Library, Case and Draper Collection, ASL-

P39-0673; P.45, bottom, University of Washington, Alaska and Western Canada Collection, AWC1385; P.46, top, Alaska State Library, Place File Collection, ASL-Haines-Housing-4; P.46, bottom, University of Alaska Fairbanks, Vertical File Photograph Collection, UAF-1983-171-2; P.47, University of Washington, Alaska and Western Canada Collection, AWC1045; P.48, top, University of Washington, Freshwater and Marine Image Bank, Facing page 83; P.48, bottom, University of Washington, Freshwater and Marine Image Bank, Facing page 87; P.49, top, University of Washington, John E. Thwaites Collection, THW118; P.49, bottom, University of Alaska Fairbanks, Albert Johnson Collection, UAF-1989-0166-170; P.50, library.thinkquest.org/ 11313 media goldfields; P.51, top, University of Washington, Eric A. Hegg Collection, HEG011; P.51, bottom, University of Washington, Eric A. Hegg Collection, HEG134.

CHAPTER 4: BORDER DISPUTE HEATS UP

P.53, www.mapquest.com; P.54, University of Washington, Eric A. Hegg Collection, HEG397; P.55, top, Alaska State Library, Wickersham State Historic Site, ASL-P277-001-018; P.55, bottom, University of Washington, Alaska and Western Canada Collection, AWC0436; P.56, University of Washington, Eric A. Hegg Collection, HEG616; P.57, University of Washington, Frank H. Nowell Collection, NOW262; P.58, Frank and Frances Carpenter Collection, Courtesy Library of Congress; P.59, University of Washington, Eric A. Hegg Collection, HEG383; P.60, "Boundaries," The Encyclopedia of Canada , Vol. I, Toronto, University Associates of Canada, 1948; P.61, top, Courtesy National Oceanic and Atmospheric Administration Photo Library; P.61, bottom, Courtesy National Oceanic and Atmospheric Administration Historic C&GS Collection, image ID theb1633; P.63, Alaska State Library, Early Prints of Alaska Collection, ASL-P297-280.

CHAPTER 5: GOLD-RUSH ENTERTAINERS ARRIVE

P.64, www.americancinematheque.com; P.65, University of Washington, Portraits Collection, POR0124; P.66, University of Washington, Veazie Wilson-Special Collections, NA2637; P.67, University of Washington, Alaska and Western Canada Collection, AWC1160; P.68, University of Washington, Alaska and Western Canada Collection, AWC0853; P.69, University of Washington, Eric A. Hegg Collection, HEG720; P.70, University of Washington, Eric A. Hegg Collection, HEG522; P.71, Parks Canada, Canadian Imperial Bank of Commerce Collection, Larss and Duclos 19/118; P.72, top, University of Washington, Eric A. Hegg Collection, HEG591; P.72, bottom, University of Washington, J. Willis Sayre Collection, SAY00250; P.73, Alaska State Library, William R. Norton Collection, ASL-P226-842; P.74, University of Washington, Eric A. Hegg Collection, HEG715; P.75, Historicphotoarchive.com, CT-053; P.76, top, Anchorage Museum of History and Art, O.D. Goetze Collection, AMRC-b01-41-263; P76, bottom, Alaska State Library, B.B. Dobbs Collection, ASL-P12-141.

CHAPTER 6: GOLDEN HEART CITY GROWS

P.78, University of Alaska Fairbanks, Vertical File Photograph Collection, UAF-1989-12-102; P.79, Alaska State Library, Wickersham State Historic Site, ASL-P277-004-014; P.80, University of Washington, Transportation Collection, TRA642; P.81, University of Alaska Fairbanks, Walter and Lillian Phillips Collection, UAF-1985-72-131; P.82, University of Alaska Fairbanks, Frederick B. Drane Collection, UAF-1991-46-503; P.83, University of

Alaska Fairbanks, Vertical File Photograph Collection, UAF-1966-9-7; P.84, Anchorage Museum of History and Art, Crary-Henderson Collection, AMRC-b62-1-a-120; P.86, University of Alaska Fairbanks, Albert Johnson Collection, UAF-1989-0166-29-Print; P.87, Map gold field, Special publication "The Tanana Gold Fields" published May 1904, Library Call No. Rare Book C0067; P.88, Anchorage Museum of History and Art, O.D. Goetze Collection, AMRC-b01-41-294; P.89, University of Alaska Fairbanks, R.C. Force Papers, UAF-2003-174-513; P.90, top, Anchorage Museum of History and Art, John Urban Collection, AMRC-b64-1-66; P.90, bottom, University of Alaska Fairbanks, John Zug Collection, UAF-1980-68-6; P.91, top, University of Washington, Frank H. Nowell Collection, NOW215; P.91, bottom, University of Alaska Anchorage, Charles E. Claypool Collection, UAA-hmc-0015u-7; P.92, top, University of Alaska Fairbanks, George and Lilly Clark Collection, UAF-1986-109-7; P.92, bottom, University of Alaska Fairbanks, Albert Johnson Collection, UAF-1989-0166-30-Print; P.93, top, University of Washington, Asahel Curtis, CUR1919; P.93, bottom, University of Washington, Alaska and Western Canada Collection, AWC0499; P.94, top, University of Alaska Fairbanks, Albert Johnson Collection, UAF-1989-0166-191-Print; P.94, bottom, University of Washington, Asahel Curtis, CUR1865; P.95, top, University of Washington, Asahel Curtis, CUR1992; P.95, bottom, University of Alaska Fairbanks, Albert Johnson Collection, UAF-1989-0166-192-Print; P.96, top, University of Alaska Fairbanks, Albert Johnson Collection, UAF-1989-0166-101; P.96, bottom, University of Alaska Fairbanks, Buzby and Metcalf Collection, UAF-1963-0071-63; P.97, top, University of Alaska Fairbanks, Buzby and Metcalf Collection, UAF-1963-0071-34; P.97, bottom, University of Alaska Fairbanks, Buzby and Metcalf Collection, UAF-1963-0071-21; P.98, top, Alaska State Library, George A. Parks Collection, ASL-P240-478; P.98, bottom, University of Alaska Fairbanks, Buzby and Metcalf Collection, UAF-1963-0071-20; P.99, top, University of Alaska Fairbanks, Albert Johnson Collection, UAF-1989-0166-84; P.99, bottom, University of Alaska Fairbanks, Clausen Family Collection, UAF-2002-134-3; P.100, University of Alaska Fairbanks, Albert Johnson Collection, UAF-1989-0166-55-Print; P.101, University of Alaska Fairbanks, Albert Johnson Collection, UAF-1989-0166-256-Print; P.102, top, Anchorage Museum of History and Art, Alaska Engineering Commission Collection, AMRC-aec-j102; P.102, bottom, University of Washington, Asahel Curtis, CUR1853; P.103, University of Alaska Fairbanks, Albert Johnson Collection, UAF-1989-0166-220-Print; P.104, University of Washington, Alaska and Western Canada Collection, AWC0555; P.105, top, Anchorage Museum of History and Art, John Urban Collection, AMRC-b64-1-266; P.105, bottom, University of Washington, Asahel Curtis, CUR1866; P.106, top, University of Alaska Fairbanks, Albert Johnson Collection, UAF-1989-0166-241-Print; P.106, bottom, University of Alaska Fairbanks, Albert Johnson Collection, UAF-1989-0166-95; P.107, top, University of Alaska Fairbanks, Buzby and Metcalf Collection, UAF-1963-0071-70; P.107, bottom, University of Alaska Anchorage, Estelle and Philip Garges Collection, UAA-hmc-0381-series2-22-2; P.109, top, University of Alaska Fairbanks, Albert Johnson Collection, UAF-1989-0166-183-Print; P.109, bottom, University of Alaska Fairbanks, Albert Johnson Collection, UAF-1989-0166-73-Print; P.110, Anchorage Museum of History and Art, General Photograph File, AMRC-b80-41-69; P.111, University of Washington, John E. Thwaites Collection, THW338.

CHAPTER 7: TURN-OF-THE-CENTURY JUSTICE
P.112, Library of Congress.

CHAPTER 8: TOMBSTONE TEMPORARILY TRANSPLANTED

P.114, Alaska State Library, Wickersham State Historic Site, ASL-P277-017-001; P.115, Alaska State Library, Wickersham State Historic Site, ASL-P277-017-024; P.116, Library of Congress; P.117, National Oceanic and Atmospheric Administration; P.118, University of Washington, Eric A. Hegg Collection, HEG272; P.119, University of Washington, Eric A. Hegg Collection, HEG425; P.120, www.archives.gov.

CHAPTER 9: ALASKA'S FIRST LAWMEN

P. 122, Library of Congress; P.123, University of Washington, Asahel Curtis, CUR1142; P.124, legendsofamerica.com; P.125, top, University of Washington, Eric A. Hegg Collection, HEG254; P.125, bottom, University of Washington, Eric A. Hegg Collection, HEG256; P.127, University of Alaska Fairbanks, Robert Collier Collection, UAF-1981-192-61; P.128, Courtesy National Park Service; P.129, Courtesy U.S. Coast Guard; P.130, Alaska State Library, Dr. Daniel S. Neuman Collection, ASL-P307-0095; P.131, University of Washington, Arthur Churchill Warner Collection, WAR0449; P.132, Courtesy U.S. Coast Guard; P.133, Courtesy Boston College; P.135, Courtesy U.S. Coast Guard.

CHAPTER 10: JUDGE'S LIGHT SHINES ON

P.136, Anchorage Museum of History and Art, Crary-Henderson Collection, AMRC-b62-1-1335; P.137, Alaska State Library, Wickersham State Historic Site, ASL-P277-007-107; P.138, University of Washington, Alaska and Western Canada Collection, AWC0313; P.139, University of Washington, Eric A. Hegg Collection, HEG428; P.140, University of Washington, Frank H. Nowell Collection, NOW128; P.143, Alaska State Library, Wickersham State Historic Site, ASL-P277-004-135; P.144, Alaska State Library, Wickersham State Historic Site, ASL-P277-009-087; P.145, Alaska State Library, Wickersham State Historic Site, ASL-P277-011-060; P.146, University of Alaska Fairbanks, Mike Ersig Album, UAF-1970-0028-276; P.147, Alaska State Library, Wickersham State Historic Site, ASL-P277-019-075.

CHAPTER 11: *CITY OF SEATTLE* TURNS TO PIRACY

P.148, University of Washington, John N. Cobb Collection, NA2703; P.149, University of Washington, Eric A. Hegg Collection, HEG241; P.150, University of Washington Collection, UW8571.

CHAPTER 12: INMATE NO. 594

P.151, University of Washington, John E. Thwaites Collection, THW219; P.152, University of Washington, John E. Thwaites Collection, THW225; P.153, Alaska State Library, Winter and Pond Collection, ASL-P87-0882; P.155, Courtesy National Park Service; P.156, alcatrazhistory.com.

CHAPTER 13: ALASKA'S FIRST SERIAL KILLER

P.157, Petersburg, University of Washington, John E. Thwaites Collection, THW355; P.158, University of Washington, John N. Cobb Collection, COB168; P.160, Alaska State Library, Skinner Foundation Collection, ASL-P44-03-022; P.161, University of Washington, John E. Thwaites Collection, THW218; P.162, University of Alaska Anchorage, Justice Department.

CHAPTER 14: ARIZONA EDITOR MAKES MARK ON ALASKA

P.163, National Oceanic and Atmospheric Administration; P.164, Courtesy National Park Service; P.165, University of Washington, Asahel Curtis, CUR1139; P.166, University of Washington, Transportation Collection, TRA718; P.167, Anchorage Museum of History and Art, O.D. Goetze Collection, AMRC-b01-41-34; P.168, U.S. Post Office, by B.L. Singley, Inspector and Lecturer; P.169, top, University of Washington, Eric A. Hegg Collection, HEG117; P.169, bottom, University of Washington, Arthur Churchill Warner Collection, WAR0402.

CHAPTER 15: ALASKA'S PIONEERING POSTMEN

P.171, Yukon National Archives; P.172, Aunt Phil's Files; P.173, Yukon National Archives; P.174, University of Washington, Arthur Churchill Warner, WAR0390; P.176, University of Washington, Eric A. Hegg Collection, HEG275; P.177, University of Washington, Wilhelm Hester Collection, HES237; P.178, Yukon National Archives; P.180, University of Washington, Arthur Churchill Warner Collection, WAR0515; P.181, Alaska State Library, Asa C. Baldwin Photographs, ASL-P71-Album; P.182, University of Washington, Arthur Churchill Warner Collection, WAR0513; P.184, University of Alaska Fairbanks, Albert Johnson Collection, UAF-1989-0166-121-Print; P.185, University of Alaska Fairbanks, Edward Lewis Bartlett Collection, UAF-1969-95-464; P.186, Anchorage Museum of History and Art, Ward W. Wells Collection, AMRC-wws-1867-C-82; P.188-189, University of Texas Library.

CHAPTER 16: THE TRAPPING LIFE

P.190, Alaska State Library, Wickersham State Historic Site Collection, ASL-P277-017-035; P.191, Alaska State Library, Wickersham State Historic Site Collection, ASL-P277-017-018; P.192, University of Alaska Fairbanks, Fabian Carey Collection, UAF-1975-0209-58; P.193, University of Alaska Fairbanks, Alaska Steamship Company Collection, UAF-1987-175-525; P.194, University of Alaska Fairbanks, Lawyer and Cora Rivenburg Collection, UAF-1994-70-295; P.195, University of Alaska Fairbanks, Fabian Carey Collection, UAF-1975-0209-91; P.196, top, University of Washington, Industries and Occupations Collection, IND0145; P.196, bottom, University of Alaska Fairbanks, Lawyer and Cora Rivenburg Collection, UAF-1994-70-164; P.197, University of Alaska Fairbanks, Lawyer and Cora Rivenburg Collection, UAF-1994-70-192; P.198, Seward Community Library, Sylvia Sexton Collection, SCL-1-1217; P.199, top, University of Washington, John E. Thwaites Collection, THW330; P.199, bottom, University of Alaska, Fabian Carey Collection, UAF-1975-0209-81; P.201, University of Alaska Fairbanks, Fabian Carey Collection, UAF-1975-0209-94; P.202, Anchorage Museum of History and Art, O.D. Goetze Collection, AMRC-b01-41-99.

CHAPTER 17: DALTON TURNS TIMBER INTO GOLD

P.204, University of Washington, William E. Meed Collection, MEE151; P.205, University of Washington, Alaska and Western Canada Collection, AWC0528; P.206, top, University of Washington, Frank La Roche Collection, LAR233; P.206, bottom, Alaska State Library, William A. Kelly Collection, ASL-P427-19; P.207, University of Alaska Fairbanks, Jim Oyler Collection, UAF-1986-37-28; P.208, Alaska State Library, Early Prints Collection, ASL-P297-049.

CHAPTER 18: ROUTES TO GOLD, COPPER AND COAL

P.210, Alaska State Library, Case and Draper Collection, ASL-P39-1025; P.211, top, National Park Service; P.211, bottom, University of Washington, Eric A. Hegg Collection, HEG032; P.212, University of Washington, Eric A. Hegg Collection, HEG663; P.213, Anchorage Museum of History and Art, Alaska Engineering Commission Collection, AMRC-aec-g1027; P.214, Anchorage Museum of History and Art, General Photograph File, AMRC-b63-16-32;

CHAPTER 19: GLACIER TRAIL BIRTHS VALDEZ

P.216, Anchorage Museum of History and Art, General Photograph File, AMRC-b62-1-2036; P.217, top, Anchorage Museum of History and Art, Crary-Henderson Collection, AMRC-b62-1-1448; P.217, bottom, Anchorage Museum of History and Art, General Photograph File, AMRC-b69-13-26; P.218, University of Alaska Fairbanks, Albert Johnson Collection, UAF-1989-0166-132-Print; P.219, Anchorage Museum of History and Art, General Photograph File, AMRC-b62-1-1451; P.220, Anchorage Museum of History and Art, Crary-Henderson Collection, AMRC-b62-1-a-430; P.221, Anchorage Museum of History and Art, General Photograph File, AMRC-b62-1-634; P.222, University of Alaska Anchorage, National Geographic Society Katmai Expeditions Collection, UAA-hmc-0186-volume4-4021; P.223, top, Anchorage Museum of History and Art, General Photograph File, AMRC-b78-65-22; P.223, bottom, University of Washington, Alaska and Western Canada Collection, AWC1426; P.224, University of Washington, Frank H. Nowell Collection, NOW231; P.225, Alaska State Library, Wickersham State Historic Site, ASL-P277-007-008; P.226, University of Washington, John E. Thwaites Collection, THW274.

CHAPTER 20: CORDOVA: A TOWN BORN OF STRIFE

P.228, top, University of Washington, John E. Thwaites Collection, THW299; P.228, bottom, Alaska State Library, History Collection, ASL-P340-001; P.229, University of Washington, Eric A. Hegg Collection, HEG369; P.230, Anchorage Museum of History and Art, General Photograph File, AMRC-b83-159-32; P.231, Anchorage Museum of History and Art, General Photograph File, AMRC-b62-1-2194; P.232, Anchorage Museum of History and Art, Crary-Henderson Collection, AMRC-b62-1-a-282; P.233, Alaska State Library, Portrait Files, ASL-PCA-20-11; P.234, Alaska State Library, Ray W. Moss Collection, ASL-P11-037; P.236, University of Washington, John E. Thwaites Collection, THW302; P.238, Alaska State Library, Ray W. Moss Collection, ASL-P11-036; P.239, University of Washington, John E. Thwaites Collection, THW291; P.240, top, University of Washington, John E. Thwaites Collection, THW308; P.240, bottom, Anchorage Museum of History and Art, General Photograph File, AMRC-b83-159-45; P.241, top, University of Washington, John E. Thwaites Collection, THW270; P.241, bottom, University of Washington, Alaska and Western Canada Collection, AWC1472.

CHAPTER 21: SEWARD'S RESURRECTIONS

P.242, Seward Community Library, Robert McEaneney Collection, SCL-38-10; P.244, Seward Community Library, DC Brownell Collection, SCL-28-1; P.245, Seward Community Library, Stauter-Mongin Collection, SCL-4-162; P.246, Seward Community Library, Silvia Sexton Collection, SCL-1-131; P.247, Seward Community Library, DC Brownell Collection, SCL-28-5; P.248, Seward Community Library, Silvia Sexton Collection, SCL-1-491; P.249,

Seward Community Library, Robert McEaneney Collection, SCL-38-28; P.250, Anchorage Museum of History and Art, General Photograph File, AMRC-b62-1-1482.

CHAPTER 22: SLED DOGS LEAD THE WAY

P.251, Anchorage Museum of History and Art, Crary-Henderson Collection, AMRC-b62-1-1992; P.252, Anchorage Museum of History and Art, John Urban Collection, AMRC-b64-1-462; P.253, top, Anchorage Museum of History and Art, Crary-Henderson Collection, AMRC-b62-1-a-223; P.253, bottom, Anchorage Museum of History and Art, Crary-Henderson Collection, AMRC-b62-1-a-74; P.254, Anchorage Museum of History and Art, General Photograph File, AMRC-b81-19-18; P.255, Anchorage Museum of History and Art, General Photograph File, AMRC-b88-11-19.

CHAPTER 23: BLAZING THE IDITAROD TRAIL

P.256, Anchorage Museum of History and Art, John Urban Collection, AMRC-b64-1-714; P.257, Anchorage Museum of History and Art, General Photograph File, AMRC-b65-15-71; P.258-259, Aunt Phil altered Bureau of Land Management map, The Iditarod National Historic Trail, September 1988; P.261, www.rootsweb.com; P.262, University of Alaska Fairbanks, Fred Herms Jr. Collection, UAF-1974-42-8.

CHAPTER 24: IDITAROD TRAIL PHOTO ESSAY

P.263, University of Washington, John E. Thwaites Collection, THW203; P.264, University of Washington, John E. Thwaites Collection, THW023; P.265, top, University of Washington, John E. Thwaites Collection, THW024; P.265, bottom, Anchorage Museum of History and Art, General Photograph File, AMRC-b67-1-133; P.266, Anchorage Museum of History and Art, Alaska Engineering Commission Collection, AMRC-aec-g935; P.267, Anchorage Museum of History and Art, Alaska Engineering Commission Collection, AMRC-aec-g639; P.268, University of Alaska Fairbanks, Mary Whalen Photograph Collection, UAF-2000-197-4; P.269, top, University of Alaska Anchorage, John E. Baker Collection, UAA-hmc-0065-seriesf-1-c; P.269, bottom, Anchorage Museum of History and Art, John Urban Collection, AMRC-b64-1-171; P.270, top, University of Alaska Fairbanks, Albert Johnson Collection, UAF-1989-0166-210-Print; P.270, bottom, University of Alaska Fairbanks, Fred Herms Jr. Collection, UAF-1978-14-1; P.271, top, Alaska State Library, Wickersham State Historic Site, ASL-P277-004-110; P.271, bottom, University of Alaska Fairbanks, Fred Herms Jr. Collection, UAF-1974-42-7; P.272, University of Alaska Fairbanks, Fred Herms Jr. Collection, UAF-1974-42-4; P.273, Seward Community Library, Robert McEaneney Collection, SCL-38-30; P.274, University of Alaska Fairbanks, George and Lilly Clark Collection, UAF-1986-109-15; P.275, Anchorage Museum of History and Art, Ickes Collection, AMRC-b75-175-194; P.276, Anchorage Museum of History and Art, Ickes Collection, AMRC-b75-175-213; P.277, Anchorage Museum of History and Art, O.D. Goetze Collection, AMRC-b01-41-117; P.278, top, Seward Community Library, Sylvia Sexton Collection, SCL-1-685; P.278, bottom, Anchorage Museum of History and Art, General Photograph File, AMRC-b81-19-2.

CHAPTER 25: BEACONS IN THE WILDERNESS

P.280, University of Alaska Fairbanks, Charles E. Bunnell Collection, UAF-1958-1026-

803; P.281, Alaska State Library, Wickersham State Historic Site, ASL-PCA-277; P.282, University of Alaska Fairbanks, Lawyer and Cora Rivenburg Collection, UAF-1994-70-337; P.283, University of Washington, Alaska and Western Canada Collection, AWC0495; P.284, University of Fairbanks, Richard Frank Collection, UAF-193-71-4; P.285, Alaska State Library, Wickersham State Historic Site, ASL-P277-017-002; P.286, University of Washington, Arthur Churchill Warner, WAR0556; P.288, University of Fairbanks, North American Transportation and Trading Company Collection, UAF-1995-190-35.

CHAPTER 26: VOICE OF THE YUKON
P.290, University of Washington, William E. Meed Collection, MEE132; P.292, University of Washington, Frank La Roche Collection, LAR283; P.293, University of Washington, William E. Meed Collection, MEE160; P.294, Anchorage Museum of History and Art, General Photograph File, AMRC-b88-3-98; P.295, University of Alaska Fairbanks, Barrett Willoughby Collection, UAF-72-116-334; P.296, University of Washington, Wilhelm Hester Collection, HES043; P.297, University of Washington, Eric A. Hegg Collection, HEG246; P.298, University of Washington, Eric A. Hegg Collection, HEG334; P.300, Anchorage Museum of History and Art, General Photograph File, AMRC-b70-61; P.301, University of Washington, Alaska and Western Canada Collection, AWC1220.

CHAPTER 27: SOURDOUGH PREACHER PAINTER
P.303, University of Washington, Eric A. Hegg Collection, HEG429; P.304, University of Alaska Museum of the North, Gerald Fitzgerald (donor), UA1970-306-2; P.306, University of Alaska, Walter and Lillian Phillips Collection, UAF-1985-72-19; P.308, University of Alaska Museum of the North, Robert Claus Estate, UA2003-018-001; P.309, University of Alaska, Walter and Lillian Phillips Collection, UAF-1985-72-141; P.311, University of Washington, Modern Photographers Collection, MPH285; P.312, University of Alaska Museum of the North, Grace Berg Schaible Collection, UA1991-017-001.

CHAPTER 28: ELIAS: TOUGH EVERY FOOT OF THE WAY
P.313, Courtesy National Park Service; P.314, findagrave.com; P.316, Library of Congress; P.317, worldroots.com; P.318, Alaska State Library, Asa C. Baldwin Photographs, ASL-P71-515; P.320, Alaska State Library, Asa C. Baldwin Photographs, ASL-P71-247; P.321, U.S. Geological Service; P.322, U.S. Geological Service, Bering Glacier and Mount Saint Elias.

CHAPTER 29: DENALI: THE HIGH ONE
P.324, Federal Aviation Administration; P.325, Alaska State Library, Wickersham State Historic Site, ASL-P277-018-043; P.327, top, Anchorage Museum of History and Art, John Urban Collection, AMRC-b64-1-796; P.327, bottom, Frederick A. Cook Society; P.328, Ohio State University, Fredrick Cook Society Collection, 34-18e; P.329, Ohio State University, Fredrick Cook Society Collection, 34-29a; P.330, Ohio State University, Fredrick Cook Society Collection, 34-18a; P.331, Ohio State University, Fredrick Cook Society Collection, 34-18s; P.332, National Park Service; P.333, University of Alaska Fairbanks, Mount McKinley Expedition 1964, UAF-2004-0162-61; P.334, University of Alaska Fairbanks, R.C. Force Papers, UAF-2003-174-514; P.336, University of Alaska Fairbanks, Historical Photograph Collection, UAF-2005-26-1; P.337, Episcopal Diocese of Alaska; P.338, University of Alaska, Walter and Lillian Phillips Collection, UAF-1985-

72-54; P.339, Courtesy Jan Harper Haines; P.340, Anchorage Museum of History and Art, John Urban Collection, AMRC-b64-1-323; P.341, Alaska State Library, Skinner Foundation Collection, ASL-P44-05-002.

CHAPTER 30: KATMAI ERUPTS

P.342, Anchorage Museum of History and Art, General Photograph File, AMRC-b80-104-9; P.344, University of Alaska Anchorage, National Geographic Society Katmai Expeditions Collection, UAA-hmc-0186-volume1-3940; P.345, University of Alaska Fairbanks, Amelia Elkinton Collection, UAF-1974-175-384; P.346, University of Washington, John E. Thwaites Collection, THW154; P.348, top, University of Alaska Fairbanks, Amelia Elkinton Collection, UAF-1974-175-399; P.348, bottom, University of Washington, John E. Thwaites Collection, THW169; P.349, University of Alaska Fairbanks, Amelia Elkinton Collection, UAF-1974-175-376; P.350, Seward Community Library, Robert McEaneney Collection, SCL-38-6; P.351, University of Washington, Alaska and Western Canada Collection, AWC1475; P.352, University of Washington, Alaska and Western Canada Collection, AWC1591; P.353, University of Alaska Anchorage, National Geographic Society Katmai Expeditions Collection, UAA-hmc-0186-volume3-1207; P.354, top, University of Alaska Anchorage, National Geographic Society Katmai Expeditions Collection, UAA-hmc-0186-volume1-3843; P.354, bottom, University of Washington, Alaska and Western Canada Collection, AWC1474; P.355, University of Alaska Anchorage, National Geographic Society Katmai Expeditions Collection, UAA-hmc-0186-volume5-5087; P.356, University of Alaska Anchorage, National Geographic Society Katmai Expeditions Collection, UAA-hmc-0186-volume4-3693; P.357, University of Alaska Anchorage, National Geographic Society Katmai Expeditions Collection, UAA-hmc-0186-volume3-1176.

PREVIEW AUNT PHIL'S TRUNK: VOLUME 3

P.375, top, Anchorage Museum of History and Art, General Photograph File, AMRC-b78-14-74; P.375, middle, Anchorage Museum of History and Art, General Photograph File, AMRC-b73-43-2; P.375, bottom, Anchorage Museum of History and Art, Alaska Engineering Commission Collection, AMRC-aec-h80; P.376, top, Anchorage Museum of History and Art, General Photograph File, AMRC-b63-19-8; P.376, second, National Museum of Health and Medicine; P.376, third, Alaska State Library, Mary Nan Gamble Collection, ASL-P270-639; P.376, bottom, Minnesota Department of Transportation.

Preview of Aunt Phil's Trunk: Volume 3

Scheduled to be on bookstore shelves in April 2008, "Aunt Phil's Trunk: Volume 3" highlights stories about the birth of Anchorage, the blossoming of the Matanuska Valley with an influx of depression-era colonists and other exciting tales about Alaska's colorful past.

Railroad spurs Anchorage

The U.S. government sparked a stampede of hard-working railway workers to Cook Inlet when it chose to build a railroad from Seward to the coal fields of the Matanuska Valley.

Anchorage rises from timbers

What would become the territory's largest city was in its infancy in 1915 along Ship Creek in Southcentral Alaska. It soon became a thriving railroad town.

Anchorage's oldest unsolved murder

Anchorage officials appointed John "Jack" Sturgus its first chief of police (first jail shown here) in December 1920. Two months later, he was dead from a single gunshot wound to his chest. The case has never been solved.

Joe Spenard's story

A feisty little man named Joe Spenard moved into the new railroad town at Ship Creek in 1919, and he operated the City Express, pictured left.

Flu epidemic hits Alaska

Soldiers coming home from World War I brought back more than battlefield memories. The flu epidemic of 1918 devastated many Alaska villages.

Colonists settle Alaska's wilderness

Tents and gardens popped up all over the Matanuska Valley in 1935 after the U.S. government offered homesteads to farmers from the depression-riddled Midwest.

Black fog over Barrow

When rescuers arrived on the scene of an airplane crash near Point Barrow on Aug. 15, 1935, they found Will Rogers and Wiley Post dead. The last word written on Rogers' typewriter, found in the wreckage, was "death."